The
'SCIENCE OF MAN'
in the Scottish Enlightenment
Hume, Reid and their Contemporaries

The
'SCIENCE OF MAN'
in the Scottish Enlightenment

Hume, Reid and their Contemporaries

edited by
Peter Jones

Edinburgh University Press

© Edinburgh University Press 1989
22 George Square, Edinburgh

Set in Linotron Plantin
by Photoprint, Torquay, and
printed in Great Britain by
Redwood Press Limited,
Trowbridge, Wilts

British Library Cataloguing
  in Publication Data
The "Science of man" in the Scottish enlightenment :
Hume, Reid and their contemporaries.
1. Scottish philosophy
I. Jones, Peter, 1935–
192
ISBN 0 7486 0109 0
      0 7486 0146 5 pbk

CONTENTS

PREFACE

The essays in this book are based on lectures given during the 1986 Institute Project on the Scottish Enlightenment (IPSE 86), organised by the Institute for Advanced Studies in the Humanities of the University of Edinburgh. All of the authors were either Fellows or Visiting Scholars of the Institute during the Project. More than eight thousand members of the public attended over two hundred such addresses during the summer months of 1986, and it is our hope that this collection will enable many of them to reflect on the nature and implications of the new interpretations that are offered.

I am immensely grateful to all of the authors for their patience, enthusiasm and encouragement; without them and their colleagues, the 1986 Project would not have been the success it evidently was, nor would general understanding of our heritage have been so significantly advanced.

PETER JONES

ANNETTE C. BAIER is Professor of Philosophy at the University of Pittsburgh, and author of *Postures of the Mind* London 1985.

HARVEY CHISICK is Professor of History at the University of Haifa, and author of *The Limits of Reform in the Enlightenment: Attitudes toward the Education of the Lower Classes in 18th Century France*, Princeton, 1981.

THOMAS CRAWFORD was formerly a Reader in English at the University of Aberdeen. Among his numerous publications are *Love, Labour and Liberty: The 18th Century Scottish Lyric*, Cheadle, 1976: *A Study of Society and the Lyric*, Edinburgh, 1979.

PETER JONES is Professor of Philosophy at the University of Edinburgh. Among his many publications are *Hume's Sentiments*, Edinburgh, 1982.

MANFRED KUEHN is Professor of Philosophy at Purdue University, and author of *Scottish Common Sense in Germany*, Montreal, 1987.

KEITH LEHRER is Professor of Philosophy at the University of Arizona. He is the author of numerous articles and books, including *Knowledge*, Oxford, 1974.

DONALD W. LIVINGSTON is Professor of Philosophy at Emory University, and author of *Hume's Philosophy of Common Life*, Chicago, 1984.

JOHN PASSMORE is Professor Emeritus of Philosophy at the Australian National University. Among his many books are *Hume's Intentions*, London, 1952, and *Science and its Critics*, London, 1978.

RÜDIGER SCHREYER is Professor of English at the Aachen Institute. The author of numerous articles in learned journals.

Page references to Hume's works (or letter number, in the case of letters) are to generally available editions, abbreviated as follows:

A   *An Abstract of A Treatise of Human Nature*, ed. J.M. Keynes & P. Sraffa, Cambridge, 1938

D   *Dialogues Concerning Natural Religion*, ed. N. Kemp Smith, Indianapolis, n.d.

Es   *Essays Moral, Political, and Literary*, ed. Eugene F. Miller, Indianapolis, 1985

EU   *An Enquiry Concerning Human Understanding*, ed. L.A. Selby-Bigge, revised by P.H. Nidditch, Oxford, 1975

EM   *An Enquiry Concerning the Principles of Morals*, ed. L.A. Selby-Bigge, revised by P.H. Nidditch, Oxford, 1975

L   *The Letters of David Hume*, ed. J.Y.T. Greig, Oxford, 1932

NHR   *The Natural History of Religion*, in *David Hume: The Philosophical Works*, ed. T.H. Green & T.H. Grose, London, 1875, Vol 1V

T   *A Treatise of Human Nature*, ed. L.A. Selby-Bigge, Oxford, 1888.

There is no single, widely available edition of Hume's *History of England*, and all the authors have had to use whatever editions they could find. In each case the author cites the relevant edition in the Notes.

French writers who spoke of 'the science of man', such as Malebranche, together with their English-speaking successors, such as Hume, never formally defined the notion. There is no difficulty, however, in identifying their concern to undertake a systematic investigation of man's nature, practices and social arrangements, parallel in rigour and comprehensiveness to the investigations of the natural world with which they were becoming familiar. Until very recently, the scope of their enquiries has been neglected by modern scholars, no doubt in part because later ages parcelled up and allocated their questions to different professional disciplines.

This book presents a number of new perspectives on thought and attitudes in the eighteenth century, designed to show both their range and their contribution to 'the science of man'. The themes which recur throughout the book dominated the minds of the Enlightenment thinkers, and influenced almost all of their conclusions: religion, the nature of society, knowledge and belief, the nature of philosophy itself. All of the authors draw intriguing parallels between major figures of the eighteenth century, and contrast them with our own times.

The first three papers explore aspects of Hume's thought which help us to understand the considerable gap between his day and ours. We are shown that his views on the common people, on women, and on art, however unusual for their time, are nevertheless at some remove from our own. Harvey Chisick examines Hume's attitudes towards the common people who made up the vast majority of the population amongst which he lived. Because Hume defines them in terms of their ignorance, and because he argues that responsible politics requires extensive education, he feels entitled to debar the people from any such role. Chisick argues that Hume did not recognise the existence of a distinct popular culture with its own motifs and values, largely because the only culture that he acknowledged was the classical 'high' culture of the European élite to which he belonged. Chisick further suggests that Hume's own practicality and reasonableness locked him within the conservative domain of an unchanging world, and one which the Industrial Revolution showed to be inadequate. By contrast, Rousseau posited an ideal for the people which helped to create conceptual space for change. Livingston, in a later chapter, argues that Hume's conservatism is by no means discredited by subsequent events, and that its true nature has yet to be fully grasped.

Annette Baier examines Hume's views on female human nature, on marriage and its duties. She argues that a twentieth-century charge of 'sexism', although anachronistic, can nevertheless be rebutted, since Hume's account of women is radical in several ways. Hume identifies the roots of the social inferiority of women, points out the power women have to change the situation, should they resent it, and underlines the strength of women's sexual desires.

Peter Jones argues that Hume located his own reflections on the arts in the framework of our social life, but that he was also writing at a time when there was no British tradition of criticism of painting, and indeed, scarcely an informed audience for it, or for architecture or music. But Hume is one of the first thinkers to recognise that response to the arts requires awareness of the context in which we find ourselves. Moreover, he holds that neither the meaning nor the value of the arts can be discerned without interpretation of some kind. Hume does not allow for any notion of constant re-interpretation, however, and even follows some French suggestions that criticism can become insidiously parasitic. Like most of his contemporaries, his own views about the arts seem to be based almost exclusively on literature.

On his death-bed, Hume is reported as declaring that he had not completed the task of delivering his countrymen from 'the Christian Superstition'. The next two chapters explore his views on religion, and on philosophy as emancipated from its influence. Donald Livingston shows how, by developing what could be called a pathology of the philosophical intellect, Hume released philosophy from its historical and religious inheritance, and at the same time, separated himself from thinkers of the French Enlightenment, such as Diderot. Traditionally, philosophers had sought for a complete, final and exclusive understanding of all that there is, in ways independent of other enquiries. Hume argues that these demands are incoherent with human nature, and that everything man does is grounded in custom and habit. These habits and customs pervade thought, language, social arrangements, political ideals. By ranging over all of Hume's writings, including the *History*, Livingston draws attention to many aspects of Hume's thought, including his sociology of knowledge, that seem to have been overlooked even by contemporaries such as Ferguson.

John Passmore develops Livingston's discussion of true, false and philosophical religion. He shows that, in the end, Hume cannot give a clear psychological account of the enthusiast's state of mind. Although, like other writers, Hume also speaks of poetical enthusiasm, referring to the capacity of literature to arouse beliefs and feelings, it is the technical religious notion which attracts his attention, and reprobation. Hume holds that the typical beliefs of an enthusiast count neither for knowledge nor even for rational belief; indeed, they barely count as beliefs at all. Such a view inevitably encourages him to associate enthusiasm not only with fanaticism, but also with hyprocrisy; but his historical reflections that enthusiasm and superstition may be humanly ineradicable, and that enthusiasm has occasionally advanced the cause of freedom leave us with a final paradox.

The next two papers effect a transition between Hume and his contemporaries. In the first, Keith Lehrer takes up in detail an issue underlined by Passmore, when discussing Hume's analysis of religious belief; for Lehrer explores Thomas Reid's criticisms of Hume's overall account of human conception and belief. Reid postulates certain innate conceptual operations of the mind that he takes to be necessary in order to explain the supposed facts of thought. As Lehrer points out, Reid's own interpretation of Hume is, and remains, controversial but, as Manfred Kuehn shows, Reid's discussions were immensely influential on the Continent. Kant's own philosophy is shown to be directed against Reid's followers in Germany who, like Reid himself, he believed, had misunderstood Hume. Kant felt that he had to solve both the sceptical challenge thrown down by Hume, and to show that Reid's 'common-sense' attempt to rebut it was inadequate. Reid and Kant, although in crucially different ways, seek to solve Hume's problems by appeal to innate and *a priori* principles which he could never accept. In the end, they too are concerned to characterise the nature of philosophy itself.

Rüdiger Schreyer takes discussion of Reid a stage further. He contrasts the views of Reid and Adam Smith on the nature of language. Many eighteenth-century thinkers realised that language plays an essential part in the progress of the human mind, and in the development of society and its institutions. Schreyer shows that Reid and Smith shared a number of basic assumptions, and that they both sought to locate their enquiries into the origins of language in the larger scientific context of their time. Many of their claims might strike us as mere speculation, but they were intended and received as important contributions to the science of man. Contemporary readers who wish to detach and discard certain views from a system they are then willing to repair face a serious intellectual challenge.

Thomas Crawford suggests that the contradictions in Boswell's character and work in part derive from the complex context in which he grew up in the 1750s. Boswell was interested more in people than ideas, and it is notable that his very first interview – with Hume, who was later to be his landlord – makes almost no reference to the philosopher's tenets. And yet Hume himself argued that man was to be understood more as a creature of passion than of rational intellect, and as a being who achieved full realisation only in society and activity. Do we need a series of psycho-biographies, of Hume and Boswell and other men of sentiment, in order properly to grasp their nature and achievement? Or does Boswell differ fundamentally from the historians, philosophers and scientists whose work in eighteenth-century Scotland is only now beginning to be appreciated in a fuller context?

The authors in this book examine in detail the writings of our great predecessors. In so doing, they demonstrably increase our understanding of the context in which those writers lived and thought. But it would be a mistake to conclude that an interest in such analyses remains exclusively or even essentially historical. When philosophers speak of 'perennial' problems they sometimes imply that the very same questions are tackled over widely spread periods of time, and in very different contexts. It can be argued, however, that without seeking to establish the precise identity of issues throughout history, human beings often do raise similar issues to those of their ancestors; and that it is immensely beneficial to be aware of earlier attempts to reflect on those issues, albeit in different contexts, and with different intellectual commitments. Earlier thinkers can help us to focus or re-focus problems of our own time, and in that way release us from contemporary prejudices and habits of thought. By sensitively analysing the thought of Hume and his contemporaries, the contributors to this volume bring us significantly closer to their work and their achievements.

HARVEY CHISICK

David Hume and the Common People

After a period of relative neglect, David Hume and his philosophy have become the focus of an extensive and expanding body of critical literature. This scholarship is for the most part devoted to explicating and analysing key problems raised by Hume's complex texts, especially in the areas of epistemology and ethics.[1] In this paper I wish to address an issue that cannot properly be said to be part of Hume's philosophy, and which Hume himself never treated systematically. This is his attitude toward what would today be called the lower classes, but in the eighteenth century was referred to as the 'common people'. Hume's attitude toward the lower classes and their situation can be pieced together from comments scattered throughout his writings. The picture of the people that emerges from the usually brief remarks in Hume's philosophical tracts, essays, history and letters is not altogether coherent. It should not be taken as part of a comprehensive social philosophy, but rather as representing a set of attitudes that Hume held. And the attitudes of a philosopher, it need hardly be said, cannot reasonably be expected to show the uniformity of his formal thought. What is at issue here, then, is not a system of social philosophy developed by one of the great thinkers of the eighteenth century, but more simply the views of David Hume, gentleman, man of letters and subject of the British crown, on his social inferiors.

Since the terms 'people' and 'common people' are more ambiguous than the contemporary 'lower classes', which is itself not unequivocal, it may be useful to begin by defining them. In the eighteenth century the common people were understood to stand in contrast to social groups that were not 'common'. The juridical mark of un-commonness throughout Europe during this period was privilege, or more correctly, personal privilege. The two groups best defined in terms of their privileges at this time were the clergy and nobility.[2] On this first, rather literal definition, then, the people were all those who were neither nobles nor clerics.

A second use of the term 'people' in the eighteenth century was borrowed from classical sources and meant roughly the citizen body (*demos*, *populus*). In the monarchies of eighteenth-century Europe, the term 'citizen body' had no direct application, and was important largely for its historical associations and cultural resonance. This use is not altogether in accord with the first, as it includes members of the aristocracy who may enjoy legal or constitutional advantages within the citizen body, while it excludes slaves or resident aliens who were usually engaged in 'common' pursuits. This overlap in meaning is no doubt responsible for some of the imprecision in the use of the term 'people' at the time.

A third use of the term takes the people to be those engaged in some form of productive or menial economic activity and would include wealthy merchants, clerks, artisans, servants and peasants. J.F.C. Harrison states that the 'commonalty' begins below the level of the gentry and includes the great majority of the population occupied as 'freeholders (yeomen), farmers, shop-keepers, artisans, tradesmen, soldiers and sailors, labourers, servants, cottagers and paupers. They were the "plain mean people" among whom the Puritan divine Richard Baxter had been bred.'[3] Moving from the upper to the lower classes in his sketch of eighteenth-century English society, Roy Porter notes, 'Beneath the moneyed men were the craftsmen and artisans, the labourers and the poor. There was nothing homogeneous about the lower orders, who ranged from weavers to watermen, from ostlers to shepherds, from ploughmen to piemen, from crossing-sweepers to coal-miners.'[4]

Eighteenth-century writers would speak of the people or common people as consisting of all or any of the above groups in any combination, depending on the context. The term was broad and malleable enough to accommodate all these usages. When Hume's contemporaries wished to be more precise they often used epithets such as 'low', 'vile', or 'ignorant', or substituted synonyms, such as 'rabble', 'populace', or 'multitude'. By itself the term 'people' was normally the equivalent of lower classes but could also be taken in the sense of citizen body, usually in the context of ancient history or political theory. The common people were usually understood to be the labouring population, or, as we shall see, the poor, which amounted to the same thing.[5]

During the eighteenth century, then, the terms 'people' and 'common people' could be used in a variety of ways which were not always compatible. The people, however, were never thought to exist in a vacuum, but in some social framework, and within this framework were opposed to 'non-people'. In juridical terms, as we have seen, the people were opposed to the privileged. In social terms, the people may be said to stand against an élite, or complex of élites. If we borrow Pierre Goubert's rough division of the society of the old regime into three broad groups, the dominant, the independent and the dependent,[6] we would find that in France the élites comprised the top 2%–5% of the population, the common people the dependent 75% or 85%, together, in most cases, with the economically independent 10% or 15%. England, it seems, was better off than the Continent in the sense that the economically independent social groups were larger there.[7]

A nexus of wealth, status, office and power identifies a composite élite of landowners, financiers, legal and administrative functionaries and wholesale merchants which, by its economic and political power, as well as by its social prestige, dominated eighteenth-century society. The people stood against this complex élite, inferior, subordinate, dependent. Between the dominant few and the common people come Goubert's independent groups – well-off farmers, comfortable artisans and merchants, members of the liberal professions, *rentiers* – groups which have variously been called the bourgeoisie, bourgeois of the old-regime type, and 'middling sort' or 'middling ranks'[8]. This independent group also contained established or successful intellectuals (university professors, clerics with good livings or benefices, popular authors), but certainly not all, or even most, intellectuals. The social position of these economically independent groups was ambivalent. In the eyes of the aristocracy of wealth and power, they belonged to the people. The labouring population, on the other hand, saw them as social superiors. Most members of these intermediary groups, if they felt inferior to the dominant élites, nevertheless aspired ultimately to rise socially and be integrated into them. And they viewed the poor and labouring population with mistrust.

The people are the subject of frequent comment in the literature of the eighteenth century. But members of the lower classes almost never speak in their own voices in this literature. Those who write about the people, even those who write in the name of the people, are almost invariably members of the élites or of the independent groups in society. While it is theoretically possible for members of the people to write about their own experiences and aspirations, in the eighteenth century this rarely happens.[9] In their attempts to listen to the authentic voice of the people during this period, historians have examined police and court records, popular literature, and of course *cahiers de doléances*.[10] The results have seldom been satisfying. The obvious alternative of examining the writings of authors who began life among the lower classes –

Rousseau, Diderot, Marmontel, Restif de la Bretonne in France, William Cobbett, Robert Burns and others in Britain – suffers from the equally obvious drawback of these men having modified their outlooks and values as they rose in society. Having been co-opted into the élites, they to a greater or lesser degree adopted élite values and assumptions. In the eighteenth century, then, the people cannot, and do not, speak for themselves. It is their social superiors who speak about them. In the case of David Hume, it is worth remarking, we are dealing with an intellectual who began his career as one of the middling sort, but with good connections and a combination of office-holding, successful pension hunting and even more successful publication, became financially independent and indeed wealthy. Socially and intellectually he was close to the ruling élites and may be said to have shared their interests and aspirations.[11] His view of the common people is very much a view from above. And in its broad outlines, I wish to argue, it is representative of the dominant and independent strata of eighteenth-century society.

As Hume nowhere systematically discusses the common people, I have chosen to analyse his views in the areas of economics, culture and politics. Though Hume himself might not have found these categories congenial,[12] they will serve to provide a framework for explicating his scattered comments on the silent majority of his contemporaries.

ECONOMICS

What distinguished the common people from an economic point of view was their dependence and greater or lesser degree of poverty. In the western world today, it is probably fair to say that the chief cause of poverty is unemployment. In the eighteenth century the greater part of the working population was regarded as poor by definition. This was because wages for unskilled labour were seldom much above subsistence, because work was often seasonal, and there were no relief schemes for the unemployed, though the Poor Law might offer significant assistance to those settled in a parish. Hume thus denies that 'a poor peasant or artizan' could freely travel to another country if he were dissatisfied where he lived, both because he would not know another language and because living 'from day to day, by the small wages which he acquires' he would not have the necessary reserves (Es. 475).[13] What distinguished rich from poor in the eighteenth century was not the opportunity to work, but ownership of a significant amount of property.

Without property, receiving low wages, and subject to periodic unemployment, the working population would have to live modestly, and would frequently be reduced to need. Hume is aware that the poor cannot normally afford meat, and that their diet consists largely of grains and potatoes, while their dress is often wretched (Es. 356, 387). The agricultural labourer, probably the most typical representative of the people in the eighteenth century, had, according to Hume, no greater aspiration than to assure his subsistence. In his own words, '. . . the beggarly peasant has no means, nor view, nor ambition of obtaining above a bare livelihood' (Es. 299). Hume's assessment here seems accurate. Social historians have shown that in the harsh socio-economic and demographic climate of the old regime, remaining above the level of subsistence involved an uneven and unremitting struggle against forces over which the peasant or labourer had no control.[14] Illness, unemployment, a too-large family, bad weather with attendant poor harvests and high prices could by themselves or severally plunge the poor into extreme want and even starvation. Hume speaks of famine a number of times in his *History*. The causes he ascribes are war[15] and bad weather,[16] and he takes famine in peace-time as proof of backward or declining agriculture,[17] even though crop failure due to bad weather was by far the most common cause. Hume's main conclusion on this subject is that attempted regulation of prices exacerbates the problem, and that the best and indeed only way of dealing with grain shortages is to rely on the mechanism of the market, for '. . . in reality, the increase of prices is a necessary consequence of scarcity; and laws, instead of preventing it, only aggravate the evil, by cramping and restraining commerce.'[18]

But leaving the extreme case of famine aside, as authors in the eighteenth century tended to do, Hume describes the ideas associated with poverty as 'want, penury, hard labour, dirty furniture, coarse or ragged cloathes, nauseous meat and distasteful liquor', and the response these images call up in the observer is 'contempt', just as wealth and the ideas associated with it elicit 'regard' and 'esteem'.[19]

How does Hume believe that we should respond when confronted with those reduced to poverty? Certainly not with indiscriminate almsgiving. In his discussion of benevolence in the *Enquiry Concerning the Principles of Morals* he writes:

> Giving alms to common beggars is naturally praised; because it seems to carry relief to the distressed and indigent: but when we observe the encouragement thence arising to idleness and debauchery, we regard that species of charity rather as a weakness than a virtue. (EM. 180)

Contrasting the character of justice, which benefits society as a whole, and acts of beneficence or generosity, which immediately benefit the person receiving them, Hume is careful to emphasise that such acts must not be indiscriminate, and can properly be directed only toward the 'industrious and indigent' and those who are 'not undeserving' of them (T. 580).

It seems that Hume's behaviour in private life was consistent with the views he expressed in his theoretical writings. Having been asked by a friend to pass on a guinea to a woman both knew, Hume undertook to carry out the commission, but noted that the woman, whom he had not seen for years, was said to have become 'a common Prostitute' and added, 'I commend your Humanity; though perhaps, it is misplac'd on the present Occasion. Not but dissolute People are a proper Object of Compassion; but no Assistance or Relief does them any Service.'[20] Hume's statement here is perplexing. As a gift of money to a poor person could procure them food or clothing, such a gift could certainly be a 'service'. What Hume seems to imply, his commendation of his friend's humanity and his recognition that 'dissolute People are a proper Object of Compassion' notwithstanding, is that 'the dissolute' will not use alms well, and so should not be given them.[21]

In a discussion of Roman history, Hume criticised the practice of distributing corn to the people of Rome without charge, and in the same passage condemned the *sportula*, or gifts made by lords to their clients, on the grounds that such gifts tended to produce 'idleness, debauchery, and a continual decay among the people' (Es. 457). Giving his text contemporary relevance, he added, 'The parish-rates have at present the same bad consequence in England.'[22]

Hume's aversion to almsgiving on the grounds that it encourages idleness seems to be based on his view of human nature. In the *Dialogues* he has Philo say that Nature has made man so that 'nothing but the most violent necessity can oblige him to labour . . .'[23] In the same passage Philo asserts both that 'Almost all the moral, as well as natural evils of human life arise from idleness', and that in order to remedy 'most of the ills of human life' it would be enough for man to have 'a greater propensity to industry and labour; a more vigorous spring and activity of mind; a more constant bent to business and application.'[24]

Hume's aversion to almsgiving, then, should not be ascribed to meanness, but to a vision of the world as a harsh place and man as a slothful creature who has no choice in the long run, but to wrest his livelihood from nature by painful labour. Indeed, Hume explicitly regards scarcity as the normal condition obtaining in the world and maintains that in conditions of abundance both the virtue of justice and the right of property would lose their meaning (T. 494–6). Any measures that ignore or seek to sidestep these basic facts encourage habits and attitudes that vitiate the poor man's ability to cope with his situation. Yet if Hume is reluctant to tamper with what he regards as the natural order of things, he has no sympathy for measures that, by lack of foresight or by self-interest, might exacerbate the naturally harsh condition of the greater part of the population. A case in point concerns taxation.

Hume maintained that 'The best taxes are such as are levied upon consumptions, especially those of luxury; because such taxes are least felt by the people' (Es. 345). By contrast, the worst taxes are arbitrary ones, for 'They are commonly converted, by their management, into punishments on industry; and also, by their unavoidable inequality, are more grievous, than by the real burden which they impose' (Es. 345–6). Hume similarly criticises not so much the weight, as the methods of levying taxes in France, for it is as a result of this 'expensive, unequal, arbitrary and intricate method' that 'the industry of the poor, especially of the peasants and farmers, is, in a great measure, discouraged, and agriculture rendered a beggarly and slavish employment' (Es. 95). The poor, Hume seems to be saying, have both the need and the right to work, so that any policy that discourages their industry, from whatever motive, is blameworthy. Intentionally shifting the tax burden from the common people was another matter. Hume objected to Turgot's view that taxation should fall exclusively on proprietors of land, preferring instead to retain indirect taxation, the burden of which falls on the consumer.[25]

CULTURE

Though it is possible to examine Hume's views on the culture of the common people, one should do so without expecting any significant contribution to the current debate on popular culture.[26] Indeed, I have found little evidence that Hume recognised the existence of a distinct popular culture with its own motifs and values. Apart from the argument that the religious views of the many tend toward superstition and idolatry and are based on the attempt to propitiate unseen and unknown forces, an argument made most fully in The Natural History of Religion, Hume seems to recognise the existence of a distinct popular culture only in a letter in which he deals with the authenticity of the Ossian poems. He there asked Hugh Blair 'to get positive testimony from many different hands, that such poems are vulgarly recited in the Highlands, and have there been long the entertainment of the people.'[27] To the best of my knowledge, however, Hume nowhere else speaks in terms of a distinct popular culture. Rather, he sees the lower classes living beyond the civilising and moderating influences of the only culture that he recognised, namely, the culture of the 'great tradition',[28] characterised by a high level of literacy, usually complemented by proficiency in the classical languages, that was shared by the élites of Europe during this period.

When Hume refers to cultural aspects of the people, it is usually in negative terms. The people, Hume observes repeatedly, are disorderly. They are superstitious, undisciplined, seditious and ignorant.[29] Indeed, Hume's comments on the culture, or lack of culture, of the people tells us a good deal more about David Hume and the élites of the eighteenth century than about the lower classes of the period.

It is ignorance more than anything else that characterises the people for Hume. In the *Treatise*, the two *Enquiries*, the *Dialogues* and 'The Natural History of Religion' the 'vulgar' are consistently opposed to philosophers, or those capable of a scientific and dispassionate understanding of things.[30] It is, for example, among the most ignorant that belief in miracles takes root most easily and spreads most quickly (EU. 120). The people tend naturally to polytheism and idolatry, for the regularity of natural phenomena, which might lead to the notion of a single ordering force in the universe, fails to arouse the curiosity of the multitude, who are impressed by the dramatic and exceptional.[31] When the people come to adopt monotheism it is for the wrong reasons,[32] and whoever thinks otherwise 'would show himself little acquainted with the ignorance and stupidity of the people.'[33] Hume does not restrict his discussion to the distant past, but asserts that 'idolatry has prevailed, and still prevails, among the greatest part of uninstructed mankind.'[34] In the course of a discussion of the development of religion from a lower to a higher form, Hume states that 'it may safely be affirmed, that many popular religions are really, in the conception of their more vulgar votaries, a species of daemonism; and the higher the deity is exalted in power and knowledge, the lower of course is he frequently deprest in goodness and benevolence . . .'.[35] It would seem that for Hume, the religion of the common people is little more than the objectification of their fear and ignorance.

Nor is the boundless ignorance of the people a matter of chance or of misconceived policy. It follows from the very nature of

things. Hume counted it one of the principal advantages of those
belonging to the 'Middle Station' that they can be 'suppos'd
susceptible of Philosophy' (Es. 546). The very wealthy and the
poor could not, for 'The Great are too much immers'd in Pleasure;
and the Poor too much occupy'd in providing for the Necessities
of Life, to hearken to the calm voice of Reason' (ibid.). In his
essay 'Of National Characters', Hume matter-of-factly explains
that, 'poverty and hard labour debase the minds of the common
people, and render them unfit for any science and ingenious
profession . . .' (Es. 198). In the *Treatise* he states that:

> The skin, pores, muscles, and nerves of a day-labourer are
> different from those of a man of quality: So are his sentiments,
> actions and manners. The different stations of life influence
> the whole fabric, external and internal; and these different
> stations arise necessarily, because uniformly, from the necess-
> ary and uniform principles of human nature. (T. 402)

Hume cannot, of course, be taken to mean that the upper and
lower classes are genetically different.[36] His point is that we are
the products of the societies and ranks to which we belong, the
occupations we exercise, and the opportunities which we enjoy or
from which we are excluded. But it remains the fundamental
differences among men that are central for Hume.

When Hume uses synonyms for 'common people' or related
terms, he frequently chooses expressions that underscore their
ignorance and his contempt. He observes that 'the gazing populace
receive greedily, without examination, whatever sooths superstition
and promotes wonder' (EU. 126). He refers to the 'ignorant and
thoughtless part of mankind,' to the 'raw and ignorant multitude'
and to the 'ignorant vulgar' when he might as easily have spoken of
the majority.[37] When deposed, Vitellius is handed over not to the
Roman people, but to a 'merciless rabble' (EM. 253). A carpenter
capable of building ships might be admired for his skills. Hume,
however, emphasises his lack of creativity and orginality, and
dismisses him as a 'stupid mechanic'.[38] The French peasants
during their rising of 1358 are called 'furious malcontents' and
'savages',[39] while English peasants of the 1381 rebellion are desig-
nated the 'lowest populace' and 'enraged multitude'.[40]

This is coloured and emotive rather than analytical language,
and reveals much about Hume's attitude toward the lower classes.
But in using this rhetoric of disdain and in regarding the common
people with contempt, Hume is not alone. Like many of his
contemporaries, Hume was educated upon, and throughout his
life continued to study, the Greek and Roman classics. This was a
literature produced almost exclusively by aristocratic authors

whose distate for and mistrust of the common people, however
justly or unjustly founded, was insuperable. An eminent literary
critic has argued that the classical authors were, by virtue of their
world view, incapable of sympathy with the people.[41] Be that as it
may, the rhetoric of disdain with regard to the common people
would appear to be an integral part of the classical tradition, and
is found in full bloom in the humanists of the sixteenth century,
including men such as Erasmus and Pius II, though it is largely
lacking in Machiavelli. The dictionaries of the seventeenth and
the first half of the eighteenth centuries are imbued with the same
fear of, and disdain for, the people.[42] Though not so influential as
the classical tradition in shaping attitudes toward the lower
classes, the tradition of chivalry should also be taken into account
here. As Jean Delumeau has pointed out, the literature expressing
the values of medieval chivalry normally portrays the noble
warrior as a man distinguished by his individual bravery, and
contrasts him with the masses, who live in collective fear.[43]
Together these traditions predominated at least through the
seventeenth century, and cannot be said to have been eclipsed
before the nineteenth century, if indeed then.

A change is perceptible during the 1750s, however, and
discussions of the people in their productive capacities during the
second half of the century resulted in a positive revaluation of the
lower classes.[44] Most of Hume's works were written and published
before the end of the 1750s, and he seems to have been largely
untouched by the new attitudes.[45]

POLITICS

Summarising the argument to this point, we find that for Hume,
the chief economic characteristic of the common people was its
constant occupation in some form of business or manual work,
and that its principal cultural characteristic was ignorance. If
successful application to the art of government required extensive
education, cool judgement, sufficient means to assure independence, and considerable leisure, it followed that the people had no
place in politics. Hume did not hesitate to draw this conclusion.
In doing so he was in harmony with both contemporary practice
and mainstream eighteenth-century theory, which allowed the
people no active role in politics.[46] Hard work, honesty, resignation
to their lot and obedience to their superiors are all that could be
expected or required of the great majority of mankind (Es. 546).

Hume's objections to the people having an active role in politics
are comprehensive. The purpose of his essay 'Of the Original
Contract' was to show that the notion of a social contract, and

with it the principle of popular sovereignty, are untenable. They are untenable partly for historical reasons, partly because the people have not the capacity, according to Hume, to organise or administer themselves. He states that 'When we assert, that all lawful government arises from the consent of the people, we certainly do them a great deal more honour than they deserve, or even expect and desire from us' (Es. 478). In the essay in which he sketches an outline of an ideal government, Hume restricts his proposed franchise to substantial members of the community, and by means of a property qualification eliminates the people from even primary electoral assemblies at the parish level. In revising this essay, Hume increased the sum by virtue of which a freeholder would qualify for a place in the local assembly from ten to twenty pounds.[47] This suggests that his mistrust of the people grew with time. In any case, he intended to grant a deliberative voice in politics to at most 10% and more probably only 5% or fewer heads of families.[48]

Perhaps the strongest statement of Hume's aversion to popular participation in politics is to be found in his essay, 'Of the Original Contract'. There he writes:

> In reality, there is not a more terrible event, than a total dissolution of government, which gives liberty to the multitude, and makes the determination or choice of a new establishment depend upon a number, which nearly approaches to that of the body of the people: For it never comes entirely to the whole body of them. Every wise man, then, wishes to see, at the head of a powerful and obedient army, a general, who may speedily seize the prize, and give to the people a master, which they are so unfit to chuse for themselves. (Es. 472)

It is hard to think of a more forceful assertion of the political nullity of the people than that contained in the phrase 'unfit to chuse for themselves.'[49]

Hume, then, believed that the people could not be trusted to make important decisions, even concerning themselves. More than this, he believed that they could not support, and so should not be told, the truth as it was perceived by the enlightened. This point comes out forcefully in a letter in which Hume argued that a young man whose religious convictions were less than firm should accept a clerical position which his patron might get for him. He writes:

> It is putting too great a respect on the vulgar, and on their superstitions, to pique one's self on sincerity with regard to them. Did ever one make a point of honour to speak truth to

children or madmen? If the thing were worthy of being treated gravely, I should tell him, that the Pythian oracle, with the approbation of Xenophon, advised everyone to worship the gods [. . . for the good of the state]. I wish it were still in my power to be a hypocrite in this particular. The common duties of society usually require it; and the ecclesiastical profession only adds a little more to an innocent dissimulation, or rather simulation, without which it is impossible to pass through the world. Am I a liar, because I order my servant to say, I am not at home, when I do not desire to see company?[50]

Here again the people are presented as sub-rational, as children who have not yet reached the age of reason, and as madmen who are without, or who have lost, their reason. Defining the people in these terms is of course to prejudice the argument. If the people are perceived as minors or as insane, it follows that for their own good they must remain the wards of their rational and enlightened superiors. Hume is here giving his views on a subject that was often discussed by men of learning in the eighteenth century, namely, whether it is permissible to mislead the people.[51] Far from standing outside the mainstream of Enlightenment thought, in refusing to regard the common people as rational and responsible, Hume is representative of the enlightened élitism that predominated among the progressive thinkers of the time.[52]

Hume's theoretical reservations about the political capacities of the people could have found support in, if they were not in fact based upon, classical history. Thucydidyes and Tacitus, Xenophon and Polybius, all chronicle the process by which small city-states, usually democracies, destroy each other, or having weakened each other, were conquered by larger states. Hume, whose knowledge of the classical authors was both comprehensive and precise, frequently has recourse to them. He observes that throughout antiquity the people responded with 'perpetual discontents and seditions' to proposals to establish property qualifications for office (Es. 415). In his view, the radical democracy of Athens governed 'without regard to order, justice, or prudence' (Es. 368–9), while the unregulated power of the Roman citizenry made the replacement of the republic by the 'despotic power of the Caesars' inevitable (Es. 16). The classics of course formed a major part of the cultural heritage of the men of the Enlightenment. Hume's use of them was typical.[53]

Hume's comments concerning the people in contemporary politics are consonant with the views he expressed in his theoretical writings. Excluded from office and, except at its highest levels, excluded too from the electoral process, the common people were obliged to make their politics in the street or market place. The chief instrument of popular politics was the crowd, and there was no shortage of crowd actions in either England or Scotland over the eighteenth century.[54] Hume's correspondence reflects little concern with such events until the Wilkes Riots of the late 1760s and early 1770s. It is not necessary to enter into a detailed account of the career of John Wilkes and his success in galvanising a disparate group of supporters, including small freeholders, City merchants, modest shopkeepers, craftsmen and workers, around a set of issues that included freedom of the press and personal freedom, but which remained closely tied to Wilkes's person.[55] Historians are agreed that the popular slogan 'Wilkes and Liberty' served as a rallying point for economic as well as political grievances, and that Wilkes himself became a symbol of opposition.[56] In a letter to Hugh Blair in March 1769, Hume said that though the Wilkes affair had initially aroused indignation, it now appeared ridiculous. Yet writing about Wilkes, he seemed seriously concerned. 'Think of the Impudence of that Fellow,' he directed Blair, 'and his Quackery; and his Cunning; and his Audaciousness; and judge of the Influence he will have over such a deluded Multitude [the London mob].'[57] Hume's dislike of Wilkes and his followers emerges clearly nearly two years later, when he regarded the movement as finished as a political force. 'It is a pleasure', he wrote to his friend and publisher William Strahan, 'that the Wilkites and Bill of Rights-men are fallen into total and deservd Contempt. Their noise is more troublesome and odious than all the Cannon that will be fird on the Atlantic.'[58] What troubled Hume was that, in mobilising the common people of London and Middlesex, Wilkes had introduced a force into politics that threatened the stability of the government, and indeed the state. Referring to the riots of 1768 as 'the late Mobs', Hume observed that 'the Laws and Constitution and the King were openly insulted with Impunity', and he later asserted that 'There must necessarily be a Struggle between the Mob and the Constitution . . .'[59] In October 1769 he further expressed the view that:

> Our government has become an absolute Chimera: So much Liberty is incompatible with human Society: And it will be happy if we can escape from it, without falling into a military Government, such as Algiers or Tunis. The Matter will only be worse, if there be no shooting or hanging next Winter: This Frenzy of the people, so epidemical and so much

> without a Cause, admits only of one Remedy, which however
> is a dangerous one, and requires more vigour than has
> appeared in any minister of late.[60]

Hume's mistrust of the people is heightened at this time by his
concern that the government was not prepared to handle the
danger with the necessary firmness. He complained to Strahan in
January 1771 that 'our Ministry are more afraid of the despicable
London Mob than of all Europe.'[61] Two months later he criticised
government policy on the Falklands and attributed it to 'the
Timidity of our Ministry, who dread more the contemptible
Populace of London than the whole House of Bourbon.'[62] Like
most conservatives, Hume was committed to strong government
as well as to certain principles of government. He recalled these
principles following some of the more severe of the Wilkes Riots.
Hume wrote to the Comtesse de Boufflers that he would like very
much to come to France to visit her again, and added:

> . . . though indeed the prospect of affairs here is so stange
> and melancholy, as would make any one desirous of with-
> drawing from the country at any rate. Licentiousness, or
> rather frenzy of liberty, has taken possession of us, and is
> throwing everything into confusion. How happy do I estime
> it, that in all my writings I have always kept at a proper
> distance from that tempting extreme, and have maintained a
> due regard to magistry and established government, suitably
> to the character of an historian and a philosopher.[63]

If we turn from contemporary politics and Hume's theoretical
writings to his *History of England*, we find a measure of continuity
in the way he speaks about the common people, but also that new
themes appear. According to Hume, events in France leading to
Etienne Marcel's uprising and the Jacquerie of 1358 '. . . had
produced in that country a dissolution, almost total of civil
authority, and had occasioned confusions, the most horrible and
destructive that had ever been experienced in any age or nation.'[64]
The 'dissolution of government' which had aroused such fear in
'Of the Original Contract' is here said to have been realised, and
the Jacquerie is described by Hume as a return to the state of
nature.[65] He describes the way the peasants hunted down,
tortured and killed nobles, but he also prefaces this description
with the observation that, 'The peasants, formerly oppressed and
now left unprotected by their masters, became desperate from
their present misery . . .'[66] This does not excuse the outrages
committed by the peasants, but it does help explain them, and it
introduces an element of objectivity. Hume similarly prefaces his
account of the Peasant Rebellion of 1381 in England with the
observation that:

All history abounds with examples where the great tyrannise over the meaner sort: But here the lowest populace rose against their rulers, committed the most cruel ravages upon them, and took vengeance for all former oppressions.[67]

Hume proceeds to give a fairly sympathetic account of the rising, noting the haughtiness of the nobility and the currency of egalitarian doctrines at the time. He gives a charming description of the actual outbreak of the revolt, which was initially directed against a new tax.[68] Though he describes the leaders of the rising, Wat Tyler, Jack Straw and the rest, as 'the most audacious and criminal' of the rebels, Hume finds their demands for a pardon, the abolition of slavery, freedom of market towns (i.e. reduction or elimination of taxes on goods being brought to market) and the replacement of feudal dues with real rents as 'extremely resonable in themselves'.[69] Hume clearly had no sympathy for the aspiration of the rebels for a 'general levelling of society',[70] yet he does not gloss over the harshness of the repression. We come to understand Hume's relative indulgence for the people in the light of the moral he points when summarising the rebellion:

It was pretended that the intentions of the mutineers had been to seize the King's person, to carry him through England at their head, to murder all the nobility, gentry, and lawyers, and even all the priests except the mendicant friars; to dispatch afterwards the King himself; and having thus reduced all to a level, to order the kingdom at their pleasure. It is not impossible, but many of them, in the delirium of their first success, might have formed such projects: But of all the evils incident to human society, the insurrections of the populace, when not raised and supported by persons of higher quality, are the least to be dreaded: The mischiefs consequent to an abolition of rank and distinction, become so great, that they are immediately felt, and soon bring affairs back to their former order and arrangement.[71]

In other words, purely popular movements do not constitute a serious threat to society. Because of their excessive radicalism and extreme naïveté they are self-destructive. Only when the people find leaders from the upper classes capable of distinguishing what is practicable from what is not and guided by reason rather than blind passion do they pose a real social threat – as they did, in Hume's view, virtually throughout antiquity. Left to themselves, the people, precisely because of their ignorance and incompetence, do not pose a serious long-term threat to society.

Hume is, I think, right about the naïveté and virtual certainty of failure of purely popular movements, at least in the early modern period.[72] But his views on the role of the people in politics extend beyond the arguments that the people, because of its ignorance, ought not to participate in politics, and that if it does, it is bound, again because of its ignorance, to fail. Hume does concede the people a role in politics, albeit a restricted and largely passive one.

In his discussion of the conflict between the houses of York and Lancaster, Hume observes:

> By the gradual progress of arts in England, as well as other parts of Europe, the people were now becoming of some importance; laws were beginning to be respected by them; and it was requisite, by various pretences, previously to reconcile their minds to the overthrow of such an ancient establishement as that of the house of Lancaster, ere their concurrence could reasonably be expected.[73]

The significance of this passage is considerable, for we find in it recognition both of the new importance of public opinion (the need to 'reconcile the mind' of the people to important changes) and of the people as a political force whose consent ('concurrence') is necessary for effecting significant changes. The 'people' – Hume almost certainly has in mind the top 20% of the non-noble population – henceforth appears repeatedly in the *History* and plays an important, if secondary, role. Though in Hume's words only 'an empty shadow of a king', Henry II, initially at least, was not harmed by his enemies because of his popularity, while Raleigh was said to owe his condemnation to his unpopularity.[74] Though the Duke of Gloucester's popularity did not save his life, it made his assassination a serious matter for the crown, which was generally believed to have had a hand in it.[75] Similarly, it proved necessary to reconcile the citizens of London to the execution of Hastings because he was 'very popular' among them.[76]

By exercising a sort of *de facto* veto through the threat of direct action if popular politicians were harmed or popular causes slighted, the people moderated the internecine violence of the great nobility, which was extreme from the fourteenth to the sixteenth centuries. Indeed, the nobles, whose struggles for power and preeminence during the medieval and early modern periods repeatedly spilled over into civil wars, causing untold misery to ordinary people and undermining or even preventing the development of a strong central power, are arguably the villains of the bulk of Hume's *History*.[77] The people take on a positive value not so much for any virtues they might have, but because they act as a counterweight to the anarchic influence of the nobility. The people may not be aware of their power, and they are liable to be manipulated by ambitious or unscrupulous members of the upper classes (Es. 522), but the force they represent is real. As Hume noted in the *Treatise*, 'Popular fame may be agreeable even to a man, who despises the vulgar; but 'tis because their multitude gives them additional weight and authority' (T. 324).

By way of summary we may say that Hume's attitude toward the common people was in no way flattering, yet nor was it devoid of sympathy. He used the rhetoric of disdain in referring to the lower classes, as did almost all representatives of the humanist tradition, and while emphasising the ignorance of the people and the dangers of their being actively involved in politics, he could also, like Machiavelli, objectively evaluate the political force he believed them to represent. If Hume's aversion to almsgiving appears harsh, it should be borne in mind that it was not uncommon at the time, and was, moreover, a logical extension of the policy of laissez-faire that Hume recommended consistently. Liberal economics extended a new freedom to the individual in the marketplace, but at the same time it denied all responsibility for the individual's well-being. The concomitant of the freedom to grow wealthy by industry was the freedom to starve when that industry miscarried or failed. Traditional conservatism recognised the religious obligation of charity and the secular obligation of paternalism. Hume, it seems, recognised neither. There is a fine expression of traditional conservatism in Samuel Johnson, who, while agreeing with Hume on the importance of rank, order and subordination, and disagreeing with him on much else, is reported to have said that 'a decent provision for the poor is the true test of civilization.'[78] Hume, I think, would have regarded the terms in which Dr Johnson expressed himself as outmoded, for he recognised no obligation on the part of society or of any individual to provide for another.[79]

Hume is, finally, adamant in denying the common people any positive or direct role in politics. In this he differed fundamentally from another thinker of whom Dr Johnson disapproved, namely, Jean-Jacques Rousseau. Rousseau was no wild-eyed reformer, as anyone who has looked at his projects for the governments of Poland and Corsica knows. But in his political theory Rousseau assumed that the people might become, or might ideally be posited to be, what they in fact were not. By imagining the people as what they clearly were not, Rousseau added a dimension to his political thought and helped create the conceptual space for change. That is, by positing an ideal set of circumstances he provided a criterion by which the real world could be judged, and implicitly, a model for changing it. Hume, because he was so concerned with what he saw around him and with things as they were, refused to make any such conceptual leap. And this surely was reasonable. But his practicality and reasonableness here led him to remain locked in a world conceived in one dimension, a world which, in its main social and economic features, was expected to remain fundamentally unchanged.[80] This, I repeat, was a reasonable and practical outlook for a thinker of the eighteenth century. It is also an outlook the implications of which are profoundly conservative. Yet if the premises of this conservatism are largely sound for a pre-industrial society such as Hume lived in, they are overtaken by events somewhere on the other side of the Industrial Revolution.

NOTES

I wish to thank Annette Baier, Joseph Ellin, Ed Hundert and Roger Emerson for having read and most helpfully commented on earlier drafts of this paper. The remaining errors and imperfections are entirely my own.

1. See R. Hall, *Fifty Years of Hume Scholarship: A Bibliographical Guide* (Edinburgh U.P., 1978). Hall's guide contains no reference to the people, the poor or poverty in its index. Nor does E.C. Mossner's basic *Life of David Hume* (London, 1954). Among scholars who have touched on Hume's attitudes toward the lower classes in the context of broader studies, W.L. Taylor maintained that Hume showed an 'unflagging concern with the problem of raising the standard of living' of the labouring population and favoured high real wages (*Francis Hutcheson and David Hume as Predecessors of Adam Smith*, Durham, N.C., 1965, 107–8), while C.N. Stockton has argued that Hume accepted extreme hardship for the working population as inevitable and beneficial to economic growth ('Economics and the Mechanism of Historical Progress in Hume's *History*,' in D. Livingston ed., *Hume: A Re-evaluation*, New York, 1976, 315). Taylor's view, I believe, is more generous than warranted. Stockton's, while harsh and perhaps requiring some qualification, seems to reflect Hume's outlook more accurately.

2. The issue of privilege is highlighted in such general histories of Europe in the eighteenth century as George Rudé, *Europe in the Eighteenth-Century: Aristocracy and the Bourgeois Challenge* (London, 1972); William Doyle, *The Old European Order: 1660–1800* (Oxford, 1978); O. Hufton, *Europe: Privilege*

and Protest: 1730–1789 (London, 1980). The privileges of the English nobility during this period were far less extensive and less important than those of the continental aristocracies. Hume's experience, however, was European rather than narrowly Scottish or British. He twice lived for extended periods in France (1734–7 and 1763–6) and he travelled in Germany and Italy (1748–9). He also frequently resided in London. Hence his comments on the people ought not to be taken to refer specifically to Scotland or England, unless explicitly said to do so.

3. J.F.C. Harrison, *The Common People: A History from the Norman Conquest to the Present* (Aylesbury, 1984), 116.

4. Roy Porter, *English Society in the Eighteenth Century* (Bungay, 1982), 99.

5. For France see Harry Payne, *The Philosophes and the People* (Yale U.P., 1976), ch. 1 and H. Chisick, *The Limits of Reform in the Enlightenment: Attitudes to the Education of the Lower Classes in Eighteenth-Century France* (Princeton U.P., 1981), chs. 1 and 5. For England see Dorothy Marshall *The English Poor in the Eighteenth Century* (London, 1926); G.D.H. Cole and R. Postgate, *The Common People: 1746–1946* (London, 1971); K.D. Snell, *Annals of the Labouring Poor: Social Changes and Agrarian England, 1600–1900* (Cambridge U.P., 1985), as well as the works of Porter and Harrison cited above.

6. Pierre Goubert, *The Ancien Régime*, translated by Steve Cox (New York, 1973).

7. Gregory King's calculations of the social and economic breakdown of England for 1688 suggest that this is so. King shows just over 51% of the total population of 5,500,520 consuming more than it earned, so this section of the population, comprised of common seamen, labouring people and servants, cottagers and paupers, common soldiers and finally vagrants, must be regarded as living in poverty, and hence dependence. Unfortunately, the categories used by King are not so clear-cut as to allow us to assert that the rest were independent. King places all artisans (240,000) together, without distinguishing between masters and journeymen, and he similarly fails to distinguish between better-off and more humble shopkeepers and tradesmen (225,000). It is virtually certain that the majority in both categories were economically dependent. In the case of lesser freeholders (660,000) and farmers (750,000), it is much more likely that we are dealing with groups that in the main enjoyed economic independence, but even here families with small holdings or those suffering downward mobility would also have to be classed among the economically dependent. Even so, King's figures suggest that at least a third and possibly four-tenths of the population enjoyed economic independence.

King's figures are too early to be directly applicable to

Hume's time. Patrick Colquhoun's for 1814 are late, but also
suggestive, and may serve to balance King's. His categories are
also more easily used for our purposes. The élites of England
account for three of Colquhoun's seven categories, but only
1.56% of the total population of 17,096,803. The dependent
population is concentrated in the sixth class of 'Working
Mechanics, Artisans, Handicrafts, Agricultural Labourers and
others who subsist by labour in various employments with
their families' (8,792,800), the sub-category menial servants
(1,279,923), and the seventh class of paupers and vagrants
(1,828,170) and the separate category of non-commissioned
officers and men in the army and navy (862,000). The dependent
population, then, certainly comprised three-quarters (74.65%)
of the whole. Colquhoun's fourth class, consisting among
others of 'respectable Freeholders, Ship Owners, Merchants
and Manufacturers of the second class, Warehousemen and
respectable Shopkeepers, Artists, respectable Builders, Mechanics and Persons living on moderate incomes, with their
families' (1,168,250) seem to have been economically independent. With respect to the fifth class, which included 'Lesser
Freeholders, Shopkeepers of the second order, Inn-keepers,
Publicans and Persons engaged in miscellaneous occupations or
living on moderate incomes, with their families' (2,798,475),
we can be less sure. The same considerations which led us to
question the economic standing of lesser freeholders and small
shopkeepers in the 1688 document also hold here. Assuming
that only a third of Colquhoun's fifth class failed to achieve
relative economic success, then roughly 80% of the population
would have to be reckoned dependent. This is clearly less
favourable than the figures suggested by King, but still better
than the situation on most of the continent. King's and
Colquhoun's figures are conveniently available in Harrison, *The
Common People*, 114–15 and 232–34.

  While King's figures for population have been widely accepted
by scholars, his social categories have been subject to criticism.
In particular, he has been said to have significantly underestimated both the numbers and the wealth of the highest levels
of the social hierarchy, to have similarly underestimated the
numbers, wealth and variety of merchants, shopkeepers and
tradesmen, to have varied his estimates for farmers and freeholders by a factor of 3 (from 240,000 to 740,000) and to have used
excessively loose categories of classification, such as 'gentlemen'.
(G.S. Holmes, 'Gregory King and the Social Structure of Pre-
Industrial England', *Transactions of the Royal Historical Society*,
fifth series, vol. XXVII, 1977, 41–68). According to a recent
attempt to revise and correct King's tables, the seventeenth-
century statistician underestimated the numbers and wealth
of the better off and 'overstated the numbers in agriculture,

common labor and poverty'. (P.H. Lindert and J.G. Williamson, 'Revising England's Social Tables: 1688–1812', *Explorations in Economic History*, XIX, 1982, 390). If this is so, then the proportion of the comfortable and independent strata of English society would be greater than suggested by King's figures. Colquhoun's statistics are generally regarded as more reliable than King's, and if in need of revision, then in the opposite direction (ibid, 399). Colquhoun's figures for 1814, however, which were cited above, are considered less reliable than his 1801–3 figures, in that the statistics for the later period include Ireland, the data for which are questionable.

8. Nicholas Phillipson has recently emphasised the importance of the 'middling sort', which he carefully distinguished from the traditional bourgeoisie, in his IPSE lecture, 'A Social Historian's View of the Scottish Enlightenment'.

9. One notable exception for England is the autobiography of a textile worker who successfully set up as a bookseller. See William Hutton, *The Life of William Hutton* (London, 1817). I am indebted to Roger Emerson for bringing to my attention the memoirs of the servant John Macdonald, and the autobiographical writings of the clergyman John Brown of Haddington and James Hogg, both of whom began life among poor families. Daniel Roche has recently published the memoirs of a vitrier who belonged wholly to the lower classes. See *J.L. Ménétra: Journal de ma vie* (Paris, 1982).

10. See the extensive bibliogaphy in Peter Burke, *Popular Culture in Early Modern Europe* (London, 1968).

11. Hume is described as belonging to the gentry by J.B. Stewart, *The Moral and Political Philosophy of David Hume* (Westport, 1977), 7, and David Miller, *Philosophy and Ideology in Hume's Political Thought* (Oxford U.P., 1981), 2. In his brief autobiography, Hume proudly states that he was of 'good family' on both sides, and that his father's family belonged to the nobility, being 'a branch of the Earl of Home's'. 'My Own Life', in Es. xxxii.

12. The term 'politics' would no doubt have been acceptable to Hume, as he used it himself (as in the full title to the *Essays*), but he tended to put most social phenomena under the common rubric 'moral', which at the time was distinguished from the 'natural'. Hence the common opposition in the eighteenth century of the natural to the moral sciences. In the Introduction to the *Treatise*, Hume asserts that the sciences of logic, morals, criticism and politics include 'almost every thing' that it is important for man to know. (*A Treatise of Human Nature; Being an Attempt to Introduce the Experimental Method of Reasoning into Moral Subjects*, xx.) The full title of the work is indicative. I argue below that Hume would not readily have agreed that the people should be said to have a 'culture'. For Hume, culture

meant politeness or what we call 'higher culture', so that the notion of popular culture would have seemed to him a contradiction in terms.

13. Hume's statement here is descriptive. Elsewhere he writes prescriptively, 'Every person, if possible, ought to enjoy the fruits of his labour, in a full possession of all the necessaries, and many conveniences of life. No one can doubt, but such an equality is most suitable to human nature, and diminishes much less from the *happiness* of the rich than it adds to that of the poor' (Es. 265). This statement has been taken by W.L. Taylor and Edgar S. Furniss as proof that Hume wished to raise the standard of living of workers (see above, n.1; Furniss, *The Position of the Laborer in a System of Nationalism: A Study in the Labor Theory of the Later English Mercantilists*, Boston and New York, 1920, 180). Before accepting this interpretation, one should consider Hume's statement that ' 'Tis always observed, in years of scarcity, if it be not extreme, that the poor labour more, and really live better, than in years of great plenty, when they indulge themselves in idleness and riot' (Es. 635). This statement appears in all editions of 'Of Taxes' published between 1752 and 1768, but was removed from the 1770 edition. This may mean that Hume changed his mind on this point as he neared old age. For his views on the propensity toward idleness among men in general and the working population in particular, see below.

14. See, for example, Geoffrey Taylor, *The Problem of Poverty: 1660–1834* (London, 1969); Porter, *English Society*, 28–30 and 99–112; Harrison, *The Common People*, ch. 4; J.P. Gutton, *La Société et les pauvres en Europe: XVI–XVIIIe siècles* (Paris, 1974); and O. Hufton, *The Poor of Eighteenth-Century France: 1750–1789* (Oxford U.P., 1974).

15. David Hume, *The History of England* (London, 8 vols., 1812), vol. I, 360. Henceforth cited as *History*.

16. Ibid., 142; II, 364.

17. Ibid., I, 142; 227–8; II, 266.

18. Ibid., II, 365.

19. Hume, EM. 247–8. This is not a chance comment on Hume's part. He states in the *Treatise* that 'Nothing has a greater tendency to give us an esteem for any person, than his power and riches; or a contempt, than his poverty and meanness . . .' (T. 357). These sentiments are aroused naturally by the mechanism of '. . . *sympathy*, by which we enter into the sentiments of the rich and poor, and partake of their pleasures and uneasiness' (T. 362). As a direct response of our senses, these feelings are unconditioned and involuntary: ''Tis not with entire indifference we can survey either a rich man or a poor one, but *must* [my emphasis] feel some faint touches, at least, of respect in the former case, and of contempt in the latter' (T. 393).

20. *New Letters of David Hume*, 104; to Colonel Edmonstoune, 17 March 1771.

21. There seems to be a conflict here between Hume's sympathy for his friend and his conviction that charity should be given only to the 'not underserving'. Hume's saying to Edmonstoune that the woman in question had 'by all accounts degenerated very much from the primitive Innocence, in which you found her, and, I hope, left her . . .' (NL. 104) raises the possibility that his friend was perhaps responsible for her fall. This may in turn have influenced Hume's attitude to the case.

22. In the *History*, Hume fails to comment on the effect and implications of legislation on the poor passed in 1552, except to note that too extensive discretionary powers were granted the clergy in collecting the levy to finance the law (*History*, IV, 356). He is curiously silent on the Elizabethan poor law, noting simply that it was passed (*History* V, 483).

23. Hume, *Dialogues Concerning Natural Religion*, 208. Hume also approvingly cites William Temple to the effect that 'men naturally prefer ease before labour, and will not take pains if they can live idle . . .' (Es. 344). To judge by comments of Arthur Young and Joseph Townsend that 'Everyone but an idiot knows that the lower classes must be kept poor or they will never be industrious' and 'Hunger will tame the fiercest animals . . . In general, it is only hunger which can spur and goad the poor on to labour . . .' (cited in Porter, *English Society*, 146), Philo's opinion here seems unexceptional. John Wesley's assertion that the 'common opinion' that poverty was the result of idleness was unfounded (ibid., 102), suggests that it may well have been representative. Historians have pointed out that attitudes to work in pre-industrial societies were often loose, and that workers in fact often preferred leisure to increased income. See Harrison, *The Common People*, 144–5 and Porter, *English Society*, pp. 105–6. Moreover, Furniss, in the most extensive study of this question to date, finds a hardening of attitudes toward labourers over the eighteenth century which came to be expressed in widespread demands for 'rigorous life conditions to discipline the laborer and purge his character of the evil habits of "luxury" and "sloth" . . .' (*The Position of the Laborer*, 107). For the background to this discussion see ibid., chs. 5 and 6, and R.C. Wiles, 'The Theory of Wages in Later English Mercantilism', *Economic History Review*, second series, XXI (1968), 113–26, who argues that Furniss presents too pessimistic a picture of mercantilist wage theory.

24. *Dialogues*, 208. One cannot say with certainty which character in the *Dialogues* speaks for Hume, or whether indeed any one can be identified with him. However, the statements just cited go without contradiction or challenge from the other speakers.

25. *The Letters of David Hume*, 345; to Turgot, 5 August 1766. In his essay 'Of Taxes', Hume notes that it is usually assumed that increasing indirect taxes on commodities used by the people results either in depressing their standard of living or in raising wages, then adds, 'But there is a third consequence, which often follows upon taxes, namely, that the poor encrease their industry, perform more work, and live as well as before' (Es. 343). Hume further maintained that 'No Man is so industrious but he may add some Hours more in the Week to his Labour: And scarce any one is so poor but he can retrench something of his Expence' (L. 351; to Turgot, September 1766). During the eighteenth century the British government shifted the tax burden from landed proprietors to ordinary people by increasing indirect taxes (Porter, *English Society*, 29).

26. Burke, *Popular Cuture*.

27. Hume, L. 215; to Hugh Blair, 19 September 1763.

28. Burke follows R. Redfield in distinguishing between a literary 'great tradition' of the élites and a largely oral 'little tradition' of the people. *Popular Culture*, 23–4.

29. See also Payne, *The Philosophes and the People*, ch. 2.

30. Hume recognises that in 'ordinary things' philosophers do not differ from the 'vulgar' and that the people and philosophers sometimes share the same opinions (EU. 106, 89). Indeed, when misled by false doctrines, philosophers may well be farther from the truth than the 'vulgar'. For the most part, however, Hume contrasts the rational and critical capacities of philosophers to the ignorance, superstition and incapacities of the many.

31. Hume, 'The Natural History of Religion' in *Four Dissertations* (London, 1757; facsimile edition, New York, 1970), 6.

32. The many are brought to accept theism or monotheism not by reason, but by, 'the adulation and fears of the most vulgar superstition' (ibid., 46), and they are said to be 'incapable of conceiving those sublime qualities, which they seemingly attribute to the deity' (ibid., 51).

33. Ibid., 42.

34. Ibid., 20.

35. Ibid., 98.

36. Hume did, however, suggest that Negroes might be 'naturally inferior to the whites' (Es. 208, n. 10).

37. Es. 169; 'The Natural History of Religion', 6; and Es. 140. Hume does, however, frequently use the neutral phrase 'the generality of mankind' to designate the majority.

38. *Dialogues*, 167. In the eighteenth century a distinction was commonly made between the liberal and mechanical arts, and a carpenter certainly exercised one of the latter. The modifier, however, seems gratuitous.

39. *History*, II, 464; 463.

40. *History*, III, 6; 10. In the light of these expressions I would hesitate to accept Donald W. Livingston's assertion that 'Hume did not have the classical aristocrat's disdain for the masses', an assertion which he bases largely on the following citation from Hume's *Essays*: 'It has also been found, as the experience of mankind increases, that the *people* are no such dangerous monsters as they have been represented' (*Hume's Philosophy of Common Life*, Chicago U.P., 1984, 327). There were other contexts, however, in which Hume did indeed believe the people to be dangerous.

41. Erich Auerbach, *Mimesis*, translated by W.R. Trask (Princeton U.P.), 33–8.

42. Chisick, *Limits of Reform*, 48–52.

43. Jean Delumeau, *La Peur en occident* (Paris, 1978), 14–16.

44. Chisick, *Limits of Reform*, 52–68 and ch. 5. A.W. Coats traces the origin of this change in attitudes to the early part of the century in his article, 'Economic Thought and Poor Law Policy in the Eighteenth Century,' *Economic History Review*, series II, XIII (1960–61), 39–51. See also his related article, 'Changing Attitudes to Labour in the Mid-Eighteenth Century', in *Economic History Review*, series II, XI (1958). Gertrude Himmelfarb maintains that poverty stopped being taken for granted and began to be perceived as a problem around 1750 or 1760 (*The Idea of Poverty: England in the Early Industrial Age*, New York, 1985, p. 18).

45. The only passage I have found in which Hume emphasises the productive role of the lower classes is in the second volume of the *History*, which was published relatively late in his career, in 1762. There he speaks of rulers throughout Europe having 'embraced the salutary policy of encouraging the more industrious orders of the state; whom they found well disposed to obey the laws and the civil magistrate, and whose ingenuity and labour furnished commodities requisite for the ornament of peace and the support of war' (*History*, II, 273).

46. Payne, *The Philosophes and the People*, 165–9.

47. Es. 516. In fact, Hume raised the property qualification twice. In the 1752 edition of this essay he allowed all freeholders in the country and rate-payers in the towns, to attend primary assemblies. In the 1754 edition he required a ten pound minimal freehold for farmers and 200 pounds worth of property for townsmen. He retained these figures until 1768, when he again raised them. Ibid., 647. The significance of these figures is perhaps best explained by noting that in the second half of the eighteenth century, a freeholder of forty shillings (two pounds) was entitled to vote in parliamentary elections (J.S. Watson, *The Reign of George III: 1760–1815*, Oxford U.P., 1964, 132).

48. During the eighteenth century most unskilled labourers

in Britain earned on the average about fifteen pounds a year. Cole and Postgate, *The Common People*, ch. 6. See also Porter, *English Society*, 107–9.

49. Montesquieu maintained that though they were not capable of doing much else, the people could at least do this, *De l'Esprit des loix*, Bk II, ch. 2. In the 'Idea of a Perfect Commonwealth' Hume conceded that the people were good enough judges of the character of their immediate neighbours, or those close to them in rank (Es. 522). Elsewhere he observes, 'For though the people, collected in a body like the Roman tribes, be quite unfit for government, yet when dispersed in small bodies, they are more susceptible both of reason and order; the force of popular currents and tides is, in a great measure, broken; and the public interest may be pursued with some method and constancy' ('Of the First Principles of Government', Es. 36).

50. Hume, L. 238; to Colonel Edmonstoune, April 1764.

51. The question 'Est-il utile de tromper le peuple?' was proposed by the Berlin Academy as the subject of its essay contest for 1780. The responses in French were published by W. Krauss, *Est-il utile de tromper le peuple? Ist der Volksbetrug von Nutzen? Concours de la classe de philosophie spéculative de l'Académie des Sciences et des Belles-Lettres de Berlin pour l'année 1780* (Berlin, 1966).

52. Harry Payne has pointed out that the Enlightenment favoured a responsible élitism (*The Philosophes and the People*, 188–90). It remains a thoroughgoing and undemocratic élitism none-the-less.

53. This is certainly the view of Peter Gay in *The Enlightenment: an Interpretation* (New York, 2 vols., 1966–9). See especially the first chapter of volume one, 'The Useful and Beloved Past'.

54. For crowd actions in London in the eighteenth century see George Rudé, *The Crowd in History* (New York, 1964) and *Paris and London in the Eighteenth Century: Studies in Popular Protest* (Bungay, 1978). Roger Emerson has pointed out that there were riots in Edinburgh in 1705, 1725, 1736, 1766 and 1779.

55. On Wilkes's supporters see Rudé, *The Crowd*, 52, 61 and 267 and Watson, *The Reign of George III*, 64, 131 and 139. Two full-length studies of Wilkes are G. Rudé, *Wilkes and Liberty: a Social Study of 1763 to 1774* (Oxford U.P., 1962) and A. Williamson, *Wilkes: 'A Friend to Liberty'* (London, 1974).

56. Rudé, *The Crowd*, 219; Watson, *The Reign of George III*, 134, 139. Wilkes, however, had attacked Scots in general, and Hume in particular. Mossner, *Life*, pp. 552–3.

57. Hume, L. 427; to Hugh Blair, 28 March 1769.

58. L. 454; to William Strahan, 11 March 1771.

59. L. 422; to Baron Mure of Caldwell, 18 October 1768; L. 441, to William Strahan, 13 March 1770.

60. L. 434; to William Strahan, 25 October 1769.

61. L. 453; to William Strahan, 21 January 1771.

62. L. 455; to William Strahan, 25 March 1771. Hume may, as Donald Livingston asserts, have seen the Wilkes riots as 'a violent eruption of metaphysics into politics' (*Hume's Philosophy*, 324–5), and he may, too, have included the 'entire Whig literary and political establishment' in epithets such as mob and scum (ibid., 328). But surely he was chiefly troubled at the prospect of the common people, who, in his view, had no place in politics, playing a role there.

63. L. 423; to the Comtesse de Boufflers, 23 December 1768.

64. *History*, II, 461.

65. Ibid., 463.

66. Ibid.

67. *History*, III, 6.

68. Ibid.

69. Ibid., 8. He objected, however, to their being imposed by force. Ibid., 9.

70. Ibid., 10–11.

71. Ibid., 11.

72. See, for example, the Peasant Code in Roger Mettam (ed.) *Government and Society in Louis XIV's France* (Toronto, 1977), 246–8.

73. *History*, III, 196–7.

74. Ibid., 205; VI, 93.

75. Ibid., III, 183.

76. Ibid., 275.

77. See, for example, ibid., II, 342–3 and III, 45–6 and 142.

78. Boswell, *Life of Johnson*, Everyman Edition, pp. 395–6.

79. Benevolence, in Hume's view, cannot be compelled. Nor can it be much relied on. He observes that '. . . private benevolence is, and ought to be, weaker in some persons than in others: And in many, or indeed most persons, must absolutely fail' (T. 483). He also asserts that experience teaches that '. . . the generosity of men is very limited, and that it seldom extends beyond their friends and family, or, at most, beyond their native country' (T. 612).

80. Hume actually does posit a state of society radically different from that obtaining at his time. This is the anarchic condition, referred to above, of a dissolution of society that breaks down all order and renders life utterly precarious. This, of course, is a negative utopia whose purpose is to make us value the existing order more highly.

We might also note that the essay 'Idea of a Perfect Commonwealth' contains the suggestion of a fundamental change, in making wealth the criterion of political enfranchisement while quietly ignoring rank and privilege. Though the demand for rule by the wealthiest 10% or so of the population is retrograde today, it was not so in the eighteenth century. At Hume's time, far less than 10% of adult males had any role in politics, while privilege was decisive. Thus Hume's suggestion that enfranchisement be based on property, which can be taken as a measure of ability in a way that birth cannot, was, in the context of the time, progressive. It may also be worth remarking that Hume's proposal for a franchise based on the ownership of property is in substance the same as those put forward by Turgot in his 'Mémoire sur les municipalités' and by Holbach in the article 'Representatives' in the *Encyclopédie*.

2

ANNETTE C. BAIER

Hume on Women's Complexion[1]

I begin with two quotations from Hume's *Essays: Moral and Political*, of 1741–2. Writing against polygamy, after making a sort of case for it, he says, 'it may be urged with better reason that this sovereignty of the male is real usurpation, and destroys that nearness of rank, not say equality, which nature has established between the sexes' (Es. 184).[2] In 'The Rise and Progress of the Arts and Sciences', discussing the way the stronger, such as young adults, will not, in a 'polite' society, flaunt their superior strength disagreeably over the weaker, such as the old, but will display a studied deference, to allay the weaker's fears of contempt, he goes on: 'Gallantry is nothing but an instance of the same generous attention. As nature has given *man* the superiority above *woman*, by endowing him with greater strength both of mind and body; it is his part to alleviate that superiority, as much as possible, by the generosity of his behaviour, and by a studied deference and complaisance for all her inclinations and opinions' (Es. 132–3).

So *has* nature established a nearness of rank, not to say equality, between the sexes, or was that remark mere gallantry? A pall of gallantry obscures much that Hume published about women, and what survives of what he wrote to women. Some of *their* letters to *him*, by contrast, show an assumption of equality unmarred by excessive politeness. 'Most satisfactory, dear Phil, is your account of all your animal functions. God long preserve thy five wits . . .' writes that merry widow, Alison Rutherford Cockburn, in 1768,[3] responding to a letter we (or I) do not have, and which may, by the reply it elicited, have avoided gallantry. In all Alison Cockburn's letters to Hume the tone is intimate, affectionate, and disrespectful. Earlier, in 1764, during his 'French affair', after describing herself as 'the uncultured daughter of Caledon', she writes warning her 'dear Phil' of the dangers of foreign flatterers: 'Idol of Gaul, I worship thee not . . . Idol of a foolish people, be not puffed up!' She signs herself 'the sincere friend and willing servant of Mr. Hume, A Cockburn', then adds a

postscript saying 'your tall cuz Miss Hume is now Countess of
Hume. Most of our Misses pay dear for their coronets, as they are
yet ignorant of the polite method of mending what is amiss at
Home . . .', then in a second postscript, she innocently adds
'Compliments to Madam Bouflours'.[4] When in 1766 Hume is
expected back from Paris, she writes, 'but what shall we do with
you? You are spoiled; its impossible for me to retain you. I am a
Christian. I neither paint nor fricassy. My wit is much abated, but
I can play at quadrille and sleep with you. Will that do? . . .'[5] No
wonder that Hume (in a letter to Hugh Blair of 1 July 1766, L.
334) expresses uneasiness about the consequences for his reputation
of his correspondence with such a formidable and free Scotswoman,
one whom he suspects of circulating copies of his letters to herself
and her friends, especially those concerning his dealings with
Rousseau, which had high current news or gossip value. (He
seems to have succeeded in preventing the circulation of his
letters to her. None are known to survive.) Hume consults her
about what house to take (she rules out one of Allan Ramsay's
houses for its sunless north aspect), and apparently also about
what woman to marry – she at any rate writes back to him in
1768, 'You see I have answered all your commissions faithfully. I
want the size, complexion, age and fortune of your wife. Send me
that, and the thing is done . . .'[6] That she had any commission to
find Hume not merely a house, but also a wife, is highly doubtful,
although there is a letter from Hume to Baron Mure, two years
later, once he has decided to build a house in the new St Andrews
Square, in which he says: 'I am engag'd in the building of a
house, which is the second great Operation of human Life: for the
taking of a Wife is the first, which I hope will come in time . . .'
(L. 451). Greig, the editor of the letters, takes this hope to refer to
Nancy Orde, as it may well. It seems that it took Hume most of
his lifetime (he was in his sixtieth year when he wrote this letter)
to get the resolve to embark on the first great operation of life.
(His earlier entanglement with Hyppolyte de Saujon, Comptesse
de Boufflers-Rouverel, seems free of any matrimonial intentions,
certainly on her part and probably on his also.) I shall later
suggest that, after his own exposé of the artifice of Christian
marriage as it existed in his time, he had every reason, as a
benevolent and sympathetic person, to hesitate to take on the role
of husband, a role he had analysed with ruthless clarity in the
Treatise, and whose variants he continues to scrutinise in essays
such as 'Of Polygamy and Divorces', 'Of Love and Marriage',
'A Dialogue'.

I have cited one woman's views of her 'dear Phil', David

Hume, before proceeding to look at his views about 'the weak and pious sex, as David Hume calls us',[7] because it is only right and properly Humean to add their views of him to his of them. I have chosen Alison Rutherford Cockburn's views because of their refreshing directness, so different from the epistolatory 'petite voix flutée' (as Madame du Deffand maliciously described it)[8] of the Comptesse de Boufflers to her 'cher Maître'. Where the latter combines sycophancy with relentless egotism, Alison Cockburn combines disrespect with affectionate concern. She mocks Hume's religious scepticism and moral fatalism, and her actions seem to bear out her suspicion that 'for all the adulation you have met with amongst them [French women], that I am infinitely more your affectionate friend and servant . . .'.[9] She strikes the reader as a more trustworthy witness than her main French rival. In her own verse self-portrait she accuses herself of some failings, but not of insincerity or selfishness. Her failings were, she says, ones that 'neither the Bible has taught me to amend them, Nor David Hume to be easy under them'.[10] (Her friend Lord Alemore amends or supplements this with: 'But neither hath the Bible taught me to dread a future state, Nor David Hume to be indifferent about it.')[11]

So what were the views of this near universal favourite of the women who knew him[12] concerning female human nature? The first thing to be clear about is that Hume combined a conviction that there were constants in human behaviour, that there is such a thing as human nature, with the conviction that 'the different stations of life influence the whole fabric, external and internal; and these different stations arise necessarily, because uniformly, from the necessary and uniform principles of human nature' (T. 402). There will always be, he believed, some equivalent of day labourers, whose work will be different from, say, a lawyer's work, and whose 'skin, pores, muscles and nerves' will therefore be different. He seems to see women as also occupying a special 'station' that affects their skin, muscles and nerves. 'There are different trees, which regularly produce fruit, whose relish is different from each other; and this regularity will be admitted as an instance of necessity and causes in external bodies. But are the products of *Guienne* and of *Champagne* more regularly different than the sentiments, actions, and passions of the two sexes, of which the one are distinguish'd by their force and maturity, the other by their delicacy and softness?' (T. 401) This regularly occurring greater delicacy and softness however, must not be thought to be necessarily any *inferiority*, since 'delicacy' of taste, if not always of sentiment, is a Humean virtue in any person, and

Hume valued what he saw as the 'softness' of women for its civilising influence on those whose 'force' might otherwise become 'rough and boisterous' (Es. 6).

> 'What better school for manners than the company of virtuous women; where the mutual endeavour to please must insensibly polish the mind, where the example of female softness and modesty must communicate itself to their admirers, and where the delicacy of that sex puts every one on his guard lest he give offense by any breach of decency?' (Es. 134)

'Delicacy' and 'softness' seem more suitable terms for the Comptesse de Boufflers, as portrayed by Carmontelle, than for Alison Rutherford Cockburn, who fancied that she looked like Elizabeth of England, dressed to accentuate that likeness, and whose manner seems to have verged on the boisterous and bossy, for all her contentment to remain in a domestic station, and to leave not merely most of the writing but also the critical judging of writing to the men.[13] Hume relished the liveliness of his Scottish women friends, as well as the more 'polished' conversation of his Paris women admirers, but he does not seem to have expected women to be full participants at 'the feast of reason'. After the above quoted remarks about the beneficial effects of female company, he added, in some editions of that essay:

> 'I must confess, That my own particular choice rather leads me to prefer the company of a few select companions, with whom I can, calmly and peaceably, enjoy the feast of reason, and try the justness of every reflection, whether gay or serious, that may occur to me. But as such a delightful company is not every day to be met with, I must think, that mixt companies, without the fair-sex, are the most insipid entertainment in the world, and destitute of gaiety and politeness, as much as of sense and reason. Nothing can keep them from excessive dulness but hard drinking; a remedy worse than the disease' (Es. 626).

These 'confessions' show that although Hume expected women readers, and had women translators,[14] he no more expected women to be included in that select group who would help him try the justness of his reflections than he expected them to be among the hard drinkers. Is this because of the sort of upbringing and education they received in his day, or because of some less variable difference between them and his select male companions? Did he think that women were excluded from the feast of reason by historical and changeable factors, or by their 'natural' difference of station from men? In recommending the study of history to women, in one of the essays he later suppressed, he speaks to and of them as 'debarred the severer studies, by the tenderness of their complexion and the weakness of their education' (Es. 565). Is it their natural complex of essential characteristics, or the weakness of their eighteenth-century education, which excludes them from the feast of reason? And how, if they *are* excluded, can they have a 'nearness of rank, not to say equality' with men? It is Hume's answer to this question, of what female weaknesses are due to variable historical factors, what to unvarying causes, that is hardest to discern.

A 'trivial and anatomical observation' of the different roles of male and female in human reproduction enables us, Hume writes, to derive 'that vast difference betwixt the education and duties of the two sexes' (T. 571). Because women bear children, and men do not, a man requires an 'artificial' guarantee of his parenthood of a given child that no woman requires (at least not at the moment of birth). A wife's duty is to be chaste, because of her husband's underprivileged epistemological position, when it comes to certainty of parenthood, along with his 'limited generosity' when it comes to child rearing. Unwilling to 'labour for the maintenance and education' (T. 571) of their wives' children unless assured that those children are also 'really their own', and unable to get any natural assurance to this effect, they need the social artifice of female chastity 'to give them some security in this particular' (ibid.). All women's sexual freedom must thus be severely abridged so that men can remain free to refuse to participate in the rearing of children who are not reasonably deemed to be 'really their own'. As Hume analyses it, the rationale of the artifice of marriage, with its double standard, is to provide children with parental care from parents of each sex, by unnaturally curbing women's sexual freedom, rather than by forcing men to be less choosy about which children are supported by their 'fatigues and expenses' (T. 570). Hume does not even contemplate an artificial virtue of male 'fatherliness' as an alternative to the artificial virtue of female modesty and chastity. Indeed he presents the matter as the problem of 'inducing the men to impose on themselves this restraint', namely the restraint of remaining with the mother of their 'own' children long enough to assist in bringing up those children. The men are 'restrained', it seems, by *any* paternal responsibilities, so that both sexes are unnaturally restrained by marriage, by Hume's account of it. The women are made to be unnaturally chaste, and the men made to be unnaturally cheerful about child rearing responsibilities. To ask them to be generous in assumption of responsibility as well as

cheerful in discharge of it would be to ask too much, more than
male human nature would stand. So the only viable artifice which
can hope to provide children with full parental care is that of
female modesty and wifely chastity.

Several features of this account of marriage and marital duties
are noteworthy. First is Hume's agreement with the Christian
tradition that the 'end' of marriage is the production and care of
children. It is an artifice for the proper regulating of human
reproduction. Everything Hume writes about it, both in this first
discussion and later, keeps paramount the question of the good of
children. Hume's first reason for opposing voluntary divorce and
against treating marriage as simply a contract, whose terms could
vary from case to case, is that adopting such measures would be
'putting it into the power of parents, upon every caprice, to
render their posterity miserable' (Es. 188). The children's good is
the main thing to be kept in view.

Secondly, we should note that for Hume, as for Grotius and
Pufendorf before him, the root cause of asymmetrical marital
duties is men's natural uncertainty concerning paternity, an
uncertainty Hume may himself have experienced in the Agnes
Galbraith affair.[15] However, where Grotius and Pufendorf see the
remedy for this uncertainty to be the subordination of wife to
husband, so that she is under his control,[16] Hume makes no
mention of any artificial virtue of wifely obedience, but takes
female *chastity*, not wifely submission, to be the artificial remedy
for the male epistemological predicament. It is society as a whole,
not individual husbands with authority over their wives, who
demand chastity of mothers and mothers-to-be, on the Humean
story. The institution of marriage that Hume describes in the
Treatise as socially useful does impose more restraints on wives
than on husbands, but does not incorporate any individual male
right to rule, nor any duty of wifely submission. These conventional Christian rights and duties are not endorsed in any of
Hume's versions of a reflectively affirmable morality.

Thirdly we should note Hume's economic assumptions: that
fathers will be needed to shoulder the expenses of child rearing.
Hume later considers (in 'Of Moral Prejudices') the possibility
that an independently wealthy mother could do without this
particular paternal contribution to successful reproduction, but
he portrays no mothers who work and earn outside the home.
Some women become queens, thus govern as well as become
wives and mothers, others may inherit enough wealth to be
economically independent of the fathers of their children, but
Hume does not explore the possibility that mothers might them-

selves bring home the bacon, rather than cure it in the home, or engage in more genteel domestic pursuits while waiting for their fathers, brothers, or husbands to bring it home. Women's station, as Hume usually sees it, is domestic, whatever else it may be or become. (I will later discuss one place where this assumption may be seen as questioned.) In his essay 'Of the Immortality of the Soul' he jokingly accuses 'the religious theory' of having an inadequate account of 'the inferiority of women's capacity'. If both sexes are in for an eternal life of spiritual exertion, then 'the one sex has an equal task to perform with the other: their powers of reason and resolution ought also to have been equal, and both of them infinitely greater than at present', whereas 'on the theory of the soul's mortality, the inferiority of women's capacity is easily accounted for: Their domestic life requires no higher faculties either of mind or body', (Es. 593). Hume here is clearly teasing the religious, by turning on them the charge of social radicalism, or taunting them with the contradiction between their official theory and their actual practices towards women. It is hard from this passage to know much of what he himself thought about women's powers of reason and resolution, but no other passages directly challenge the assumption that women's life must be domestic. The assumption is one about a fixed division of station. Given that women are bearing and breast-feeding children, then home may have seemed to be the logical place for them, for at least those child-bearing years of their life, and, as Hume notes in the *Treatise*, 'tho' all these maxims have a plain reference to generation, yet women past child-bearing have no more privilege in this respect, than those who are in the flower of their youth and beauty. . . . The general rule carries us beyond the original principle' (T. 573), so the place of women of whatever age is seen to be primarily the home. There they may spin or weave, if more leisured they may read Hume's *History*, or translate it into French, or even paint or write a little song or essay themselves, or, if the home is a palace, have to govern a nation as well as a family, but they are *not* expected to be lawyers, judges, members of the clergy, professors, physicians, politicians, or commercial entrepreneurs, nor to occupy any other position in that 'middle station of life' which Hume valued so highly as 'favourable to the acquiring of *Wisdom* and *Ability* as well as of *Virtue*' (Es. 547). 'A man so situate' has no reason to envy others, Hume says, but no women are thought to be so happily situated. The best women can hope for, it seems, is to be the daughters, wives, mothers, the readers, translators, or portrait painters[17] of such lucky lamps of enlightenment and depositories of civilisation.

Having noted the domesticity limitation, which I take to be an assumption on Hume's part concerning bio-socio-economic constants in human society, I turn now to the psychological assumptions Hume makes in his account of marriage. As the passage cited from 'Of the Immortality of the Soul', as well as many another passage suggests, Hume expects a correlation between station and psychology. If not divine design, then at least some sort of natural selection or role adaptation by causal conditioning, will ensure that there be a sort of 'fit' between psychology and station. Is women's 'softness' a functional virtue in a domestic companion? Is female 'inferiority of mind' a natural concomitant of socially induced female modesty? Before answering those questions about female psychology, as Hume finds it in a marriage-regulated society, first we should note the assumptions Hume makes about female psychology in his story about the origin and rationale for marriage itself. He assumes, first, that women are 'ductile' (T. 572), capable of being trained to an unnatural modesty, which enables them to resist 'the strongest imaginable' (T. 571) temptation to 'a pleasure, to which nature has inspir'd so strong a propensity' (T. 572). These quotations reveal not just the assumed docility of women, but also the second assumption Hume makes, one concerning the healthiness of women's sexual appetites. 'Modest women', for Hume, are certainly not indifferent to sexual pleasure. The companion volume to *The Whole Duty of Man*, against which Hume tells us he developed his ethics,[18] was a now forgotten amusing little volume by the same anonymous author, entitled *The Ladies' Calling*, and prefaced with the biblical proclamation that 'a Woman that Feareth the Lord, she shall be praised'. In its chapter 'On Modesty' we find the claim that, in all sound philosophers and divines:

> 'an Impudent woman is look'd on as a kind of Monster, a thing diverted and distorted from its proper form. That there is indeed a strange repugnancy to nature needs no other evidence than the struggling, and difficulty in the first violations of Modesty, which alwaies begin with regrets and blushing, and require a good deal of Self-denial, much of vicious Fortitude, to encounter with the recoilings and upbraidings of their own minds'.[19]

Where this puritan author, remembered now mainly for Hume's disdain for him, sees the sexually bold woman as a 'monster', and sexual intercourse as initially requiring female self denial and fortitude, Hume sees female modesty as a 'conspicuous instance' (T. 570) of social artifice, a going against nature that requires considerable self denial on the part of normal naturally sensual and promiscuously inclined women. Thirdly, women's maternal feelings are assumed to be strong and generous. They do not, like fathers, have to 'restrain' themselves in order to take on the care of children. A 'fond mother' (EM. 300) gladly ruins her health for her sick child, and may die of grief when 'freed, by its death, from the slavery of that attendance' (ibid.).

We must here be careful not to exaggerate the difference Hume supposes there to be between maternal and paternal concern. He does indeed suppose that fathers have a 'natural affection' (T. 478) for their children, an affection that will lead them not to neglect them. Paternal solicitude is a *natural* virtue – the moral sentiment endorses the natural tendency of fathers to love and care for their children. But fathers are nevertheless described as having to impose a 'restraint' on themselves in order to 'prolong their union' with their children's mothers long enough to help in child rearing. A man does naturally have both a desire for 'propagation of his kind' (EM. 191) and a 'natural instinct' to 'give a loose to love and tenderness' to those he believes to be his children, but this latter instinct wars with his equally natural promiscuity, his instinct for non-monogamy. As Hume puts it in 'Of Polygamy and Divorces', 'the heart of man delights in liberty' (Es. 187), and enjoys 'that *variety* that is so agreeable in love' (ibid.), so that any 'confinement' of the objects of the amorous passion will be by artifice not nature. This is as true of women as of men, on Hume's account, but women do not 'naturally' (that is, in the hypothetical state of nature) have to choose, as men may, between indulgence of parental and of amorous affection. Hume assumes, like most writers (Hobbes, Rousseau) that the children will 'naturally' remain with the mother, whether she is chaste or not, and whether or not the father stays. The artifice of marriage reverses this asymmetry. It enables fathers to know and keep their children, while indulging, outside marriage, their wish for agreeable variety of sexual partner;[20] while it threatens mothers with separation from their children should they be found to have been unchaste. The psychological assumptions that Hume makes in this account about men's and women's natural motivation are that while both sexes are instinctively promiscuous, welcoming erotic pleasure from a variety of sexual partners, and instinctively concerned for the welfare of those they take to be their own children, in men the former instinct tends to dominate the latter, especially when there is any doubt about paternity. Marriage, and training for marriage, warps female human nature more than it warps male human nature, but then women are 'ductile'. Marriage gives women full indulgence of their maternal affections, at the cost of regulating or thwarting their erotic instincts. (Hume thinks that 'whoever dreams of raptures and extasies beyond the honey-month, is a fool' (Es. 628).) It artificially encourages men's paternal instincts while only weakly restraining their erotic instincts. If all goes well it satisfies both men's and women's natural wish for lasting friendship. 'So sober an affection . . . as friendship, rather thrives under constraint, and never rises to such a height, as when any strong interest or necessity binds two persons together, and gives them some common object of pursuit. We need not, therefore, be afraid of drawing the marriage-knot, which chiefly subsists by friendship, the closest possible' (Es. 189) writes Hume, making his case against divorce by mutual consent. The 'constraint' imposed by marriage is greater on wives than on husbands, but both are constrained. Women may be more 'ductile' than men, but men too can adapt to circumstances: 'the heart of man naturally submits to necessity, and soon loses an inclination, when there is an absolute impossibility of gratifying it' (Es. 188). Contented marriages for life are therefore deemed possible, even if 'I have often had thoughts of . . . writing a panegyric upon marriage: But, in looking around for materials, they seemed to be of so mixed a nature, that at the conclusion of my reflections, I found that I was as much dispos'd to write a satyr' (Es. 558).

Hume's version of marriage, in the *Treatise*, and later, is no panegyric. Is it a 'satyr'? What evaluation does he make of the artifice whose variants continued to interest him throughout his writings? (His first extant writing is a student essay on courtly love, and in his last-written volume of the *History of England* he dwells with fascination on canon law, incest prohibitions, and breaches of them. In chapter II, for example, he tells of the passion and the horrible fate of the royal cousin-spouses Elgiva and Edwy.) To have condemned the social institution of marriage would have been radical indeed, perhaps more radical than his condemnation of 'priestly inventions' and their 'monstrous doctrines' (T. 524). Although Christian marriage is affected by monstrous doctrines of priestly invention, other forms of marriage are not found to be any better, by Hume's standards, and he finds no alternative to marriage, no superior method of looking after the interest society has and must have in the proper care of children. As I read him, his attitude to marriage is pessimistic resignation to an imperfect artifice, tempered now and again with a more radically inspired gentle challenge to women, as if he were saying to them 'are you *really* so ductile that you will put up with this?'.

At the conclusion of the *Treatise* account, Hume says that lack of chastity in women, or at least in wives and would-be wives, is disapproved of by 'those who have an interest in the fidelity of women' and that 'those, who have no interest, are carried along with the stream' (T. 572. He later added, 'and are also apt to be affected with Sympathy for the general Interests of Society'. See T. 671.) This, he says, is the whole explanation of the status of female chastity as a virtue. It suits the interest of *some* that women be chaste, and a general interest of society is served by requiring them to be chaste. Who have an interest in the fidelity of women? The women themselves? Or are they 'carried along with the stream'? In as far as mothers want the fathers of their children to help support them, this artifice could be one that women reasonably want, provided that this is the best way of ensuring paternal care. Is it, for female as well as male children, an 'infinitely advantageous' artifice (T. 498) to be given paternal care at the cost of unnatural restraint imposed on all women and girls? It seems to me pretty clear that clear-sighted Hume had his doubts about that, as well as about male sovereignty in marriage.[21]

He began his account of the artificial virtues with the claim that such virtues consisted in obedience to conventions which were the constitutive rules of social artifices that were 'infinitely advantageous to the whole and every part' (T. 498) of society. He made this claim for property rules, the claim, that is, that despite inequities and basically 'frivolous' principles determining property rights, every proprietor, even the unluckiest, when he considers institution of private property as it exists, as compared with the absence of any settled property rights, 'must find himself a gainer, on ballancing the account' (T. 497). Does Hume believe that, on balancing the account, every woman will find herself a gainer from the institution of marriage as he knew it? Or is this a case of the sort he recognised to be possible in the *Enquiry Concerning the Principles of Morals*, where an artifice exploits the powerlessness of some of those it affects? (EM. 190–2). He there says that women cannot be in this position, victims of an artifice that sacrifices their interests to those of others, since they are not powerless, and have the means to make felt the effects of any resentment they see cause to feel. He then significantly goes on to remind us that no individual possesses 'within himself every faculty, requisite both for his own preservation and for the propagation of his kind' (EM. 191), so that 'mutual regards and forebearance' are only prudent. The 'conjunction of the sexes' is established in nature, and from it arises justice and 'the gradual enlargement of our regards to justice' (ibid.). One could scarcely get a stronger hint of what sort of 'power to make the effects of their resentment felt' women have, nor of what prudent considerations should assist men to enlarge their conceptions of justice.

Nor is this an isolated radical passage. Ten years earlier, in Vol. II of *Essays Moral and Political* (1742), Hume published an incendiary little essay entitled 'Of Moral Prejudices', in which he describes two departures from sexual stereotype: a man overly dependent on wife and daughter, and a woman exhibiting an extreme degree of independence from men. Her story, presented as a report in a letter from a French friend, was to be later taken up and discussed by Diderot in his letters to Sophie Volland. It is the story of a wealthy aristocratic young 'philosophical heroine' (Es. 543), who is determined to avoid marital servitude, but wants a child. So she selects a suitable father (picking him out of a crowd in the parterre of a theatre, and inviting him to call), subjects him to various intelligence and character tests which he passes, then encourages him in intimacies which lead to her pregnancy. He is then turned out – with reluctance, since 'gladly wou'd she have continu'd her Friendship with the Father; but finding him too passionate a Lover to remain within the Bounds of Friendship, she was oblig'd to put a Violence upon herself' (Es. 543). She denies him any access to herself or their child, claiming in an ensuing lawsuit that this had been their agreement. The case is left still before the courts. Hume the author precedes the tale with the ironic(?) remark that 'it contains such an Instance of a Philosophic Spirit as I think pretty extraordinary, and may serve as an Example not to depart too far from the receiv'd Maxims of Conduct and Behaviour, by a refin'd Search after Happiness or Perfection' (Es. 542). This pretty extraordinary essay of Hume's was quickly withdrawn. He writes to Charles Erskine that he withdrew it, along with 'Of Essay Writing' and 'Of the Middle Station in Life', as 'frivolous and finical' (L. 63), but in this case he might also have had reasons of prudence. Did it cause an outcry in 1742? We (I) do not know. 'Of Essay Writing' contains his somewhat patronising reference to 'the Fair Sex, who are the Sovereigns of the Empire of Conversation. I approach them with Reverence . . .' (Es. 535), and to his self appointment as 'a Kind of Resident or Ambassador from the Dominions of Learning to those of Conversation' (ibid.). This essay may have been rightly withdrawn as 'frivolous', and offensively gallant, but 'Of Moral Prejudices' surely avoids gallantry. More likely Hume's professorial ambitions and prudence explain this radical essay's short public life, in his own lifetime. At the same time that he was withdrawing it from the 1748 edition, however, he was engaged in writing the *Enquiry Concerning the Principles of Morals,* and perhaps thought he had succeeded there in inserting his radical feminist ideals in more decent disguise.[22] For, after all, there is a paragraph break between his claim that women have the power to defeat any male conspiracy against them, and his pointed remarks about the need for the two sexes to co-operate if any male individual is to succeed, and know he has succeeded, in 'the propagation of his kind'.

Hume has a clear eye for power relations and their determinants. He lays bare the facts about production, reproduction, and access to knowledge, facts which determine the relationship between men and women, and leaves it for the reader, especially the female reader, to draw her own conclusions. This may be a more realistic policy than that, say, of J.S. Mill, who naïvely seemed to have thought that male moral tracts urging men to share power and privileges with women would effect any change. Hume saw that change would come only when the oppressed felt resentment, and used what power they have to make the oppressors feel the effects of their resentment. He saw very clearly both the causes of women's social inferiority, and what could alter that.

It is not surprising that the Hume who wrote the *Treatise* chapter on chastity and modesty, the essays 'Of Moral Prejudices', 'Of Love and Marriage', and the chapter on justice in the *Enquiry Concerning the Principles of Morals,* should hesitate to take on the role of husband. What of the older Hume, the ex-diplomat, the historian, and the one who at least pretended to be looking for a wife to share his St Andrews Square house? Had he changed his mind? Does the *History* show a different attitude to female human nature than the *Treatise,* early essays, and *Enquiries?*

Hume's remarks about the attractive 'softness' of Mary Queen of Scots and the lack of that softness in Elizabeth of England, have been cited by feminist critics of Hume as proof of his sexism. Speaking of Mary, he says:

> Ambitious and active in her temper, yet inclined to cheerfulness and society; of a lofty spirit, constant, and even vehement, in her purpose, yet polite, and gentle, and affable in her demeanour; she seemed to partake only so much of the male virtues as to render her estimable, without relinquishing those soft graces which compose the proper ornament of her sex (H. ch. XLII, year 1587).

Elizabeth, by contrast receives this comment: 'When we contemplate her as a woman, we are apt to be struck with the highest admiration of her great qualities and extensive capacity; but we are also apt to require some more softness of disposition, some lenity of temper, some of those amiable weaknesses by which her sex is distinguished' (H. end of ch. XLIV). But this is said to be what those influenced by a durable and natural *prejudice* 'founded on consideration of her sex' are apt to think, and Hume contrasts such a judgement with 'the true method of estimation, to lay aside all these considerations, and consider her merely as "a rational being plac'd in authority, and intrusted with the government of mankind"' (ibid.). Looked at this way, she counts for Hume among the eight English sovereigns of great capacity out of twenty-eight, since the Norman Conquest (Es. 548). She had, he says in the *History*, 'singular talents for government'. Nor is the quoted passage about Mary's amiable weaknesses intended as summary praise of Mary on Hume's part. For he goes on to say how this amiable woman with her soft graces 'abandoned herself to the guidance of a profligate man', so that 'an account of her conduct must in some parts wear the aspect of severe satire and invective', (continuation of earlier quoted paragraph from H. ch. XLII). Hume's treatment of Mary outraged many Scots, and neither his judgement about her nor about her Calvinist enemies[23] was a favourable one. What he is saying about these two women is that one was *not* to most men's fancy as a wife or mistress, but governed superbly, the other was well suited to please men (while also exciting the violent but perhaps also pleasurable denunciation of the Calvinists) but her amiable weaknesses led to murders, mutiny, and her own execution. As a rational being put in authority over others she performed badly. Her special position enabled her to indulge her amorous inclinations without the usual female fear of 'bad fame', but she did this without enough concern for political and national consequences. Hume as historian distances himself from the puritan criticisms of her sexual self indulgence, but not from criticisms of her imprudence and her irresponsibility in her public role.

Queens at work were the only 'working women', in the sense that excludes domestic work, that Hume discussed or assessed. In his assessment of women governors he shows neither gallantry nor other forms of that 'durable because natural prejudice' that would restrict women to domestic roles. Or rather, he at least notes and discounts any such prejudice when he allows it expression. And he notes as a peculiar oddity that form of the prejudice which would not recognise the legitimacy of any woman ruler. As Hume reproves the anti-Semitic rulers such as Edward I, not just for cruelty but for their stupidity in not welcoming the contribution Jews were making to the nation's life (H. chs. X, XII, XIII), so he regards discrimination against women rulers as plainly foolish.

But he assumes, like everyone else, that sons will succeed ruler parents before daughters do, this being the time-honoured custom, as is the custom that older sons have precedence over younger sons. *Some* rules of precedence are unavoidable, and some arbitrariness in these rules is also seen as unavoidable. Women take second place to men, as younger sons take second place to older sons, and as Hume the younger son had come to accept that latter rule with cheerfulness, so he assumed that most royal women would accept the customary rules of succession, and not feel slighted by them.

Perhaps the most praised woman in the *History* is Lady Jane Grey, who had the good judgement to prefer her scholarly life to that of a queen, and had to be pressured into acceptance of what soon proved a lethal crown. He praises her not for her womanly modesty, but for her 'facility in acquiring every part of manly and polite literature. She had attained a familiar knowledge of the Roman and Greek languages, besides modern tongues, had passed most of her time in an application to learning, and expressed a great indifference for other occupations and amusements usual with her sex and station' (H. ch. XXXVI). She was reluctant to desert reading Plato either for 'sport and gaiety' or for the throne; '. . . the intelligence of her elevation to the throne was in no wise agreeable to her. She even refused to accept the present, pleaded the preferable title of the two princesses; expressed her dread of the consequences attending an enterprise so dangerous, not to say criminal . . .' (ibid.). Hume clearly admires both her scholarly preferences and her (over-ridden) good sense, as well as the stoical way she faced her execution, without recriminations and 'with a steady and serene countenance' (ibid.). If there is another 'philosophical heroine' in Hume's writings, besides the extraordinary single mother of 'Of Moral Prejudices', it is the reluctant queen, Lady Jane Grey, who rose above not only the usual achievements of her 'sex and station' but the usual human vanity of power. Hume himself, although he seems to have enjoyed his years as a government official, and carefully recorded and evaluated the performance of England's governors, had no great esteem for the 'station' of ruler. As he claimed in the (soon withdrawn) essay 'Of the Middle Station in Life', it takes much greater 'Genius and Capacity' to do well as a lawyer or physician, let alone as a poet or philosopher, than to rule well (Es. 548–51). Lady Jane Grey was right in valuing her Plato more highly than the crown of England.

Hume's treatment of 'sex and station' is radical in that it sees the roots of the social inferiority of women: namely, that it is

agreeable to men that women cultivate 'amiable weaknesses', that
the general interest of society in the proper care of children be
served by confining most women to domestic roles, cultivating
domestic virtues, rather than in some alternative way. It is radical
also in pointing out the power women have to change the
situation, should they resent it. He did not endorse such a
change, perhaps because he was properly uncertain whether we
could make such a change without 'making our posterity miserable'.
In a Calvinist context (but not the French context he moved on
to) he was also unorthodox in his emphasis on the strength of
women's sexual desires, their natural proclivity to promiscuity.

Female human nature, as Hume presents it, is a nature in
which some human passions are particularly strong, and, since
they are apt to conflict with other passions, also violent. Their
strength and violence combine to make their possessors lack what
Hume calls 'strength of mind', the prevalence of calm over violent
passions (T. 418). Women are, therefore, in Hume's sense,
'weak-minded'. The weakness of mind is not lack of intelligence
but strength of violent passions. It was a characteristic that
Hume's mother is supposed to have found in her famous son, 'our
Davey . . . a fine, good natured cratur, but uncommon wake-
minded',[24] when, in his youth, he failed to persevere in any of the
professions suitable for younger sons – the law or business – but
instead indulged his ruling passion for literary fame. Women in
Hume's view, are, as he was, in this sense self indulgent, or
'weak' of mind. 'All human creatures, especially of the female
sex, are apt to over-look remote motives in favour of any present
temptation' (T. 571). What strong passions tempt typical women?
Not, in Hume's day, love of literary fame. The passions he cites
as especially strong in women are three: love of children, 'the
amorous passion', both of which I have already discussed, and a
third strong passion, one not discussed in the *Treatise* account of
marriage, which is of particular interest. In his later withdrawn
essay 'Of Love and Marriage', he imputes to women a 'love of
dominion' which can prevail over sexual desire, 'the only one that
is a proper counterpoise to it' (Es. 558). He tells of Scythian
women who conspired to blind all their men, to end their own
subjection to the wish to appear pleasing to men, and so to men's
'imperious commands'. This essay of Hume's is 'frivolous and
finical' in some of its comments on this story, and heavy-handed
in its closing allegory, borrowed from Plato's *Symposium*. But the
remarks on power, love of power, and jealousy of power, are not
so frivolous. 'No passion seems to have more influence on female
minds than this for power'. 'They will think it an unreasonable

love of it in us which makes us insist so much upon that point'
(Es. 558).

> But to be just . . . I am afraid it is the fault of our sex, if the
> women be so fond of rule. . . . Tyrants, we know, produce
> rebels; and all history informs us, that rebels, when they
> prevail, are apt to become tyrants in their turn. For this
> reason, I could wish there were no pretensions to authority
> on either side; but that every thing were carried on with
> perfect equality, as between two equal members of the same
> body (Es. 559–60).

Women's love of dominion, on Hume's analysis, even when it
takes the pathetic form of taking 'a fool for her mate, that she
might govern with less controul' (Es. 559) is the direct outcome of
women's subjection. Is he here advocating 'perfect equality'
outside as well as inside marriage? As long as the domestic sphere
is women's only sphere of operation, he seems to be saying, then
men must expect all women's frustrated human passion for power
to get expression there. The unnatural artifice of training women
only or mainly for marriage, and for chastity and obedience in
marriage, does not even serve the interests of the men very well,
since it poisons the marriage relationship, turning what ideally
should be a loving or at least friendly partnership into a battle for
dominion. Hume in this essay says fairly plainly that he, for one,
feels 'a backwardness to enter into that (matrimonial) estate',
given the jealousy of power which seems endemic to it. And he
ironically asks women if they think they themselves would be the
greatest sufferers were such backwardness to become general,
were the opportunity denied them to have a husband-master
against whom they might rebel with petty bossiness. He says he
will not misrepresent the facts about marriage as it was in his
society, since 'I must be more a friend to truth, than even to them
[women], where their interests are opposite' (Es. 558).

Did Hume think women's interests were opposed to the
interest of seeing the truth about their social station, about
marriage, and the jealousy of power involved in it? Did he think
that 'perfect equality' was impossible, or that it would 'make
posterity miserable', or that it would disserve the interests of
women? It is hard to conclude that anyone who was convinced
that a little domestic domineering was the best women could hope
for would have told the story of the Scythian women, or the story
of the Parisian 'philosophical heroine'. As a friend to truth, Hume
challenges his female contemporaries' perceptions of their interests
and of their options. He challenges the entrenched doctrine of the
'nobler' male sex with its intrinsic authority. He challenges the

assumption that the husband must be 'head' of a family, that it needs any one such head. His vote was for 'perfect equality'.

As a friend to truth, as well as to Hume's views, I should end by admitting that the evidence concerning Hume's views on the complexion and proper station of women is mixed and often equivocal. There is a report of an occasion when Hume, who had been boasting about the number of his women disciples in Edinburgh, was asked by a Dr Gregory whether he would want a wife or daughter of his own to be his disciple. 'Mr. Hume with a smile and some hesitation made this reply: "No, I believe scepticism may be too sturdy a virtue for a woman"'. This report *could* be true, for all the considerations I have advanced to show Hume's enlightenment on the woman question. He may person-ally have preferred amiable weakness to equality of rank and complexion, in the women close to him, while also acknowledging the moral dubiousness of this preference. (But would he have summed up his whole philosophy under the term 'scepticism'?) Fortunately there are good grounds for doubting the reliability of this specious report. The Dr Gregory was Dr John Gregory, Hume's not so friendly adversary (see L. 201), and the report is made by Beattie, in a letter of 1779 to Elizabeth Montague, after he had looked at and deplored Hume's *Dialogues Concerning Natural Religion*, which to him showed that Hume, to the last, had it as his aim 'to subvert the principles of truth, virtue and religion'.[25] Hume's 'bigoted silly' opponents may believe that he was a sexist, but those who read him carefully will admire the sturdy realism, the depth of insight, and freedom from prejudice with which he wrote on this very hard question. Pretty remark-able.

NOTES

1. Hume speaks in 'Of the Study of History', of women being 'debarred from the severer studies by the tenderness of their complexion and the weakness of their education'. 'Com-plexion' here has the sense the OED lists as its first, 'humours, temperament', or the third sense listed there, 'constitution or habit of mind, disposition, temperament or nature'. They cite Hume's reference in 'The Sceptic' to 'a very amorous complexion' as an example of this sense. Our contemporary sense of the term is listed as the fourth, 'appearance of the skin', but even that is to be taken as the external appearance of internal 'humours'.

2. References to (H) *History of England*, are to chapter numbers, sometimes also to years discussed in a given chapter.

RSE refers to manuscripts in the keeping of The Royal Society of Edinburgh, EUL to Edinburgh University Library.

3. See *Letters and Memoir of Her Own Life*, by Mrs Alison Rutherford or Cockburn, ed. Craig-Brown (Edinburgh, 1900), 70.

4. Cockburn, 36–40.

5. Cockburn, 54–5. 'Painting' here refers to painting the face, 'fricasseeing' could be either fancy French cooking or the latest dance, 'quadrille' is probably the card game but it too could be a dance of that name. (Alison Cockburn was a passionate dancer and arranger of private dance evenings.)

6. Cockburn, 74.

7. Cockburn, 95. The letter is to the Revd Mr Robert Douglas of Galasheels, part of an extensive correspondence. She asks him ironically how it can be that 'women and clergymen are aptest to abuse one another', as commonly alleged, if the one is weak and pious and the other the teacher of brotherly love.

8. RSE, IV, letter 68.

9. Cockburn, 45.

10. Cockburn, XXIX.

11. Ibid.

12. There were at least two women Hume knew, very different from each other, who may not have shared the general female approval of him, or at least not sustained their initial liking. The first was Agnes Galbraith of Chirnside, who named the then twenty-three-year-old Hume as father of the second of her four illegitimate children. Hume had conveniently just left for England, and Agnes Galbraith appears not to have been believed. At any rate no man wore sackcloth with her for the sin of fornication, nor shared her pillory (see E.C. Mossner, *Life of David Hume*, Oxford, 1980, ch. 7). Whatever the truth of this matter, Agnes Galbraith can not have harboured very friendly feelings for David Hume, since either she named him maliciously, or she was deserted by him (unless of course, he had generously agreed to be falsely, or possibly falsely, named, in which case she, as well as the father, or other possible fathers, were doubtless grateful). The second woman who seems to have sided with Hume's attackers, in particular with Beattie, was the original bluestocking, Elizabeth Montague, whom Hume met on various occasions. She was an accomplished woman, the author of an essay praising Shakespeare's writings, and she would doubtless have disagreed with Hume's criticisms of Shakespearean 'barbarisms', but her correspondence with Beattie suggests more fundamental (i.e., religious) causes for her coolness to Hume (see Forbes, *Life of Beattie*, Dugald Stewart Collection, EUL).

13. She herself is remembered as the author of the words of

the song 'The Flowers of the Forest'. She later wrote that 'I am very certain that no woman ought to write anything but from the heart to the heart; never for the public eye without male correction', so for all her boldness she was no feminist.

14. Octavie de Guichard, Madame Belot, later Madame de Meinieres, translated Hume's *History* into French.

15. For a brief account of this see note 12 above.

16. Grotius says that the right to command is in marriage not common, but 'is the prerogative of the husband, as being of the nobler sex', linking this nobility with men's superior rationality (*On the Laws of War and Peace*, Bk II, ch. V, sec. VIII). He takes marriage, the way by which paternity is to be made known or reasonably supposed, as 'such a cohabitation as placeth the woman under the custody of the man' (ibid.). Pufendorf is less definite about the duty of wifely submission, and sees the duty of marital chastity to fall equally on husbands and wives, but gives the man the prerogative of proposing marriage, (since it is he who wants to use the institution to have recognizable 'children of his own not spurious and suppositous') and of deciding the place of domicile. The wife must join his family, not he hers, and she must follow him at least in matters of domicile. (*Whole Duty of Man*, Bk II, ch. II. See also *Of the Law of Nature and Nations*, Bk V. ch. I.)

17. One young Scottish woman Hume probably knew, Anne Forbes, went off in 1767 to Rome to study painting with Gavin Hamilton in the Accademia di San Luca, helped by a subscription among her friends and with her mother as chaperone. But she was an exception. See Duncan MacMillan, *The Golden Age: Painting in Scotland* (Phaidon Press, Oxford, 1986), 33, 43, 49.

18. See Mossner, op. cit., 34, and Hume's 1739 letter to Hutcheson, in which he says 'upon the whole I desire to take my Catalogue of Virtues from *Cicero's Offices*, not from *The Whole Duty of Man*' (L. 34).

19. *The Ladies' Calling*, Oxford, 1695.

20. Hume in some versions of 'Of Polygamy and Divorces' tells of the remark of a Turkish ambassador to France: 'We Turks are great simpletons in comparison with the Christians. We are at the expense of keeping a seraglio, each in his own house: But you ease yourselves of this burden and have your seraglio in your friends' houses'. (Es. 628).

21. I have discussed this in 'Hume's Account of Social Artifice, Its Origins and Originality', forthcoming in *Ethics*.

22. Hume wrote in 1763 to the Comptesse de Boufflers that Rousseau, in *The Confession of a Savoyard Vicar*, 'has not had the precaution to throw any veil over his sentiments, and as he scorns to dissemble his contempt of established opinions, he could not wonder that all the zealots were in arms against him. The liberty of the press is not so secured in any country, scarce

even in this, not to render such an open attack somewhat dangerous' (L. 200).

23. In a famous delightfully playful letter to Adam Smith, congratulating him on the success of the *Theory of Moral Sentiments*, Hume ends hoping that Smith can in reply 'flatter my vanity by telling me that all the godly in Scotland abuse me for my account of John Knox and the Reformation' (L. 165). That account had referred to the 'absurd severity' of Mary's Calvinist subjects, of Knox's sermons against his 'Jezebel' of a queen as 'full of sedition . . . rage and bigotry' (ch. XXXVIII, 1558–63, 'Arrival of Mary in Scotland').

24. See Mossner, op. cit., 66.

25. Beattie's letters are to be found in William Forbes, *Life of Beattie*, op. cit. The letter to Montague is on p. 54 of Vol. II. I owe the identification of this passage (which I first encountered as a handwritten quotation, with an illegible attribution of its source, in the Burton papers in the National Library of Scotland), to the suggestion of Roger Emerson, who proved to be correct. Roger Emerson was a Fellow with me at IPSE 86, and I owe much not merely to him, but to other Fellows, and to other members of the audience when an earlier version of this paper was given at an IPSE seminar in Edinburgh in June, 1986. Among the many who helped me in Edinburgh that summer was Thomas Crawford, also an IPSE Fellow, and an expert on song-writers in eighteenth-century Scotland, including Alison Cockburn.

3

PETER JONES

Hume and the Beginnings of Modern Aesthetics

I want to begin with Chambers. Not, of course, Sir William, the architect, nor William and Robert, the publishers who, among their many works, began to bring out their encyclopedia in 1859. But Ephraim Chambers, formerly apprentice to Senex, who issued at four guineas two folio volumes in 1728 under the title *Cyclopaedia, or an Universal Dictionary of Arts and Sciences.* Attempts to translate this work into French in 1745 led to plans to improve and enlarge it; the wonderful results, under the polymathic supervision of Diderot, began to appear in 1751 as *L'Encylopedie.*

The reason for beginning with Chambers is that Hume was almost certainly familiar with the work in one or other of its first four editions, (1728, 1738, 1739, 1741) and that it helps us to understand features of the intellectual context in which Hume was himself working out his ideas. Three of Chambers's observations must suffice on this occasion, concerning criticism, writing and architecture. He tells us that criticism 'regards not only history, but also the discernment of the real works of an author, the real author of a work, the genuine reading of a text, and the art of discerning suppositions, monuments, charters, interpolated passages, etc.' In a separate article on 'grammar' he observes, nevertheless, that 'the denomination . . . of critic, now frequently [is] used as a term of reproach'. On the topic of writing he declares that an author's business is to 'consider who it is writes, what, how, why and to whom'. I want particularly to draw attention to these remarks.

I shall argue, first, that Hume incontrovertibly establishes the importance of *context* in discussions about works of art; secondly, I shall extend Chambers's point by arguing that what I call the *seven first questions of criticism* arise twice over; thirdly, I shall develop a point about criticism as an autonomous practice which worried several Scottish thinkers. Finally, I shall make some brief remarks about architecture, and at that point I shall quote Chambers's endorsement of the Roman author Vitruvius, whose writings became almost sacred to architectural theorists from the Renaissance onwards.

The details of Hume's views on art and on criticism are more familiar than they used to be, and it is not here necessary to engage in detailed textual exposition or commentary. It will be more fruitful to focus on some central, but overlooked features of Hume's thought which have consequences for our own thinking today. Hume's substantive debt to the Abbé Jean-Baptiste Dubos for his views on art and criticism needs no further argument than I have given elsewhere. Hume quotes from Dubos both in his so-called 'Early Memoranda' and in his *Essays* of 1741–2, and his essay 'Of the Standard of Taste' is heavily indebted to Dubos. Dubos published his *Réflexions critiques sur la poésie et sur la peinture* in 1719, and for the next fifty years or so it was the most influential work of its kind throughout Europe. Although very few of the ideas Dubos espoused were of his own invention, he effectively synthesised ideas that were 'in the air' and introduced a philosophical dimension into reflection upon art which Hume was himself later able to extend and deepen.[1]

The central tenets of Dubos which Hume later found so important for his own reflections are easily identified. Dubos argued that works of art raise artificial, not natural, passions, and that everyone except fellow artists and scholars reads works of art for pleasure. We should underline this contrast between fellow artists and scholars, on the one hand, and the spectator, on the other; fellow artists are interested in the know-how and technique, but as rival craftsmen and potential competitors for attention, they cannot, in that frame of mind, adopt a properly disinterested attitude (Dubos derived the notion from Shaftesbury; but *désintéressé* does not mean *dégagé*). Dubos insists that we can derive sustained pleasure from a work only if we understand it in some way, and the minimal requirement is for *ordre* – a term which might be captured nowadays by the phrase 'discernible structure'. The public, and not the professional critics, are the proper judges of art because, having no self-interest in the transaction (i.e. being disinterested), they can more easily answer the primary question of whether they have been moved or affected by a work – and that question is not the task of reason but of an internal sense called *sentiment*. The role of reason is to identify the features of a work which cause us pleasure; in this way reason justifies the verdict of sentiment. The tasks of identification and justification typically belong to the critic. Dubos contrasts, therefore, the artist who makes, the spectator who responds, and the critic who explains.

It turns out, however, that Dubos's public is a privileged group which has learned through experience to exercise comparative taste.

It is not necessary to explore further details of Dubos's work here, because enough has been quoted to indicate the extent to which Hume very largely identified himself with current ideas.

All of Hume's remarks on art are set in the framework of our social life, and that is why he considers both the making of, and the response to, works of art as human actions – and the philosophy of art as inextricably linked, therefore, to the philosophy of action. In the broadest sense, works of art are pleasurable means of communication between human beings, and so the preconditions of effective communication apply to art as much as to other means. Hume argues that the artist must consider his intended audience's needs, interests, knowledge and capacities; and, for their part, an audience must consider how the artist judged the context of his own efforts, and what he thought he was doing. Certain works please us, he holds, because of the particular properties they possess; one of our tasks, therefore, is to identify these causes of our pleasure so that we can bring other people to share in our enjoyment. The apparent simplicity of the pleasure we feel, however, masks the complexity of the task in detecting its causes; accordingly, we have to *learn* what devices might help us. We must take into account the medium, genre, style and tradition of a work; the effectiveness of means to ends, and the relations of parts to whole – these tasks confront the audience no less than the artist, because any action that we perform (*a fortiori* any intended act of communication) must have 'sufficient unity' to make it 'be comprehended'.[2] Moreover, 'the same address and dexterity which practice gives to the execution of any work, is also acquired by the same means, in the judging of it' (Es. 237).

But can the desired comprehension result from a mere encounter with causal stimuli? Can we 'comprehend' a work of art merely by being in its presence? Certainly not. Two properties that belong to human actions, and which are goals of our comprehension are *meaning* and *value*: neither of these is discernible by the five ordinary senses alone. What is necessary is the active involvement of the mind: we need interpretation. Just as *inference* beyond the present data is necessary for all factual reasoning, so interpretation is necessary to establish the meaning of what another human being has done. A spectator cannot justifiably adopt an exclusively passive attitude towards art, although the causal impact of art is one factor in our judgement on it. We should note that Hume insists that 'the same excellence of faculties which contributes to the improvement of reason . . . are essential to the operations of true taste'; moreover, 'the beauties of design and reasoning . . . are the highest and most excellent' (Es. 240). This last tenet encouraged Hume, among others, to consider art in general, and not merely literature, as importantly *propositional*, especially if its value as communication is stressed.

I quoted at the beginning Chambers's remarks that an author ought to 'consider who it is writes, what, how, why and to whom'. Such views derive, of course, from theories in classical rhetoric, and they irradiate Hume's own thinking about and practice of communication. Without answers to such questions, neither the meaning nor the value of communication can be assessed, nor can the load-bearing elements in a text be located. But the five questions Chambers asks can be supplemented, and Hume implicitly does so, to form what I call the *seven first questions* that can, and should, be asked of any text: who wrote it? for whom? about what? how? when? where? why? As we have seen, by making the spectator's tasks *symmetrical* with those of the artist, Hume realises that these questions arise *twice over*: that is, they can be asked of the original text and also of any criticism of it, since any utterance whatsoever is contextually mappable. Moreover, since the context of encounter with a work of art is constantly changing, the *second* set of answers is open to constant variation.

The audience's *questions*, I have said, are symmetrical with those the artist asks himself; but the *context* is certainly not symmetrical, and Hume becomes increasingly worried by the gap between the foresight of what he calls the 'actor' and the hindsight of the 'spectator'. His point – and it reverberates throughout the *History* – is that agents act with certain intentions, but are necessarily ignorant, when they set out, of the outcome. Observers or spectators, on the other hand, know the outcome, but are doomed merely to conjecture the intentions necessary for understanding it. We can dramatise the apparent paradox here by saying that impartiality is possible only at the expense of under-standing. Hume explains his worry in the following way. 'Men's views of things are the result of their understanding: Their conduct is regulated by their understanding, their temper, and their passions'.[3] By definition, that is, the spectator uses his understanding alone for determining the nature of another person's actions; an agent himself, however, although assisted by his understanding can never be motivated by it. But even if a spectator *uses* his own understanding, that does not require him to explain another's actions solely in terms of understanding. Hume

might hold, however, that a spectator typically emphasises the
agent's understanding both because the motivating passions are
unknown, and because it is mainly by reference to the understanding that actions become intelligible. This aside, Hume emphasises
that spectators have access to data denied to agents, namely the
long-term consequences of their acts, and the different evaluations
made of them from different perspectives.

But since Hume is so alert to the possibilities of re-interpretation
in history – and he is among the first to observe that each
generation must re-write its own histories – why does he not apply
this thought to discussions of art? Even if he was largely
unsympathetic to the idea of texts being open to legitimately
multiple interpretations, on the grounds that effective communication required determinable and determinate meaning, he could
still allow re-interpretation of the artist's contextual, historical
acts, *qua* social events. There are other reasons for his stance,
however. First, he inherits the view, as we have seen, that art
aims to give pleasure, and receives its principal justification from
success in so doing; and he too often tends to think of pleasure, on
these occasions, as merely physiological states caused by identifi-
able sensory stimuli. He is, of course, wedded to the view that
cause and effect are uniquely tied, such that no single cause can
have different effects, nor different effects have the same cause.
Second, and partly as a result of this causal stimulus view, he has
to fight hard to overcome the urge to place weight on the first
impressions that a work makes on the senses. He does resist, by
acknowledging that we are often deceived by superficial appearances, and that the lasting impact of many works rests on
extremely subtle features which are hard to identify and may take
time to do so. Third, and most importantly, Hume accepts the
inescapable roles of reasoning and interpretation. We have to
make comparative judgements of kind, genre, style; we have to
interpret what is said or done. And whilst our senses are no doubt
pleasurably stimulated by the works in question, only by using
our minds – at the very least to identify the precise causes of our
pleasure – can we hope to derive lasting satisfaction from a work.

Neither Hume nor anyone else in the first part of the eighteenth
century envisaged the multiple interpretations of works of art
which today are a commonplace of critical practice. Such promiscuity was unforeseen because the first critical requirement was to
discover the artist's own intentions, goals, aims, expectations,
and the potentially definitive answers to these were taken as over-
riding all changes in the spectators' contexts. It is notable,
however, that whilst Hume acknowledges that history records

numerous cases of agents who have been mistaken or deceived about their own intentions, particularly in the political domain, he does not consider this possibility in the context of art.

The complexity of Hume's seven first questions should be underlined, along with the query about who is able to tackle them. Moreover, since Hume implicitly bases his reflections chiefly on literature, it may be wondered how far the claim is generalisable across the arts. It was still common for literati of Hume's day to regard painters as mere artisans or craftsmen, whose primary task was the provision of pleasing decoration or luxurious furnishing. A writer such as George Turnbull, in his *Treatise on Ancient Painting* (1740), was unusual in his emphasis on the moral and educative roles of painting.

Every reader of Hume is aware that his references to arts other than literature are infrequent, and fleeting. He almost never refers to music, his asides on painting are inconsequential, and only architecture gains more than a passing mention. But while his critical views seem to have been formed with literature mainly in mind, we should nevertheless ask what opportunities he had for wider experience of paintings *prior* to his essay on taste of 1757, and from what kinds of sources he derived his opinions.

Although Allan Ramsay was a close friend, and he had access to Border houses and even the best houses in Rheims, when he was studying there in the 1730s (see L. 5, 12), Hume would have seen few paintings other than portraits until he accompanied General St Clair to Vienna and Northern Italy in 1748 (e.g. L. 64). Even by mid-century there were very few collectors in Scotland, and the market, audience and criticism of painting in England had not developed to the extent he later observed in Paris in the 1760s. There were, of course, illustrated books, and engravings, but their scale and context encouraged a literary approach. He could have known more about music in Edinburgh, since the Edinburgh Musical Society had flourished since the 1690s – although it was formally constituted only in 1728; there was also a strong tradition of dance and folk-song. And English opera arrived in Edinburgh in 1751. There was little theoretical discussion of music outside France, but Hume may well have known about the dispute between Rameau and Rousseau; and he had read Dubos.[4]

As befits someone engrossed in the debate between the ancients and moderns, however, it was architecture that captured Hume's non-literary sensibilities; he comments on it throughout his Viennese mission, was proud of the Adam family's achievements, refers to and thus presumably had read the beautifully illustrated translations of Palladio that were available from the 1720s.

Relatively few books on architecture, together with handbooks on designing small houses, were published in France and in England in the years up to 1760. Most of them insisted on utility as against ornament, convenience against decoration. But Hume does not quote from such works (by James Gibbs, or Isaac Ware, or Sir William Chambers) although he refers to Vitruvius, among other classical authors, and to French authors such as Perrault.

London witnessed a huge building programme throughout the eighteenth century, and with the increased wealth of the southern neighbour opportunities abounded for designers such as Chippendale and others to publicise their work. All of this Hume must have seen. But, of course, he regards buildings, furniture and utensils as designed to fulfil specific functions: 'Most of the works of art are esteem'd beautiful, in proportion to their fitness for the use of man' (T. 577), and the beauty of 'tables, chairs, scritoires, chimneys, coaches, sadles, ploughs, and indeed . . . every work of art' is 'chiefly deriv'd from their utility' (T. 364). For Hume, beauty of utility is always relative to species, and the conventions which govern the attribution of beauty of utility differ between cultures. Indeed, it is literature that fits most uneasily into Hume's central linking of beauty and utility. And yet it is literature that Hume has mainly in mind when canvassing the rationality of critical discussion; and that is because he regards literature itself as no more than a deviant form of discussion, in the sense that it must be the coherent expression of thought.

The development of modern aesthetics in the mid-eighteenth century is inseparable from many important intellectual, social and economic factors, including spread of wealth and ease of travel: the hardening of distinctions between the arts and the sciences; the beginning of the formal *study* of the arts, especially literature, by non-practitioners in colleges and universities, thus augmenting the informed audience; the beginning of public concerts, of public museums and of greater access to private collections; the decline of individual patronage, with the corresponding freedom available to artists to do what they wanted, or to satisfy a growing market; the consequent replacement of large public paintings by small private ones. And, of course, in the last half of the century, the beginning of the Romantic movement. The notion that I want to emphasise, however, is that of the *critic as parasite*; the disengaged non-practitioner who nevertheless passes judgement and exercises authority over the lives of both makers and spectators, and who gradually tranforms the critical role from that of a dispensable intermediary to that of an indispensable oracle. At that stage criticism has assumed autonomy as a practice in its own right, but one which fundamentally depends on the agency of others and one which itself can achieve only the most attenuated second-order agency. The 'critic' had of course been a stock-in-trade literary figure of fun for centuries, but Dubos is one of the first writers to reflect philosophically on certain inherent characteristics of the type, and he regards with horror the prospect of students formally analysing and critically assessing works in the absence of any knowledge or intention to make such works themselves.

The point is worth elaborating. The leading thinkers of the Scottish Enlightenment derided the monkish virtues of scholasticism, which celebrated learning and contemplation at the expense, allegedly, of social benefit and open communication. We should not ignore the measure of distrust towards meditation, for example. Hume, at least, perceived psychological dangers in what easily led to self-absorption, if not also self-deception. But the fascinating suggestion which hovers around these discussions and which I detect even in Dubos, can be characterised dramatically by saying that the death-wish of the humanities is to substitute text for context. Texts, that is, are regarded by Hume and others as essentially mute and inadequate records or traces of richly human experiences, ideas and responses which animate them; and no mere analysis of the texts alone can reach what gave them life and meaning. Put in this way, of course, we have the germs of a view much canvassed by Romantic poets such as Shelley, who held that the texts we mistakenly cherish are entirely inadequate and misshapen expressions of the true inspiration behind them. The Scottish point is a different one, however, and is integral to Hume's whole philosophy. Events can be understood only by reference to their relations to other events; works of art, as events contrived by human beings, can likewise only be understood by locating them in a context – not by analysing them in isolation and or staring at them, as it were, through an intellectual microscope. The point must not be misunderstood. Nothing in the overall programme precluded detailed and even minute analysis of particular problems. On the contrary, a metaphor of atomic analysis at the foundation of progress in knowledge was widely accepted. But such procedures were intended to harmonise with two other ideals, familiar in Bacon, of course, and the encyclopedists of the seventeenth and eighteenth centuries: firstly that knowledge of things in themselves, if attainable, had to be set beside knowledge of things in their relations; secondly, that all specialised enquiries would have to be brought together into a unified picture. What Dubos, and Hume, and Ferguson seemed to fear was that, in the domain of the arts, the first appeal and justification of which was the pleasure they caused, autonomous critical attention would generate specious discussion – and, anti-social attitudes. Indeed, the attitude of disinterested judgement carries with it two attendant dangers. By claiming authority for its viewpoint, it can distract attention from the artist and his work; more significantly, such detachment in no way contributes to the on-going artistic enterprise. Moreover, the critical attitude some-times claims authority precisely because it is exempt from the responsibilities of action. Hume and his contemporaries viewed any such claimed exemption as reprehensible; it precisely paralleled the speculations of the 'pure' philosophers or metaphysicians. Thinking, reasoning, reflection are, for Hume, themselves inert and incapable of motivating anyone. They are, indeed, indispens-able human attributes, and responsible social action requires their fullest contribution. But in an implicit scale of values it is *agency* that defines man, and thinking ought to be placed in the service of it.

The division of intellectual labour which was simultaneously applauded and deplored during the Scottish Enlightenment is well illustrated by Hume's thoughts on criticism which, by definition, is not undertaken in the service of agency. When discussing justice, as is well known, Hume remarks that if everyone conducted themselves 'on most occasions, by particular judgments', 'this wou'd produce an infinite confusion in human society'. Accordingly, men 'have agreed to restrain themselves by general rules, which are unchangeable by spite and favour, and by particular views of private or public interest'. He adds: 'these rules, then, are artificially invented for a certain purpose, and are contrary to the common principles of human nature, which accommodate themselves to circumstances, and have no stated invariable method of operation' (T. 532). One can plausibly argue that, for Hume, 'the *steady* and *general* points of view' we must adopt in order to cope with the fact that 'our situation, with regard both to persons and things, is in continual fluctuation' (T. 581) are equally 'artificially invented for a certain purpose': equally necessary for detachment, and equally contrived. It is precisely the limited purpose, and the artificiality, that are overlooked when the critical endeavour becomes an autonomous end in itself. We can say, therefore, that at the very beginning of modern aesthetics, several thinkers puzzled by the problems of general ideas sensed a central paradox. How is it possible to deal with the uniqueness of each case, and yet talk rationally and in general ways about it? A measure of this anxiety, which reaches its most extreme form in the Romantic movement, is well captured by a member of Aberdeen's 'Wise Club', Dr John Gregory: 'No science ever flourished, while it was confined to a set of Men who lived by it as a profession. Such Men have pursuits very different from the end and design of their art.'[5]

In his essay 'Of the standard of taste', Hume tries to make the spectator his own critic, in the sense that a proper response to any given work requires the exercise of mind in order to complete what is a collaborative endeavour of communication between artist and audience. The role of a critic is to facilitate this collaboration, and then to drop out. Hume introduces a moral criterion at the end of his essay precisely because the artist, *qua* social being, has social responsibilities in communication, and for the overall moral stance of his work.

Hume agrees with Dubos that the fine arts can develop only when subsistence conditions of existence have been transcended, and indeed only when production of the necessities of life exceeds demand. (The choices of colour, size, shape, decoration or texture of vessels or dwellings, among so-called early peoples, were never considered by contemporaries of Hume as incipient art.) But although their products are 'superfluous' in this very strict sense, Hume nevertheless regards artists as agents, and spectators as performing all the essential spectatorial roles; and our ability to learn from art is closely linked to our own inescapable duties as agents. The point which Hume so subtly discerns is much more urgently trumpeted by his friend Adam Ferguson:

Men are to be estimated, not from what they know, but from what they are able to perform. . . . It is peculiar to modern Europe, to rest so much of the human character on what may be learned in retirement, and from the information of books. A just admiration of ancient literature, an opinion that human sentiment, and human reason, without this aid, were to have vanished from the societies of men, have led us into the shade, where we endeavour to derive from imagination and thought, what is in reality matter of experience and sentiment: and we endeavour, through the grammar of dead languages, and the channel of commentators, to arrive at the beauties of thought and elocution, which sprang from the animated spirit of society, and were taken from the living impressions of an active life.

Ferguson elaborates on these thoughts:

When learned productions accumulate, the acquisition of knowledge occupies the time that might be bestowed on

invention. The object of mere learning is attained with
moderate or inferior talents. . . . When we only mean to
learn what others have taught, it is probable, that even our
knowledge will be less than that of our masters. . . . After
libraries are furnished, and every path of ingenuity is occupied,
we are, in proportion to our admiration of what is already
done, prepossessed against farther attempts. We become
students and admirers, instead of rivals; and substitute the
knowledge of books, instead of the inquisitive or animated
spirit in which they were written.

In another passage, Ferguson wisely warns the scholar:

the domestic antiquities of every nation must . . . be received
with caution. They are, for the most part, the mere conjectures or the fictions of subsequent ages; and even where at
first they contained some resemblance of truth, they still vary
with the imagination of those by whom they are transmitted,
and in every generation receive a different form. They are
made to bear the stamp of the times through which they have
passed in the form of tradition, not of the ages to which their
pretended descriptions relate. The information they bring, is
not like the light reflected from a mirror, which delineates
the object from which it originally came; but, like rays that
come broken and dispersed from an opaque or unpolished
surface, only give the colours and features of the body from
which they were last reflected.[6]

Ferguson's remarks all show one feature of the Humean
emphasis on man as a social being. Works of art are datable
human products; like other human products they can be said to
have both immediate and lasting effects – namely, the pleasure
they cause in contemporaries and their descendants. A study of
those works for their own sake, however, is not only incompatible
with agency during such study, but may discourage the student
from subsequent agency. We should not overlook, in this stern
view, the presence of *improvement* as a supervenient value in all
our endeavours. It was, after all, the clarion call of Scottish
Enlightenment philosophers, but it was to be submerged, or
rather drowned, by the nineteenth-century shouts of aestheticism
and 'art for art's sake'.

The socio-political aspect of Hume's essay on taste is important.
By reflecting on the nature and roles of art in an evolving civilised
society, he came to view the discussion and encouragement of
certain kinds of art as a more serious matter than his immediate
predecessors. Social beings share a natural interest in whatever is
found pleasing, he held, and a modicum of pleasure is necessary

both for the well-being of individuals and of society at large. And if communal pleasure in certain things is a necessary, although not sufficient, condition of harmony and progress in society, the social utility of shared critical judgements becomes clear. Hume's insistence on these matters is evident in the *Treatise*, and becomes a major theme of both his 1741 and 1752 political essays, but there is an implication for aesthetics which, I think, has been overlooked.

Hume saw artists as potential purveyors of pleasure. His views about the need for pleasure and the nature of responsible communication imply that artists occupy a relatively low social status, and also that there is a hierarchy of arts, with literature placed above painting and music. He does not include architecture within the scope of his reflections on the arts, since, like most of his predecessors and contemporaries, he required architecture to satisfy the twin requirements of function and appearance – function taking precedence. We know that Hume had read some of the recent discussions of these matters, and reference to them provides a fitting conclusion to this paper.

Chambers, in his *Cyclopaedia*, endorsed Vitruvius's list of twelve qualities 'requisite to an architect; that he be docil and ingenious; literate; skilled in designing; in geometry; in optics; arithmetic; history; philosophy; music; medicine; law, and astrology'. The pretensions of the bolder architects and their apologists, at least since Vitruvius, was not matched in literature, music, or painting.

Architecture, self-evidently, occupied and enclosed public spaces, intruded on the attention, affected people's lives in all kinds of ways, satisfied various needs and functions, required knowledge and skills of many kinds, survived through many generations, and was, in its vernacular forms, an inescapable element in daily life. Above all, it was necessarily located in the dimensions of space and time – that is, context; and one could not begin to talk about or estimate the worth of a single building without some consideration of its context. Moreover, since function was its primary purpose, one could think metaphorically of buildings as themselves agents: they did things, or directly enabled others to do them. The nervousness that Hume and his contemporaries conveyed about our responses to literature, painting and music, especially where it generated autonomous critical discussion and theory, was unlikely to surface in their thoughts about architecture: and it did not.

For our purposes we need only underline the facts that architecture plays the complex roles it does in a context of social action; Hume was writing about literature, painting and music at a time when these arts were not typically thought of in such contexts. Of course, in the nineteenth and twentieth centuries rival theories were developed which do locate *all* the arts in wider contexts, and Hume would have welcomed the conclusions if not the premises of those later theories.

It cannot be denied that there are tensions in Hume's account between his tendency to treat 'aesthetic' values as essentially sensory 'surface' qualities, and the more important qualities as residing in the meaning and the moral stance. It was perhaps surprising that with his interest in rhetoric, he did not think more about the subtle relations between form and content. Because of a tradition of ascribing beauty to nature, in the first instance, and pictorial representations of it, in the second, that predicate was too closely associated with visual arts, or with sounds. But Hume is writing at a time when non-practitioners carelessly generalise between art forms and mediums, and at a time when the social context in which people encountered painting, heard music, read literature, and travelled to other lands was changing dramatically.

'The science of man' involved a systematic investigation into everything man did, and into the ways those actions related to each other; under such a comprehensive umbrella there is no place for a radical distinction between the arts and sciences, since both are pursued by men and are conditioned and shaped by man's capacities and limitations. That is the overall context in which Hume sought to locate his thinking about art and criticism. The richness of his conclusions is only one reason for concluding that he was right to do so.

NOTES

1. I have discussed at length the texts of Hume's writings on aesthetics, and their sources, in my *Hume's Sentiments: Their Ciceronian and French Context*, Edinburgh, 1982, especially in chapter 3, but also throughout the book; my other discussions are also listed there.

2. Hume, *An Enquiry concerning Human Understanding*, sect. III, n. This note is omitted from many editions, including those by Selby-Bigge and Nidditch.

3. Hume, *History of England*, ch. LIII.

4. For details of the musical scene see: David Johnson, *Music and Society in Lowland Scotland in the Eighteenth Century*, Oxford, 1972. For the social and critical context of the arts in eighteenth century France see: Marion Hobson, *The Object of*

Art, Cambridge, 1982; Thomas E. Crow, *Painters and Public Life in 18th-century Paris*, Yale, 1985; P. Verlet, *French Furniture and Interior Decoration of the 18th Century*, London, 1967. For the British scene see: Mark Girouard, *Life in the English Country House*, Yale, 1978; John Summerson, *Georgian London*, London, 1945; Iain Pears, *The Discovery of Painting; The Growth of Interest in the Arts in England, 1680–1768*, Yale, 1988. On architecture and theory in France and Britain, see: Joseph Rykwert, *The First Moderns*, London, 1980; A. Pérez-Gómez, *Architecture and the Crisis of Modern Science*, London, 1983.

5. John Gregory, *A Comparative View of the State and Faculties of Man and those of the Animal World*, 1765 (4th edn., Dublin 1768), 112.

6. Adam Ferguson, *An Essay on the History of Civil Society*, 1767 (Edinburgh 1966), 30, 217, 76.

4

DONALD LIVINGSTON

Hume on the Natural History of Philosophical Consciousness

I

The great enemy of the Enlightenment was religion, which was viewed as the poison of society and the main barrier to an increase in knowledge and humanity. The antidote to religion was philosophy. In *The Natural History of Religion*, Hume explored the nature of religious consciousness, its origin in human nature and its pernicious effect on society. Hume had evident difficulty entering the religious mind. The spectacle of religion in history resembles 'sick men's dreams' and 'the playsome whimsies of monkies in human shape' more than a serious endeavour. It is true that Hume made a distinction between true and false religion, teaching that: 'The proper office of religion is to regulate the heart of men, humanize their conduct, infuse the spirit of temperance, order, and obedience. . .' (D. 220). But so 'pure a religion as represents the Deity to be pleased with nothing but virtue in human behavior' is spontaneous, and 'its operation is silent' (D. 220–221). When, however, true religion becomes an object of reflection and becomes institutionalised, it 'acts as a separate principle over men', departs 'from its proper sphere', and becomes 'only a cover to faction and ambition' (D. 220). So perverse is the religious mind that the establishment of true religion as an institution would destroy it: 'so inveterate are the people's prejudices, that, for want of some other superstition, they would make the very attendance on these sermons the essentials of religion, rather than place them in virtue and good morals' (NHR. 358). So true religion could never, as it were, become a religion.

The conclusion of *The Natural History of Religion* is that religion is impenetrable, 'the whole is a riddle, an ænigma, an inexplicable mystery', and Hume recommends the Stoical solution of escape into 'the calm, though obscure, regions of philosophy' (NHR. 363). In the more reformist mood of the *Treatise* and first *Enquiry*, Hume presents philosophy as 'the only catholic remedy' for the religious virus. But if philosophy can open up a 'calm' region of existence and if it is a 'catholic remedy' for religion, we might ask whether philosophical consciousness could replace religious consciousness as the dominant form of society. This was very much the project of the Enlightenment. Diderot wrote: 'Let us hasten to make philosophy popular. If we want the philosophers to march on before, let us approach the people at the point where the philosophers are'.[1] Diderot, and all who have been influenced by Enlightenment ideology since, have viewed critical philosophical reflection as an unproblematic source of light. Religion is darkness. The light should supplant the darkness, not only in the minds of the enlightened few but in the minds of the populace as well. Nearly a century after Diderot's call to make philosophy popular, Marx could write in a letter to Ruge: 'the philosophical consciousness itself has been pulled into the torment of struggle. What we must accomplish is the ruthless criticism of all that exists . . .'.[2] Critical philosophical reflection through mass consciousness-raising or even revolution should inform the fundamental institutions of society.

But it is here that Hume parted ways with the Enlightenment, for if he taught that religion appears as 'sick men's dreams', he also taught that men 'from reasonings purely philosophical' have run into 'as great extravagancies of conduct as any *Monk* or *Dervise* that ever was in the world' (T. 272). Hume explored the depths of the philosophical intellect. And although he had difficulty entering the religious mind, which for him was always an alien existence, he had no difficulty entering the philosophical mind, a mind which was his own. He found it dark indeed and capable of generating absurdities the equal of any in religion. And so Hume forged a distinction *within* philosophical reflection between true and false philosophical criticism. Unlike his Enlightenment colleagues, he saw that emancipation from religion was not enough, one must be emancipated from false philosophical criticism as well. The Enlightenment was not fully enlightened. Nor was Hume sanguine about the benefits of making philosophical criticism popular. True philosophy was as rare as true religion. And, like religion, philosophy on a popular level would most likely be of the false form not the true.

Hume never wrote a natural history of philosophical consciousness on the model of *The Natural History of Religion*, but the rudiments of an ideal natural history of philosophical criticism are worked out in Book I, Part IV, sections i-iv and vii of the *Treatise*. Using these and other passages scattered throughout Hume's writings, I wish to explore Hume's pathology of the philosophical

intellect, its origins in human nature, and its problematic relation
to society.

II

There are three principles of the human mind which make
philosophical reflection possible. I shall call these the principle of
ultimacy, the autonomy principle, and the principle of dominion,
and will take them in turn.

(1) *The principle of ultimacy.* Philosophy is an attempt to
understand the way things ultimately are. We are never content
with an empirical understanding of things but, as Hume says, we
seek to 'push on our enquiries, till we arrive at the original and
ultimate principle. . . . This is our aim in all our studies and
reflections' (T. 266). Philosophical thought can never rest until it
believes itself to have achieved an understanding that is final,
absolute, and unconditioned.

(2) *The autonomy principle.* Philosophical thinking is a radically
free and self-justifying inquiry. Anything less would reduce
philosophy to the role of handmaiden of theology, politics, or
some other prejudice. But the radical autonomy of philosophy
cannot be understood without contrasting it to that supposedly
heteronomous domain relative to which it is autonomous. That
domain is the unreflectively received order of habit, custom,
prejudice, and tradition in which the philosopher originally has
his being but which is no longer viewed as having authority. The
radical autonomy of philosophy demands that the philosopher
conceptually cease being a *participant* in the prejudices of common
life and become a *spectator* of them. He must occupy, to use
Descartes' expression, an Archimedian point outside the domain
of common life as a whole, from which critical principles can be
formulated untainted by prejudice. All the prejudices of common
life, therefore, are presumed guilty unless they can be seen to
conform to the dictates of autonomous philosophical reason.
Hume writes: 'Reason first appears in possession of the throne,
prescribing laws, and imposing maxims with an absolute sway
and authority' (T. 186).

(3) *The principle of dominion.* By the principle of ultimacy,
philosophical systems that are different are contrary. Philosophical disagreements are ultimate disagreements. By the autonomy
principle, the philosopher must, in the end, consider his own
system to be ultimately correct and to have a title to rule over
other systems; failure to do so violates his integrity as a thinker.

The sense of a fitness to rule, internal to the philosophic intellect, is transformed into a passion by an original propensity of the mind, which Hume thinks is triggered whenever men reach the level of philosophical reflection:

> such is the nature of the human mind, that it always lays hold on every mind that approaches it; and as it is wonderfully fortified by an unanimity of sentiments, so it is shocked and disturbed by any contrariety. Hence the eagerness which most people discover in a dispute; and hence their impatience of opposition, even in the most speculative and indifferent opinions. (Es. 60–1)

Plato's doctrine that philosophers should be kings is a rather natural expression of the disposition of the philosophically reflective mind to seek dominion.

Hume argues that these three principles are incoherent with other principles of our nature and that, consequently, most of the entire philosophical tradition (ancient and modern) is incoherent.[3] If critical philosophical reflection is to continue, it must reform itself. The reform issues in Hume's distinction between true and false philosophy. In Part IV of Book I of the *Treatise*, he presents the distinction in the form of a three-stage philosophical drama where philosophical reflection emerges dialectically out of the prejudices of common life; imagines itself the spectator and absolute arbiter of these prejudices; falls into self-alienation and incoherence; and through further reflection wins through to a true understanding of itself and to a reconciliation with the prejudices of common life from which it originated. We have here a natural history of philosophical consciousness, which anyone seeking philosophical self-knowledge can re-enact in his own mind. Hume describes its basic outline as follows: There are

> three opinions, that rise above each other, according as the persons, who form them, acquire new degrees of reason and knowledge. These opinions are that of the vulgar, that of a false philosophy, and that of the true; where we shall find upon enquiry, that the true philosophy approaches nearer to the sentiments of the vulgar, than to those of a mistaken knowledge. (T. 222–3)

The central thesis of true philosophy is that the autonomy principle as traditionally conceived must be abandoned. Philosophical reflection cut free from the *entire* domain of prejudice is empty and, if consistently carried out, ends in total scepticism. As Hume put it: 'the understanding, when it acts alone, and according to its most general principles, entirely subverts itself, and leaves not the lowest degree of evidence in any proposition, either in philosophy or common life' (T. 267–8). Philosophers are not, in fact, driven to scepticism, because they do not consistently adhere to the autonomy principle but unknowingly smuggle in some favourite prejudice which gives content to and hides what is otherwise an entirely vacuous way of thinking. If philosophy is to continue at all, it must reform itself by abandoning the autonomy principle and by affirming the original authority of the domain of prejudice to command judgement.

In Hume's reform we must recognise a new principle which may be called the *autonomy of custom*, which places limits on the previously unrestrained autonomy of reflection. That is, whereas false philosophy had presumed custom to be false unless certified by autonomous reflection, Hume's maxim is that custom is presumed true unless shown to be otherwise and where showing it to be otherwise presupposes the validity of custom as a whole. In this reform a revised form of the autonomy principle remains: philosophical reflection may criticise any prejudice of common life by comparison with other prejudices, and in the light of abstract principles, ideals, and models. But these critical principles, ideals, and models must be thought of as reflections of an actual order of custom. What we cannot do is seek to form critical principles from some Archimedian point from which to throw into question the order of custom as a whole. All critical principles must bear the imprint of an actual order, so that the participant of the order criticised may recognise himself in the critical principles. The false philosopher imagines himself to be the *spectator* and *sovereign arbiter* of whatever domain of custom he is reflecting upon. The true philosopher, by contrast, recognises that he is a *critical participant* in whatever domain of custom he is reflecting upon.

In Hume's reform in philosophy, the ultimacy principle remains intact. Philosophical questions are still attempts to understand the way things ultimately are. Hume is not a positivist. Philosophical beliefs are beliefs about the real. But these beliefs are now viewed with some diffidence, owing to the restrictions put on the autonomy principle, which is now reduced to critical reflection *within* the primordial customs of common life. The new principle of the autonomy of custom points out a hitherto undiscovered mode of knowledge, namely, knowledge, not through propositional reflection, but through primordial *participation*. But the recognition of the autonomy of participation is available only to those who have passed through the natural history of philosophical consciousness and have become 'thoroughly convinced of the force of the Pyrrhonian doubt' (EU. 162), that is to say, it is made possible by sceptical arguments that have the power to suspend the authority of all propositional judgement. It is only when the entire domain of propositional thought is reduced to silence that the authority of primordial participation can be heard. As Hume puts it in the Introduction to the *Treatise*, we must be in a position to see 'that we can give no reason for our most general and most refined principles, beside our *experience of their reality*; which is the reason of the mere vulgar, and what it required no study at first to have discovered. . . .' (T. xxii, italics mine). Finally, with Hume's reform in philosophy, the third principle of philosophical reflection, the principle of dominion, loses its force. Custom, and not autonomous reason, is now seen to have a better title to rule. And custom is always internal to a social order which requires deference to others.

III

The false philosopher is false not because his propositions cannot be tested by empirical reality. False philosophy is due to a failure of *self-knowledge*. The false philosophical consciousness does not recognise the constitutive role that prejudice and custom play in his own thought. Though necessarily a participant in common life, he is totally alienated from its authority by virtue of the unreformed autonomy principle. Hume explores this alienated state of mind in the Conclusion of Book I of the *Treatise*. In the first and heroic moment of philosophical reflection, the philosopher experiences that giddy arrogance of one cut loose from all bonds of custom and for whom the once familiar world has become a strange and alien object.

Hume asks: 'Where am I or what? From what causes do I derive my existence, and to what condition shall I return? Whose favour shall I court, and whose anger must I dread? What beings surround me? and on whom have I any influence, or who have any influence on me?' (T. 269). These are thought of as ultimate questions projected from an unconditioned position. The false philosopher answers them by constructing, from autonomous reason, a theoretical world in total opposition to the world of common life, what Hume calls 'a world of its own . . . with scenes, and beings, and objects, which are altogether new' (T. 271).

We now enter the dark inverted world of false philosophical consciousness. The alternative world of autonomous reason is alone held to be real, and the opposed world of custom is seen as an illusion. To give a few examples. Thales taught that everything is really just water. Berkeley taught that the physical world is just an order of experiences in a community of minds. Hobbes taught that all acts of benevolence are really acts of self-love. For Locke, no government is legitimate unless based on the consent of the people. Proudhon taught that property is theft. And Marx declared that all history, contrary to appearance, is really the story of class struggle.

All of these are cases of what Hume identified in 'The Sceptic' as the fundamental error of philosophers:

> There is one mistake, to which they seem liable, almost without exception . . . When a philosopher has once laid hold of a favourite principle, which perhaps accounts for many natural effects, he extends the same principle over the whole creation, and reduces to it every phaenomenon, though by the most violent and absurd reasoning. (Es. 159).

Philosophers do not trade in the concepts of good and evil, nor even in the concepts of truth and falsity so much as in the more fundamental concepts of *reality* and *illusion*. The good and the true must first be real. The philosopher takes part of the order of pre-reflective participation, and by an act of reflection opens up a distinction between appearance and reality, magically transforming the whole of experience into a favourite part.

In the *Enquiry* on morals, Hume described this act of critical reflection as 'philosophical chymistry' (alchemy) and in 'The Sceptic' compared it to black magic and witchcraft (EM. 297; Es. 161). This magical power of philosophical consciousness to generate an order of reality and appearance out of primordial participation, with its implied title to dominion, makes the philosopher a kind of conjuror. And he is no less a conjuror by acting in the name of something called 'reason'.

In *The Natural History of Religion*, Hume observed that the religious mind has a kind of 'appetite for absurdity' and that the more rational and systematic a religion becomes, the more absurd its doctrines and practices (NHR. 341). But philosophy has its own appetite for absurdity, generated by the interests the philosophical mind has in keeping the pre-reflective order of participation in awe. Hume writes in the *Treatise*: 'Whatever has the air of a paradox, and is contrary to the first and most unprejudic'd notions of mankind is often greedily embrac'd by philosophers, as shewing the superiority of their science, which cou'd discover opinions so remote from vulgar conception' (T. 26). Likewise, whatever causes 'surprise and admiration' gives such pleasure to the mind that it 'will never be persuaded that its pleasure is entirely without foundation' (T. 26). 'From these dispositions in philosophers and their disciples', Hume continues, 'arises that mutual complaisance betwixt them; while the former furnish such plenty of strange and unaccountable opinions, and the latter so readily believe them' (T. 26).

The inverted world of false philosophical consciousness throws the philosopher into a profound state of self-alienation, what Hume called a 'philosophical melancholy and delirium' (T. 269). False philosophical consciousness is held in tension between 'two principles, which are contrary to each other, which are both at once embrac'd by the mind, and which are unable mutually to destroy each other' (T. 215). By virtue of the autonomy principle, the prejudices of primordial participation are rejected in totality as having no original authority to command judgement (to think otherwise is to violate one's intellectual integrity). In their place an alternative world is substituted, which is arrogantly displayed as the work of autonomous reason, but is, in fact, 'the monstrous offspring' of reason and some favourite but unrecognised prejudice of common life. The alienated world of his own reason is alone considered real; yet the philosopher inescapably has his being in the very order of primordial participation, which he now, if consistent, must view as a grand illusion. Such a frame of mind, Hume says, is in 'a very lamentable condition, and such as the poets have given us but a faint notion of in their descriptions of the punishment of Sisyphus and Tantalus' (T. 223).

The dialectical tensions within the false philosopher's consciousness constitute a dynamo from which is generated the many bizarre forms of philosophical existence that have populated the historical world. We may distinguish three forms of false philosophic existence. I shall call these ascetic philosophical existence, revolutionary philosophical existence, and, for want of a better expression, guilty philosophical existence. The alienated existence of the false philosopher, caught in two contrary worlds, gives rise to alternating feelings of radical self-sufficiency and implacable hostility to the world of custom on the one hand and to feelings of morbid self-disgust for being a participant in it on the other. The ascetic and revolutionary modes of philosophical existence are different forms of what might be called the heroic moment in this natural history of philosophical consciousness. Here autonomous reason is in implacable opposition to the prejudices of common life and is determined to make no compromises with the world. Existence in the mode of philosophic guilt occurs when the philosopher participates in the prejudices of common life while at the same time disowning them. As Berkeley was to say, he speaks

with the vulgar but thinks with the learned. He declares as unreal
the very existence in which he participates. I shall discuss these
three modes of false philosophical existence in order and then
turn to Hume's conception of the mode of true philosophical
existence.

IV

The ascetic philosophical consciousness. Hume mentions Diogenes
as an ancient example and Pascal as a modern example of what I
have called the ascetic philosopher. 'The Cynics', Hume says, 'are
an extraordinary instance of philosophers, who from reasonings
purely philosophical ran into as great extravagancies of conduct as
any *Monk* or *Dervise* that ever was in the world' (T. 272). Indeed,
Hume considered Diogenes 'the most celebrated model of extravagant philosophy' (EM. 342). The ascetic philosopher endeavours
to live what Hume calls an 'artificial' life. That is, not a life lived
through the prejudices of common life and a critical reflection
upon them, but one constituted by the free play of the autonomy
principle, unspotted by what Hume calls the 'gross earthy
mixture' of custom. Such lives are lived out 'in a vacuum'. Being
the result of heroic philosophical reflection, these isolated pockets
of total alienation that erupt unexpectedly in common life are
unaccountable by reference to the common maxims of the world.
Of the ascetic philosophers Hume says: 'no one can answer for
what will please or displease them. They are in a different element
from the rest of mankind; and the natural principles of their mind
play not with the same regularity, as if left to themselves, free
from the illusions of . . . philosophical enthusiasm' (EM. 343).

The revolutionary philosophical consciousness. To understand
Hume's views on this mode of existence, we must briefly examine
his conception of the relation between philosophy and religion.
For the main (though not the only) examples of revolutionary
thinking available to Hume were those of religious philosophy.
According to Hume, philosophy, as a mode of thinking, first
appeared in a world of polytheistic religions which themselves
had no philosophical content. These religions consisted of sacred
traditions and customs which expressed the relation of the state or
tribe to the Divine. No autonomous claims were made about the
ultimate, so polytheistic religions were not experienced as contraries and could peacefully coexist.

The civic character of polytheistic religion meant that 'religion
had, in ancient times, very little influence on common life, and

that, after men had performed their duty . . . at the temple, they thought, that the gods left the rest of their conduct to themselves. . . .' (EM. 341). But with the birth of philosophy in the ancient world, a new and demanding guide to life appeared: 'In those ages, it was the business of philosophy alone to regulate men's ordinary behaviour and deportment; and . . . this being the sole principle, by which a man could elevate himself above his fellows, it acquired a mighty ascendent over many, and produced great singularities of maxims and of conduct' (EM. 341).

Informed by the principles of ultimacy, autonomy, and dominion, philosophy must and did break up into countless sects which stood in implacable opposition. It is for this reason that 'Sects of philosophy, in the ancient world, were more zealous than parties of religion . . .' (Es. 63). What made ancient religious groups less fanatical was that they had little or no philosophical content. But all of this changed with the appearance of theistic Christianity: 'as philosophy was widely spread over the world at the time when Christianity arose, the teachers of the new sect were obliged to form a system of speculative opinions . . . and to explain, comment, confute, and defend, with all the subtlety of argument and science' (Es. 62).

The result was a union of specifically philosophical thinking with religion, a union which Hume thinks has been disastrous. The reason is that philosophical consciousness demands *total control* of the thinker; hence that singularity of conduct and fanaticism that Hume discovered among philosophical sects in the ancient world. But the total dominion demanded by the philosophical consciousness was confined in the ancient world to the private sphere. With Christendom, however, philosophical consciousness gained a measure of control over the state. This meant that the alienation of false philosophy would be not simply a quirk of private sects but would actually inform public affairs. In modern times the troublesome philosophical content of Christianity has moved closer to the surface, so that the philosphical dominion confined in ancient times to private sects 'is now supplied by the modern religion, which inspects our whole conduct, and prescribes an universal rule to our actions, to our words, to our very thoughts and inclination' (EM. 341–2). But we must be very clear here that the oppressive character of modern religion is not due to its *religious* content; it is not because the religious thinker speaks of the sacred or of the divine that his thought is oppressive, it is the false philosophical content of his thought that is oppressive. Hume makes this clear in the *Enquiry* where he observes that '[modern] religion . . . is nothing but a species of philosophy'

(EU. 146). Hume could have no objection to a Christianity purged of its false philosophical content. His position seems to be that of the Athenian in the *Enquiry* who attacks 'the religious philosophers' not 'the tradition of your forefathers, and doctrine of your priests (in which I willingly acquiesce)' (EU. 135).

The philosophical impetus to dominion expressed in modern philosophic religion extends beyond the existence of the thinker to the social and political order as well. And so, Hume holds, there has emerged a new and disastrous sort of political party unique to modern times, namely, parties based not on economic interest or affection for persons and ruling households but on metaphysical principle: 'Parties from principle, especially abstract speculative principle, are known only to modern times, and are, perhaps, the most extraordinary and unaccountable phenomenon that has yet appeared in human affairs' (Es. 60). Hume's insight here is profound and prophetic. He appears to be the first to understand the modern phenonenon of metaphysical political parties, or what have come to be called ideologies. His deepest exploration of them is to be found in the volumes of the *History of England* dealing with the Puritan revolution, the overthrow of the monarchy, and the establishment of a Puritan republic under Cromwell.

Hume's study of the Puritan revolutionary consciousness presents us with the kind of mentality that will surface again in the thought of Robespierre, Babeuf, Marx, Lenin, and twentieth-century revolutionaries too numerous to mention. Indeed, Hume's *History of England* can lay claim to be the first philosophical examination of the modern revolutionary mind. The Puritan revolutionaries were not motivated by outrage over this or that wrong which could be corrected by reform. Reform always operates within the constraints of the prejudices of common life. The Puritan revolutionaries viewed the political order of common life not as the order of participation in which their own activities must operate and be disciplined but, in the manner of false philosophical consciousness, as an alien object of theoretical reflection: a complete system to be totally replaced by an alternative system. But once thought takes on the form of *total criticism*, and consistently cuts itself loose from the domain of custom, there can be no way to know when the alternative system has been instantiated, and so, as Hume observed, 'every successive revolution became a precedent for that which followed it' (H. V, 492).

While the Puritan revolutionaries were instantiating false philosophical consciousness in its religious form, Descartes was working to give it a secular form. Comparing the prejudices of common life to an old house, Descartes has Eudoxus say in *The Search After Truth*: 'I know no better remedy than absolutely to rase it to the ground, in order to raise a new one in its stead. For I do not wish to be placed amongst the number of these insignificant artisans, who apply themselves only to the restoration of old works, because they feel themselves incapable of achieving new'.[4] Descartes was aware that this conception of reason required total revolution and excluded reform, and being conservative politically, he insisted that it apply not to morals and politics but only to natural science, mathematics, and metaphysics. But this was merely a cosmetic and arbitrary manoeuvre, for Descartes' conception of reason simply makes explicit the radical autonomy implicit in philosophy from its inception and which Hume set out to reform.

And so a century and a half after Descartes' death, when false philosophical consciousness had filtered down from the philosopher's closet to the middle class, a member of the National Assembly, during the French Revolution, could address his colleagues not with the language of reform but with the Cartesian language of *total criticism*: 'All the establishments in France crown the unhappiness of the people: to make them happy they must be renewed, their ideas, their laws, their customs must be changed; . . . men changed, things changed, words changed . . . destroy everything; yes destroy everything; then everything is to be renewed'.[5] Compare this with Hume's characterization of 'the modern [philosophic] religion', which he says 'inspects our whole conduct, and prescribes an universal rule to our actions, to our words, to our very thoughts and inclinations' (EM. 341–3). The demand of false philosophical consciousness for total criticism, total destruction, and total renewal captured the work of Fourier and Marx. Fourier wrote: 'the vice of our so-called reformers is to indict this or that defect, instead of indicting civilization as a whole, inasmuch as it is nothing but a vicious circle of evil in all its parts; one must get out of this hell'.[6] And Marx taught that his criticism of society was not against 'wrong in particular' but against 'wrong in general'. The task of criticism is not to *reform* the society in which one is a participant but to totally transform an alien object: 'We are not interested in a change in private property but only in its annihilation, not in conciliation of class antagonisms but in the abolition of classes, not in reforms of present society but in the foundation of a new one'.[7] We have something here very like the inverted world of the Puritan revolutionaries in the *History* and what in the *Enquiry* on morals Hume called 'philosophical chymistry'.

The guilty philosophical consciousness. Like the heroic ascetic and revolutionary philosopher, the guilty philosophical consciousness engages in a form of thought which conceptually destroys the prejudices of common life as a whole. This leads at first to traumatic alienation and self-disgust: 'I am first affrighted and confounded with that forelorn solitude, in which I am plac'd in my philosophy, and fancy myself some strange uncouth monster, who not being able to mingle and unite in society, has been expell'd all human commerce, and left utterly abandon'd and disconsolate' (T. 264). But the guilty philosophical consciousness is not an heroic spirit; he cannot consistently carry the project of total criticism through. He does not seek to quarantine himself from the order of 'deformity' as did Diogenes; nor does he seek to totally replace it as does the revolutionary philosopher. The guilty philosopher does not have the character to free himself from the prejudices of common life; he is so far sunk in these as actually to be a participant in them, contributing to them and enjoying their benefits. His guilt is not about what he has done but about what he knows himself *to be*: a participant in custom. His reason will not allow him to affirm this participation; he has not reached that higher form of critical reflection which Hume calls true philosophy and which enables one critically to affirm the order of prejudice as having original authority. 'Fain wou'd I run into the crowd for shelter and warmth; but cannot prevail with myself to mix with such deformity' (T. 264). He looks with a fascinated and longing eye at *heroic* philosophical existence, whether ascetic or revolutionary, and is the fellow traveller of these modes of existence. But he does not have the courage to take his own reason seriously and so cannot really break with the order of deformity. Though alienated in thought from the prejudices of common life, 'I feel all my opinions loosen and fall of themselves, when unsupported by the approbation of others' (T. 265).

True philosophical consciousness. Central to Hume's conception of the true philosopher as critical participant of common life is the concept of *convention*. A Humean convention is not the result of conscious contrivance but evolves spontaneously as the unintended result of man's attempt to satisfy human needs. The paradigm convention for Hume is language. A natural language is not the result of conscious design; yet it is the work of men and is understood by men, not by rational reflection but by participation. The human world is the total set of these spontaneously evolving conventions, among which are language, law, art, religion, and justice. Though not originally constituted by reflection, it is possible through reflection to gain a speculative understanding of these conventions. For example, by reflection we may discover and make explicit the grammar of a language which we implicitly know through participation. True philosophy, for Hume, is simply an attempt to uncover the structure of the evolving conventions of common life, the grammar, as it were, of morals, science, economics, religion, and so on. As Hume describes his reform in philosophy: 'Philosophical decisions are nothing but the reflections of common life, methodized and corrected' (EU. 162).

V

This conception of true philosophy enables Hume to form links between the concepts of philosophy, history, and civilisation. To the degree that men become aware of the evolutionary process of the human world and gain some measure of control over it, they become to that degree *civilised*. Civilisation, for Hume, is not merely a matter of acting according to certain principles. It is a form of the most important self-knowledge. Civilisation is the story of 'the improvements of the human mind' and is the process whereby the conventions of common life are raised to the level of critical self-consciousness. And since Hume thinks of philosophy as a convention for reflecting on conventions, the self-knowledge of the civilised man must be seen as identical to that of the true philosopher. True philosophical understanding for Hume, therefore, is a social and historical act. As people become more civilised they necessarily become more philosophical.

Not only is philosophy a social act, a convention for reflecting on conventions, it is internally connected to all other conventions that spontaneously make up the human world. There is a sociology of knowledge in Hume which can only be touched on here: '*industry, knowledge*, and *humanity*, are linked together, by an indissoluble chain' (Es. 271). 'We cannot reasonably expect, that a piece of woollen cloth will be wrought to perfection in a nation which is ignorant of astronomy, or where ethics are neglected' (Es. 270–1). Nor 'can we expect that a government will be well modelled by a people, who know not how to make a spinning wheel, or to employ a loom to advantage' (Es. 273). Hume thought that the cultivation of philosophy had led to the superior stability of modern governments over ancient ones, and he hoped that further cultivation of philosophy would lead to further improvements (EU. 10). But all depended on whether the philosophy cultivated was the true or the false.

Hume thought that critical philosophical reflection was more widespread in his time than in any other. This was due in part to the emergence of republican government with its stress on autonomy and the rule of law: 'From law arises security; from security curiosity; and from curiosity knowledge' (Es. 118). But a deeper cause (and one in which Hume seems to have been alone in appreciating) was the historic merger of religion and philosophy in the Christianity of the ancient world. Because of this a rudimentary philosophical consciousness has become an all per-vasive part of European culture. Under modern conditions, this specifically philosophical dimension of Christendom was becoming progressively secular.

As his career developed, Hume began to see, with increasing alarm, that the secular philosophical consciousness that was replacing the religious philosophical consciousness was taking on the form of false philosophy. The fanaticism of secular philosophi-cal sects in the ancient world, which had been safely relegated to the private sphere by the civic religion, could now be played out in the modern world in the public sphere. The implacable triad of false philosophical consciousness (autonomy, ultimacy, and do-minion) and the alienated forms of ascetic, guilty, and revolution-ary philosophical existence could now actually inform political life. The result would be a modern form of oppression that would seek total control over the individual, a form of control that would inspect 'our whole conduct' and prescribe 'a universal rule to our actions, to our words, to our very thoughts and inclinations' (EM. 342). We have something here very like what Vico called 'the barbarism of reflection', the last and decadent stage of his three-stage ideal history of civilisation.[8] In this final stage, men, through philosophical reflection, become alienated from and finally destroy the pre-reflective, poetic order of common life. Hume did not work out a three-stage history of the civil world; history, for him, is open and cannot be grasped as a whole. But, as we have seen, Hume thinks of the process of civilisation as a philosophic act. In so far as false philosophic consciousness is internal to the process, civilisation carries within itself the seeds of its own destruction.

Hume sardonically described his own time as 'this philosophic age' (EM. 197n) and lamented the fact that false philosophical consciousness had captured politics: 'no party, in the present age, can well support itself without a philosophical or speculative system of principles annexed to its political or practical one' (Es. 465). We have observed Hume's teaching that metaphysical political parties are 'known only to modern times' and are 'the most extraordinary and unaccountable phenomenon, that has yet

appeared in human affairs' (Es. 60). It is common to explain
modern political ideologies as secular forms of the religious mind.
The similarities between an ideology such as Marxism and a
religion such as Christianity are too striking to ignore. Yet what
we may learn from Hume's natural history of philosophical
consciousness suggests another explanation, namely that the
rationale of modern political ideologies is internal to the philosophical mind itself.

Near the end of his life, Hume had an intimation that his age
was descending into the inverted world of false philosophical
consciousness. This awareness is expressed in the letters of the
last decade of his life concerning the constitutional crisis in
Britain, which included among other things war with the American
colonies. What these events were and how Hume conceived them
cannot be adequately discussed here. This, however, can be said.
Hume died on 25 August 1776, but he lived through the first year
of war with the colonies. The civil war which had erupted in the
Empire threatened to break out in Britain itself and to end in an
overthrow of the monarchy and the establishment of a republic.
Hume believed in republican government as an ideal, and he even
wrote an essay on the ideal form of a republic for the modern
world.[9] He also supported total independence for the colonies as
early as 1768, before the thought had occurred to most Americans
(L. 420). But for historical reasons he resisted a republican
Britain, fearing that an overthrow of the monarchy would lead to
a replay of the oppressive Puritan republic under the dictatorship
of some new Cromwell. In short, he feared the sort of thing that
did in fact occur in France thirteen years after his death.

He thought the British constitutional crisis was due not so
much to practical conflicts of interest, though these were involved,
but to the alienating power of a false philosophical consciousness.
Men were tearing the constitution apart in the name of philosophical theories of liberty, rights, and government. Here was something new. The problem was not superstition, ignorance, and
religion to be cured by the philosphical intellect. The philosophical intellect itself had become the problem. Hume makes this
point in a letter to Hugh Blair, comparing the secular philosophical
thinking which informs the present constitutional conflict with
the religious thinking that informed the Puritan revolution of the
seventeenth century. The present crisis, Hume says, 'exceeds the
absurdity of Titus Oates and the popish Plot; and is so much
more disgraceful to the Nation, as the former Folly, being derived
from Religion, flow'd from a Source, which has, from uniform
Prescription, acquir'd a Right to impose Nonsense on all Nations
and all Ages' (L. 427).

The philosophical consciousness in Hume's time, unlike religion, had not fully acquired the right to impose nonsense on mankind. Whether it has acquired it in our own time is an open question. But the age of mass philosophical self-consciousness, that Hume saw emerging and which Diderot and Marx encouraged, has in fact come to pass. The political world we live in is very much a world of contrary philosophical systems seeking instantiation in the world: liberalism, conservatism, fascism, socialism, Marxism, communism, not to mention forms of cultural criticism such as feminism, deconstructionism, and countless philosophically reflective projects of 'unmasking' and 'consciousness-raising'. Of all these, the Humean question must be asked whether the philosophical consciousness that constitutes them is the true or the false.

NOTES

The following abbreviation has been used:

H   *The History of England, From the Invasion of Julius Caesar to the Abdication of James the Second, 1688,* with the author's last corrections and improvements. 6 vols. Indianapolis, 1983.

1. Quoted in Ernst Cassirer, *The Philosophy of the Enlightenment,* Fritz C.A. Koelln and James P. Pettegrove (Boston: Beacon Press, 1955) 268–9.

2. *Karl Marx on Revolution,* 13 vols, ed. and trans. Saul K. Padover (New York: McGraw-Hill, 1971), I, 516.

3. In sections iii and iv of the *Treatise,* Hume separates his own philosophical thinking from what he takes to be the ancient *and* modern traditions of philosophy. He intended his criticism of philosophy to be radical.

4. René Descartes, *The Philosophical Works of Descartes,* trans. Elizabeth S. Haldane and G.R.T. Ross (Cambridge: Cambridge University Press, 1969), I, 313.

5. Quoted in Edmund Burke, *Reflections on the Revolution in France,* ed. Thomas Mahoney (Indianapolis: Bobbs Merrill, 1982), 196.

6. Charles Fourier, *Oeuvres complètes,* 6, xv.

7. Quoted in Eric Voegelin, 'The Formation of the Marxian Revolutionary Idea', *The Review of Politics,* XII, 301.

8. Donald Phillip Verene, *Vico's Science of Imagination* (Ithaca and London: Cornell University Press, 1981). See Chapter Seven 'Wisdom and Barbarism'.

9. See 'Idea of a Perfect Commonwealth' in Hume's *Essays, Moral, Political, and Literary.*

5

JOHN PASSMORE

Enthusiasm, Fanaticism and David Hume

'There is no enthusiasm among philosophers' (EU. 147). That forthright pronouncement from Hume's essay 'Of a Particular Providence' in his first *Enquiry* is not merely a side-remark; Hume uses it as a premise to derive the conclusion that the State can safely tolerate philosophy. (I am assuming what is, I think, reasonably plain that at this point we can safely identify the 'I', in what purports to be a dialogue, with Hume himself.) A modern reader might suppose Hume to be suggesting that philosophers are so bored with what they are doing, so apathetic, as to present no conceivable danger to anyone. But that, of course, is not his intent. Rather, Hume is here using the word 'enthusiasm' in its dyslogistic sense, standard in the theological controversies of the seventeenth and eighteenth centuries.

The same is more obviously true when in his *History of England* he writes in condemnation of 'an enthusiastic strain of devotion which admitted of no observance, rites or ceremonies but placed all merit in a mysterious species of fate, in inward vision, rapture and ecstasy' (H. iv, 29, 33). That passage, indeed, could serve as a minimal definition of religious enthusiasm. At 'the summit of enthusiasm', so Hume further tells us, the enthusiast – alternatively described by Hume as a 'fanatic madman' – goes even further than this. He comes to regard himself as 'a distinguished favourite of the Divinity' and under that illusion rejects both reason and morality as 'fallacious guides' (Es. 74). Philosophers, Hume is saying, do not go in for that sort of thing. Like his General Monk, they are 'intoxicated with no fumes of enthusiasm' and maintain 'no connexions with any of the fanatical tribe' (H. vii, 62, 274).

To sum up these already succinct descriptions, enthusiasts – here in contrast with the superstitious – reject, as a source of merit, participation in any kind of ceremony. More positively, they believe that merit consists in having been chosen as one of the elect by 'a mysterious species of fate' and that this election is made manifest in such experiences as raptures and ecstasies. In extreme instances – for enthusiasm admits of gradations – they are so convinced that they are divinely favoured that they reject all moral restraints as having no application to them and cast aside reason as useless. All truth, on their view, comes from internal revelations and the path to these revelations is faith rather than reason.

Enthusiasm, thus understood, is a technical term with a reasonably precise meaning, referring to a sub-species of religious activity. A sub-species only: not all the religious are enthusiasts, however warm their devotion. Putting together what Hume says about religion in his books, his essays and his letters, we can detect a division of religious activity into three principal types: 'true', 'philosophical' and – here the adjectives multiply – 'adulterate', 'false', 'popular' or 'vulgar'. This last is the species to which enthusiasm belongs. (I have here spoken of 'religious activities' rather than 'religions' to underline the fact that a particular historic religion, let us say Roman Catholicism, can give shelter to enthusiasts, to philosophers, and to that other species of false religion – superstition. Indeed, it may even contain a tincture of true religion. But having made that point, I shall follow Hume in using the word 'religion' to mean 'type of religious activity'.)

About the nature of 'true' religion it is hard to be confident. Sometimes, especially in the *History*, it functions as nothing more than a line of defence behind which Hume can retreat when he is accused of attacking religion. 'I included in my criticism', he can then say, 'the saving phrase "Except in the true religion"; I was only attacking false, adulterate, vulgar religion' – blithely ignoring the fact that this includes all the historic Western religions, ancient and modern, great or small. But at other times, 'true' religion does seem to have a content. His letter of June 1743 to William Mure refers to objections to 'every thing we commonly call religion' with two exceptions: 'the Practice of Morality, & the Assent of the Understanding to the Proposition that God exists' (L. 21). In his *Dialogues concerning Natural Religion* this last proposition becomes, in Philo's mouth, more than a little attenuated, reduced to 'one simple, though somewhat ambiguous, at least undefined proposition, *that the cause or causes of order in the universe probably bear some remote analogy to human intelligence*' (D. 227). Indeed, 'true' religion amounts to very little more than the practice of such virtues as tolerance, justice and humanity. Some of his successors were to call a not dissimilar view 'Christianity', but Hume's sense of history prevented him from identifying the two. It would have entailed, amongst other things, calling Confucius a Christian.

'Philosophical' religion sets out to demonstrate, by philosophical reasoning as distinct from an appeal to revelation, that at least some of the principal doctrines of a particular religion, or a particular class of religions, are true. It is, of course, the principal concern of Hume's *Dialogues concerning Natural Religion*. Since, for obvious reasons, 'philosophical' religion particularly interests philosophers, philosophical commentators have tended to concentrate on Hume's very considerable and consistently critical writings in this field. But it is 'vulgar', 'adulterate' religion, alone or commingled with philosophy, which particularly arouses his ire. Of the Reformed religion of his own day, Hume could write with approval in his *History* that it had become a religion which 'resembles more a system of metaphysics' (H. v, 38, 13), mistaken though he took that metaphysics to be. The Reformed religion as it was in the time of the late Tudors, the first Stuarts and the Commonwealth – 'inflamed to a degree of enthusiasm by novelty and persecution' – was a very different and much worse matter.

Our principal concern is with that sub-variety of 'vulgar', 'adulterate' religious activity which Hume calls 'enthusiasm', contrasting it with the other sub-variety 'superstition' and generally identifying it with 'fanaticism'. Both 'enthusiasm' and 'fanaticism' came into regular use as English words – 'enthusiasm' had a somewhat longer history as an explicitly foreign borrowing – only in the seventeenth century, with specific reference to the new Protestant sects.[1] In the minds of a classically-educated intelligentsia, 'enthusiasm' recalled Plato and Plutarch, 'fanaticism' recalled Livy; it had a stronger suggestion of political activities as well as being more consistently dyslogistic. In appropriate contexts, however, the two words were synonymous in Hume's writings – when used, that is, in condemnation of religious zealots.

That last reservation is, however, very important. For if it would certainly be a mistake to suppose that whenever Hume uses the word 'enthusiasm' he has nothing more in mind than what that word now connotes, it would be no less erroneous to suppose that he always uses it in its derogatory, religious, sense. If we do make that supposition, we shall find ourselves compelled to condemn Hume for inconsistencies on a gargantuan scale. For the very same Hume who so confidently tells us that 'there is no enthusiasm in philosophy' elsewhere condemns Pascal and Diogenes for their 'philosophical enthusiasm' and once described himself, or allowed himself to be described, as an 'enthusiast in philosophy'. To resolve these puzzles, we shall have to look with some care at the various contexts in which, and the various purposes for which, Hume uses the word 'enthusiasm'. The result, I hope, will be of some philosophical interest, not merely, although it is that, a philological inquiry.

Let us begin our philosophico-historico-philological discourse with that famous letter addressed by Hume to an unnamed physician. Hume there complains of what we should now call 'depression' but seventeenth-century writers, taking their vocabulary from medical men who had explored 'enthusiasm' as a physiological disorder, called 'cold melancholy', thus distinguishing it from 'hot melancholy', from what modern terminology calls the 'manic' stage in that 'manic-depressive cycle' so characteristic of 'enthusiasts'. He compares his condition to the 'Coldness and Desertion of the Spirit' described 'in the writings of the French Mysticks and in those of our Fanatics here', and explains this similarity thus:

> As this kind of Devotion depends entirely on the Force of Passion, & consequently of the Animal Spirits, I have often thought that their Case and mine were pretty parralel & that their rapturous Admirations might discompose the Fabric of the Nerves & Brain, as much as profound Reflections, & that warmth or Enthusiasm which is inseperable from them. (L. 3)

Some surprise may be felt that the twenty-three-year-old Hume could write thus confidently of the 'French mystics'. There is a tendency to assume that when Hume writes about religion he always has Calvinism in mind. But he had a deep interest in the variety of religious belief and practice, as this letter illustrates. Indeed, one might even suspect in Hume a kind of *nostalgie pour la boue*, a horrified fascination, such as one also finds in William James – although Hume has much less sympathetic understanding – with the wilder shores of religion.

In referring to the French mystics, he probably has in mind not so much the Huguenot Camisars who partly stimulated Shaftesbury's *A Letter concerning Enthusiasm* – in so far as it was a plea that they be dealt with, in their English exile, not with persecution but with tolerant ridicule – as the French tradition centring around at first St Francis de Sales and later Madame Guyon and her defender Fénelon.[2] Certainly that tradition particularly emphasised the dry night of the soul and certainly, too, Hume had some esteem for Fénelon. The 'local fanatics' could well have been the followers of Antoinette Bourgignon, Flemish rather than French, who enjoyed astonishing popularity in early eighteenth-century Edinburgh; so much so that, until as late as 1809, every Presbyterian ordinand was called upon formally to abjure her and her works.

These are historical speculations. Whatever particular mystics and fanatics he had in mind, the really startling thing is that Hume was prepared to compare his mental condition with theirs and was prepared to describe 'warmth and enthusiasm' as inseparable from 'profound reflections' when, after all, 'there is no enthusiasm in philosophy'.

On the first point, however, 'comparable to' is a symmetrical relation. If Hume is like the French mystics, so also are they like him. And he has no doubt that the roots of *his* trouble are to be found in physiological disturbances, that he was suffering from what would now be called a psycho-somatic disorder, by no means supernaturally induced.

As we have already suggested, there was no novelty in the view that religious enthusiasm had physiological roots, although Hume's physiology is relatively refined. To say nothing of Burton's *Anatomy of Melancholy* and the medical writers on which it relied,[3] Meric Casaubon, Henry More, Dean Swift had all drawn attention to the resemblances between the strange behaviour of religious enthusiasts and the behaviour that might be expected from those who are suffering from the effects of wine, sex, song – or flatulence.[4] Characteristically, Swift places particular emphasis on the last of these, so much so that he calls enthusiasts 'Aeolists'. (He at the same time suggests that Scotland was named from the Greek *scotia* – darkness, obscurity – on account of the prevalence of enthusiasts there.)[5]

On the second point, Hume was not the first, either, sometimes to use the word 'enthusiasm' in a narrower dyslogistic sense, sometimes in a broader sense in which it could even contain a eulogistic usage. Casaubon had divided enthusiasm into two varieties, supernatural and natural. Supernatural enthusiasm occurs when a person is actually possessed by a divinity or, alternatively, by some diabolical being. While not denying that such possessions exist, Casaubon takes them to be extremely rare. He is therefore more than a little annoyed with Plato, whom he reads as asserting in the *Ion* that the rhapsode reciting Homer is in fact divinely inspired. That dialogue, later to be so popular with the Romantics, he describes, indeed, as 'a most irrational piece, I think, as ever was written by a philosopher'.

For the rhapsode, Casaubon believes, is obviously experiencing the effects not of 'supernatural' but of 'natural' enthusiasm, defined as an 'extraordinary, transcendent but natural fervency, or pregnancy of the soul, spirits, or brain, producing strange effects, apt to be mistaken for supernatural' (TE. 22). It is this very same natural enthusiasm which is responsible, he agreed with Cudworth before him and Shaftesbury after him, for the greatest achievements of which human beings are capable: 'neither do I believe that ever any great work, that was a fruit of the brain, and that begot admiration, was atchieved, but was also the fruit of some naturall *enthusiasme*; if all elevation of the mind above ordinary thought and conceptions . . . must be so called' (TE. 193). Indeed, if the effects of natural enthusiasm are so often supposed to be supernatural, that is just because under its influence human beings do things which so surpass their normal level of achievement that they suppose themselves to have had divine assistance.

Unlike Casaubon, Hume would not grant that there is ever such a thing as genuine 'supernatural' enthusiasm. But he does want to leave room for the sort of 'natural' enthusiasm Casaubon described and he does want to say that the enthusiasm wrongly supposed to be supernatural is psychologically very like the 'natural' enthusiasm of a deep thinker.

If I have seemed to dwell at inordinate length on Hume's letter to a physician, that is because it is the only place I know of where he makes it perfectly plain that he had noted this resemblance, and so why he could at once so roundly assert that 'there is no enthusiasm in philosophy' i.e. no enthusiasm in its religious sense, and yet on another occasion describe himself, or at least without protest permit himself to be described, as 'an enthusiast without religion'.[6] He certainly did not wish to argue that there was no 'natural' enthusiasm in philosophy.

Now consider a second case, that occasion when Hume was castrating the first two books of the *Treatise* for prudential reasons. 'I was resolved', he then explained to Henry Home, 'not to be an enthusiast, in philosophy, while I was blaming other enthusiams' (L. 6). In what sense would Hume have been 'an enthusiast in philosophy' – false, then, to his maxim that there is no enthusiasm in philosophy – had he included in the *Treatise* what he then called his 'Reasonings concerning Miracles'? And in what ways, too, can the *Treatise* as it stands be described as 'blaming enthusiasms'? The word 'enthusiasm' scarcely appears in Book 1 or Book 2 of the *Treatise*, and when it does so, it is not used in its blameworthy religious sense.

To take these points in order. When Hume resolves not to be an 'enthusiast in philosophy' he means, it would seem, nothing more than this: he is not going to allow his natural enthusiasm – his warmth, his devotion – to sweep away his prudence. That is the sense, in fact, in which an anonymous writer in the *Gentleman's Magazine* had defined 'enthusiasm', as 'any exorbitant, monstrous Appetite of the human Mind, hurrying the Will in Pursuit of an

Object, without the concurrence, or against the Light of Reason, and Common Sense'.[7] It is warmth, that is, not governed by rational and commonsensical restraints, warmth gone wild.

The only enthusiasm which, if not under this name, is explicitly 'blamed' in the *Treatise* is, interestingly enough, excessive scepticism. The metaphors there employed are so characteristic of much enthusiastic literature as to underline what he had told the doctor – that intellectual enthusiasm could lead to psychological disturbances very like those that are produced by religious enthusiasm. Hume, when he allows himself to take scepticism too seriously, suffers, so he tells us, from a 'heated brain' – from, that is, 'hot melancholy'. He begins to fancy himself 'in the most deplorable condition imaginable, inviron'd with the deepest darkness, and utterly depriv'd of the use of every member and faculty' (T. 269).

This might be John of the Cross, or the French mystics, describing the 'dark night of the soul'. Characteristically, however, Hume makes his way out of his total scepticism not by being granted the vision of God but by playing backgammon with his friends; his disorder is naturally, not supernaturally, induced and naturally, not supernaturally, relieved. But it is nevertheless a disorder, not a condition in which we should try to persist. To do so would be to carry adherence to a philosophical procedure – scepticism – beyond the bounds of reason and commonsense.

It is in these terms, too, that we are to understand Hume's description, in the 'Dialogue' appended to *The Principles of Morals*, of Pascal and Diogenes as 'philosophical enthusiasts'. They are *not* enthusiasts in the sense in which 'there is no enthusiasm in philosophy'. Hume condemns Pascal for his superstition, without at all suggesting that he shared the religious attitudes of the enthusiast; Diogenes he sees as an enemy of superstition but certainly not as a religious enthusiast. They both tried to live 'artificial lives', entirely departing from 'the maxims of common reason' (EM. 343). They allowed themselves to be carried away by pushing a philosophical principle to extremes, as was also true, he thought, of some of the political activists of his own time – Wilkes, for example. They suffer from 'too extensive enthusiasm' (EM. 195), they illustrate 'the ardour of new enthusiasms, when every principle is inflamed into extravagance' (EM. 186). This, although they do not pretend to possess supernatural powers or to be divinely inspired.

To revert, however, to Hume's *Treatise*, although that work, unlike so many of his other writings, does not explicitly criticise religious enthusiasm under that name, it is throughout directed against the leading assumptions on which religious enthusiasm rests; it could carry the sub-title *An Antidote against Enthusiasm*. Consider, for example, the teachings of the Scottish Quaker, Robert Barclay. His *Apology for the True Christian Religion*, first published in 1676 and many times reprinted over the following centuries, assumed a classical status as an exposition of Quaker 'enthusiasm'. (Quakers were, for Hume, the 'most egregious' if the 'most innocent' of enthusiasts (Es. 75).) 'This Divine Revelation and inward Illumination', Barclay writes, 'is that which is evident and clear of itself; forcing, by its own Evidence and Clearness, the well-disposed Understanding to assent . . . even as the common Principles of natural *Truths* move and incline the mind to a natural Assent; as, That *the Whole is greater than its part*, That *two contradictory Sayings cannot be both true, nor both false*'.[8] It is central to Hume's argument that if the truths Barclay supposes to be thus revealed to him possess, as Barclay claims, a quasi-mathematical certainty, they would have to be, to use the terminology of the first *Enquiry*, 'relations of ideas'. But in reality, Barclay's surprisingly conventional special revelations – such revelations as 'The world was created by God' – make assertions of a causal kind and are therefore, in Hume's technical sense of the phrase, 'matters of fact'.

But is not this, the enthusiast might reply, sheer dogmatism? Why should not internal revelation be treated as a third source of knowledge, possessing all the certainty of mathematics but gaining its authority from its forcefulness, its solidity, the inner conviction which it carries? Locke had already argued, however, that the claim that a revelation is divine is not self-authenticating, that it has to be based on evidence to show that its origin is indeed divine. 'How do I know', he asked, 'that God is the Revealer of this to me . . .? If I know not this, how great soever the Assurance is, that I am possess'd with, it is groundless; whatever Light I pretend to, it is but *Enthusiasm*' (*Essay*. 701).

Hume's argument would be a little different. By the nature of the case, he would say, an inner revelation can only give us ideas; every genuine idea can be traced back to an impression; there is in the present instance no such impression. The Humean theory of knowledge, the Humean theory of causality, the Humean doctrine of experience all rule out inner revelations as a source of knowledge, or even of rational belief. That is to say nothing of Hume's scepticism, most forcibly directed against those cosmic beliefs which enthusiasts profess. But he also develops more specific arguments.

There is one point on which the critics of enthusiasm regularly insist – and Hume is certainly no exception – namely that those who claim to have experienced inner revelations do so from within a great variety of religious systems and in such a manner that they cannot all be right. To take an instance, not everyone who claims to have had it personally revealed to him that he is *the* Messiah can actually be *the* Messiah. To distinguish, in reply, between the truly inspired and those who are suffering from delusions or are diabolically, rather than divinely, inspired, enthusiasts commonly claim that *their* revelations, the genuine revelations, evidence their genuineness through miracles and particular providences.

But this only postpones the problem. For, as Hume also delights in telling us, enthusiastic sects throughout the ages, in classical quite as much as modern times, have pointed to miracles and particular providences as evidence that their particular set of revelations is to be trusted. No enthusiast, at least within monotheistic religions, would be prepared to accept as evidence every reported miracle, every reported particular providence, with whatever revelation it is associated. Then how are we to distinguish those miracles and particular providences on which a belief in divine revelations can safely be founded from those which are fraudulent or diabolical?

That was a relatively familiar line of objection. Hume's arguments against trying to found a set of religious beliefs on miracles cut deeper than this and are not solely directed against enthusiasts. The superstitious are at least as fond of miracles and particular providences as are the enthusiastic. If Hume takes a special interest in the miracles reported in his own time from the Jansenist cemetery of St Médard, that was not merely because he regarded the Jansenists as enthusiasts. His argument, rather, is that these are miracles reported from within a distinguished intellectual tradition, attested to by persons of substance, without any of the problems arising out of the transmission of testimony over lengthy periods of time. They vividly illustrate his point that even in such cases, the balance of probability was very much against a miracle having occurred. How much the more so in the normal cases where ignorant enthusiasts testify to miracles. For 'where men are heated by zeal and enthusiasm, there is no degree of human testimony as may not be procured for the greatest absurdity' (Eu. 345). If enthusiasts are not his sole target, his 'reasonings concerning miracles' are, if valid, nevertheless fatal to their pretensions.

The position is a little less obvious in respect to particular providences – reports of persons as having been saved, as a result of a divine message, from some imminent danger or as having found a new way open before them, reports very likely to come from enthusiasts, convinced that they are personal favourites of some divinity. Notoriously, that section of the first *Enquiry* entitled 'Of a particular Providence and of a future State' is in fact a preview of Hume's *Dialogues*; its concern is not with particular providences but with the philosophical conception of a Providence-governed universe. For a discussion of particular providences one has to turn to Hume's *Natural History of Religion* (Sect. 6).

There he uses philosophical religion as a counterpoise to vulgar religion. This at the same time permits him to draw attention to the enormous gap between philosophical religion and vulgar religion, the very limited degree to which philosophical religion can accurately be described as an intellectual defence of everyday religious belief and practice. Vulgar religion argues to the existence of providence not, as philosophical religion does, from the existence of order, natural laws, final causes but, on the contrary, from irregularities, striking events. Hume describes the vulgar doctrine thus: 'Ask any of the vulgar, why he believes in an omnipotent creator of the world . . . He will tell you of the sudden and unexpected death of such a one: The fall and bruise of such another: The excessive drought of this season: The cold and rains of another. These he ascribes to the immediate operation of providence'. So, Hume sums up, those events which 'with good reasoners, are the chief difficulties in admitting a supreme intelligence, are with him the sole arguments for it' (NHR. 328–9). There are several sardonic descriptions of this attitude of mind in Hume's *History of England*.

Hume's argument, once more, is not uniquely a shaft against enthusiasm, but he goes on to point more explicitly in that direction when he remarks that 'Madness, fury, rage, and an inflamed imagination, though they sink men nearest to the level of beasts, are, for a like reason, often supposed to be the only dispositions, in which we can have any immediate communication with the Deity'. Here he distantly echoes a common Cambridge Platonist argument: that if God wishes to work directly on individual human beings he will operate through their reason, the only trustworthy 'inner light', not by impelling them to extravagances of behaviour, of the sort regularly reported at the meetings of enthusiastic sects. But Hume is going much further than the Cambridge Platonists when he says that to believe in particular providences is to destroy the only philosophically plausible arguments for the existence of divine beings – quite contrary to the vulgar opinion, accepted by enthusiasts, that to *deny* particular providences is at once to be committed to atheism.

So far, Hume has been arguing that the characteristic beliefs of enthusiasts not only do not count as knowledge but do not even satisfy the requirements laid down by Hume, in his less sceptical moods, for counting as a rational belief. But in his *Natural History of Religion* he goes further than that; the enthusiast, he argues, does not – *qua* enthusiast as distinct from *qua* everyday human being – genuinely have beliefs at all, 'real beliefs' as distinct from 'counterfeit beliefs'. The foundations for this doctrine are laid in that section of the *Treatise* in which he discusses 'poetical enthusiasm'.

Whereas in theological controversies enthusiasm was universally a term of abuse – Wesley, for example, indignantly denied that he was an enthusiast – that is not so in the world of poetry. True enough, some didactic poets directed their didacticism against enthusiasm and Arthur Young, like Wesley, was indignant at the appellation, but others welcomed it, favourably contrasting 'enthusiastic heat' with what they described as the 'lukewarm' doctrines of scepticism and deism. (For the most part, they ignored the distinction between 'good' and 'bad' enthusiasm.) Taking the Platonic musings of Shaftesbury as their authority, they often suggested, indeed, that the poet himself was the bearer of a divine or semi-divine inspiration, thought of as coming from a pantheistically envisaged 'Nature' rather than from more orthodox sources. Among Scottish poets, James Thomson gave expression to this tendency as early as 1726; later in the century, that 'bigotted, silly fellow Beattie' was to be one of its principal exponents. When Hume talks about 'poetical enthusiasm', he does not have in mind, however, these pro-enthusiasm poets, but rather a particular view about poetry in general, namely that although poems are clearly products of the imagination, they are just as capable of arousing vivid ideas and deep passions as are real objects.

Hume would not have had to look far to encounter this doctrine. But I shall take as my example John Dennis; a young man as interested as Hume was in the principles of criticism would almost certainly have read so fashionable a critic. 'The enthusiasm that is found in poetry', according to Dennis, is nothing but a particular set of passions – 'Admiration, Joy, Terror, Astonishment' – 'flowing from the thoughts which naturally produce them'. And, he further tells us, 'the same sort of Passions flow from the Thoughts that would do from the Things of which these Thoughts are Ideas'.

These quotations are from *The Advancement and Reformation of Poetry* (1701). He returns to the theme in *The Grounds of Criticism in Poetry* (1704).[9] There he distinguishes 'Ideas in Meditation'

from 'the Ideas of the same object' as they are employed in
everyday conversation. So the sun in ordinary conversation 'gives
the Idea of a round, flat, shining Body of about two feet
diameter'. In meditation, in contrast, it 'gives the Idea of a vast
and glorious Body, the top of all visible Creation and the brightest
material Image of the Divinity'. The crucial point for our present
purposes is that 'the sun in meditation', although obviously an
idea of the imagination, is, according to Dennis, quite as capable
of arousing an enthusiastic passion – in this case 'Admiration' – as
either the sun itself or the conventional idea of it.

This doctrine is troublesome to Hume, in so far as it ascribes
powers to works of the imagination which, on Hume's view, only
belong to what Dennis calls 'real objects' and Hume 'complex
impressions'. In the main body of the *Treatise*, Hume simply
denies that, except in madness, ideas of the imagination can
generate real passions or serious beliefs. No more than Dennis,
who had been careful to insist that in poetical enthusiasm passion
is 'guided by judgment' would he be willing to identify poetical
enthusiasm with madness, although it is noteworthy that Hume's
discussion of it immediately follows his remarks about madness.
What he does, rather, is to ascribe to the poet, and the poet's
readers, a 'counterfeit belief', something easily dissipated by 'the
least reflection' (T. 123). Later in the *Treatise*, discussing the
passions, he denies that 'a mere fiction of the imagination' can
have any considerable effect on the passions. It lacks vividness,
just because there is no present impression to lend it vividness.
'Tis too weak to take any hold of the mind, or be attended with
passion' (T. 427).

Obviously, however, these forthright doctrines left him troubled.
It was very hard to deny that poetry could generate actual beliefs
and actual passions, as distinct from counterfeit beliefs and
counterfeit passions. Indeed, so far as the passions are concerned,
Hume might seem to be the very archetype of a forgetful author,
in so far as in the second *Enquiry* he places particular stress on
'this talent itself of poets, to move the passions' (E. 259).

But that was in a context where finer epistemological distinctions
were not called for. We should not read it as cancelling out what
he had written in his Appendix to the *Treatise*: 'How great soever
the pitch may be, to which this [the poetic] vivacity arises, 'tis
evident, that in poetry it never has the same *feeling* with that
which arises in the mind, when we reason, tho' even upon the
lowest species of probability' (T. 630). Then, too, 'the *feelings* of
the passions are very different when excited by poetical fictions,
from what they are when they arise from belief and reality'.

Indeed, this difference in the feeling of the passions is used as evidence that the ideas, too, feel different; this argument is more extensively deployed in his *Abstract* (A. 20).

'We shall afterwards have occasion to remark', he also tells us in the Appendix, 'both the resemblances and differences between a poetical enthusiasm and a genuine conviction' (T. 631). If that 'afterwards' means 'in another Appendix note', there is no such note; if it is meant to draw our attention to some later passage in the *Treatise* where Hume has already grounded this distinction, there is certainly no passage which explicitly does so. Perhaps Hume found it harder to make it than he had expected unless, indeed, he takes the whole argument of the *Treatise* to be tacitly, although not expressly, distinguishing between poetical enthusiasm and genuine conviction. As matters stand, we are fobbed off with a few remarks about 'general rules'.

Even if we do not regard it as adequate, and even if Hume himself, taking literature seriously, has some qualms on the point, we are at least quite used to the idea that literature is 'make-believe'. Poets themselves sometimes tell us that, in Hamlet's words, they write 'in a fiction, in a dream of passion' which stands very close to what Hume is saying. Religious enthusiasts, in contrast, always take themselves, whether as teachers or as disciples, to be expounding truths and to be experiencing passions of a particularly profound kind.

Nevertheless, Hume applies what he has said about poetry to religion. In spite of the dogmatism of 'religionists', he tells us, their conviction 'is more affected than real, and scarcely ever approaches, in any degree, to that solid belief and persuasion, which governs us in the common affairs of life' (NHR. XII, 348). Are we to suppose them to be hypocrites, their beliefs 'affected' for some ulterior purpose, let us say a political purpose?

On this point, Hume's position is rather complex. He certainly uses the word 'hypocrite' very freely in talking about the enthusiasts. But one principal theme of his *Natural History of Religion* is that there is scarcely any belief, however monstrously absurd, which human beings cannot believe or, at least, persuade themselves that they believe. On this showing, we have no ground for assuming to be hypocritical even the most fanatical of believers. Some further light, and a degree of darkness, is thrown on the question at two points in Hume's *History*.

At the first point, he tells us that pure hypocrisy is very rare. But so is fanaticism which is quite free from hypocrisy. Pure hypocrisy is rare because if a person, for some ulterior motive, assumes the habits and manners of a fanatic sect, their locutions, their tone of speech, their forms of worship, such a person will inevitably catch something of the fanatic's 'warmth'. Pure fanaticism without hypocrisy is equally rare because the fanatic cannot possibly keep up the level of ecstasy demanded of the enthusaist (H. n. DD to vi, 55, 427). At the second point, he describes religious hypocrisy in such a way that a person can be a hypocrite without being engaged in any kind of deliberate deception. For such hypocrisy, Hume tells us, 'is generally unknown to the person himself'. Indeed, it is for that reason particularly dangerous, even though 'it implies less falsehood' than any other 'species of insincerity' (H. vii, 62, 293). It would seem, then, that the self-deluded, as well as those who consciously pretend to beliefs they do not hold, are hypocrites. But then a problem arises. For presumably such persons are fully convinced that their religious ideas have the same degree of solidity, vivacity and the like as their ordinary ideas; they do not *to them* feel any different.

How does Hume, with no direct access to their minds, know this not to be the case, that in reality the ideas *do* feel different, as his *Treatise* assures us? Well, of course, he might argue that they *must* feel different, because in the absence of the appropriate sort of relationship to impressions, there is nowhere that the solidity, the vivacity, or what you will, could come from. But those who remain convinced that their religious beliefs are solid will no doubt reply that their experience demonstrates that there must be something wrong with Hume's theory of belief.

So Hume falls back on behavioural tests. In the passage I shall go on to quote in this connection, he is explicitly discussing superstition rather than enthusiasm. But although in some contexts that distinction is important, this is one of the many occasions on which we can run them together as Hume himself sometimes does, using the phrase 'superstition or enthusiasm'. The religious may try to persuade themselves that their religious beliefs have the same solidity, liveliness, feeling, as their everyday beliefs. But 'the usual course of men's conduct belies their words'; there is an enormous gulf between their 'verbal protestations' that their beliefs are totally certain and the way in which they actually run their lives (NHR. 362). Nature is too much for them. It will not suffer 'the obscure, glimmering light, afforded in those shadowy regions, to equal the strong impressions, made by common sense and by experience'. Then are we to say that the religious do not genuinely believe what they profess to believe? That would seem to be the outcome of Hume's argument. But he does not press the matter quite that hard. 'Their assent in these matters', he rather tells us, 'is some unaccountable operation of the mind between disbelief and conviction, but approaching much nearer to the former than to the latter' (NHR. 348).

Notice Hume's phraseology. 'Some unaccountable operation of the mind between disbelief and conviction'. Of course, this is not the *Treatise*; there are no epistemological analyses in *The Natural History of Religion*. Nevertheless, it looks as if, in an important sense, Hume has given up; he no longer pretends to be able, within his psychology, to give a clear account of the state of mind of an enthusiast. The difference between a solid conviction and a poetical, or religious, enthusiasm has to be detected in the ensuing conduct. But then one naturally raises an objection; if we do look at the enthusiast's conduct, as revealed in that persecuting zeal, that merciless ferocity, which Hume so often describes in his *History of England* does not this demonstrate the solidity of the enthusiast's conviction?

The situation, Hume suggests, is quite the contrary. The bigotry of the religionists, the violence of their asseverations, are ways in which they try to disguise from themselves their 'real infidelity' (NHR. loc.cit.). His most extended argument on this point is to be found in his *History* where he puts it in the mouth of 'the defenders of Cardinal Pole' – once again, I believe, a persona. 'Theological animosity', according to these defenders, 'so fierce and violent, far from being an argument of men's conviction in their opposite sects, is a certain proof that they have never reached any serious persuasion with regard to these remote and sublime subjects' (H. IV, 37, 358). 'Certain proof' – these are strong words; we should keep in mind Hume's disclaimer at the end of the first book of the *Treatise* of all those occasions on which he had written ' 'tis certain that' as 'extorted from me by the present view of the object' rather than as displaying a 'dogmatical spirit' or 'conceited idea of my own judgment'. Still, 'the present view' is in this instance very emphatic. 'While men zealously maintain what they neither clearly comprehend nor entirely believe', he assures us, 'they are shaken in their imagined faith by the opposite persuasion, or even doubts, of other men'. In contrast, 'wherever a man's knowledge and experience give him a perfect assurance in his own opinion, he regards with contempt, rather than anger, the opposition and mistakes of others'. If enthusiasts showed tolerance, if they no longer persecuted their opponents as 'impious and profane', that would really trouble Hume, suggesting that their beliefs were solid, sincere. But he has no fear of being refuted in that particular way.

The whole thrust of his epistemology and metaphysics, I have been suggesting, sets Hume in opposition to the enthusiast. The

same is true of his political and moral outlook. Consider this
dictum from his *Natural History of Religion*: 'no course of life has
such safety (for happiness is not to be dreamed of) as the
temperate and moderate, which maintains, as far as possible, a
mediocrity, and a kind of insensibility, in every thing' (NHR.
361–2). One could scarcely imagine a more contra-enthusiastic
statement. The stoic values it extols – safety, temperance, moderation, a kind of insensibility – are precisely what the enthusiast
spurns. And that 'happiness is not to be dreamed of' is a
conclusion the enthusiast is totally unable to accept.

In defence of his attitude, Hume points to the horrors into
which men have been led by their enthusiasm, their 'counterfeit'
belief that their actions were justified by some personal revelation,
whether to themselves or to the leader they follow. His *Dialogues*,
as I said, are principally directed against 'philosophical' religion.
No enthusiast takes part; enthusiasts are not interested in, are
incapable of, dialogue. Why discuss when the truth has been
revealed, once and for all? But towards the end, Philo directs his
fire against enthusiasm as part of a wider case against Cleanthes's
view that religion, even at its most misguided, is at least a
prophylactic against immorality. If we look at the way in which
vulgar religion actually works in society we shall find it guilty,
Hume has Philo argue, of the most appalling crimes, a point
Hume constantly underlines in his *History*. And the enthusiast
goes even further than the superstitious. It is the enthusiast
Hume has in mind when he remarks that 'amongst themselves,
some have been guilty of that atrociousness . . . of declaiming, in
express terms, against morality, and representing it as a sure
forfeiture of the divine favour, if the least trust or reliance be laid
upon it' (D. 222).

That is not all. Even when it does not go to such antinomian
extremes, enthusiasm represents, on Hume's view, a danger to
morality. In the first place, as Hume regularly argues, it is
impossible for any human being to sustain his devotion at the
level demanded by enthusiasm. Hence, enthusiasm generates
hypocrisy. Secondly, enthusiasts lay the moral stress in quite the
wrong place, away from justice, tolerance and humanity. Even if
they do not put themselves 'in direct opposition to morality' they
at the very least transvalue values. 'Where the interests of religion
are concerned, no morality can be forcible enough to bind the
enthusiastic zealot', so that at best humanity and justice are put in
second place whereas in 'true' religion they are in first place. 'A
new and frivolous species of merit' is introduced, in which justice
and humanity are less important than faith. The sharpest of all his

judgements on this point is to be found not in Hume's *Dialogues* but in his *Natural History of Religion* where he takes cover behind the Chevalier Ramsay: 'The grosser pagans contented themselves with divinizing lust, incest and adultery; but the predestinarian doctors have divinized cruelty, wrath, fury, vengeance and all the blackest vices' (NHR. 356).

'The predestinarian doctors' – this a clear enough reference to the Calvinists. Are we to assume that Hume's attack on 'enthusiasm' is, after all, no more than a covert attack on Calvinism? Certainly, he argues that 'the doctrine of absolute decrees' i.e. of election and reprobation, 'has ever been intimately associated with the enthusiastic spirit' (H. vi, Appendix to 49, 144). That doctrine, although by no means peculiar to Calvinists, was retained by them, as Hume points out, after other reformers had in practice abandoned it. And when he is discussing the Covenanters' opposition to Charles I, he describes Calvinism as 'nourishing in every individual the highest raptures and ecstasies of devotion', in the manner typical of enthusiasm (H. VI, 53, 292).

Indeed, this may explain what is otherwise rather puzzling – the discrepancy between Hume's description of the psychological type attracted to enthusiasm and what most of his predecessors had written on that theme.[10] Basically, as I said, his predecessors described the enthusiast as being what we should now call a manic-depressive. But their emphasis was on his melancholy; his manic phase was 'hot melancholy'. For Hume, in contrast, the enthusiast is subject to 'an unaccountable elevation and presumption', and that arises from 'prosperous success, from luxuriant health, from strong spirits, or from a bold and confident disposition'. That is why the enthusiast can so easily imagine himself to be 'a distinguished favourite of the Divinity'. In a way, this foreshadows Max Weber. Did Hume have in mind the bold spirits of the Scottish Covenanters?

Nevertheless, as Hume's *History* proceeds, the Presbyterians come to be respectable; they are even contrasted with enthusiasts. 'The very dregs of the fanatics', so he tells us, are 'fifth monarchy men, anabaptists, antinomians, independents' (H. VII, 61, 197). So 'enthusiast' ranges widely in its historical application.

Are we to conclude from our discussion that of all forms of religion, Hume thought enthusiasm the very worst? It is very natural to think so, given that on every point of morality and metaphysics Hume denounced enthusiasts so unsparingly. In his introduction to the *Dialogues*, Kemp Smith specifically asserts, indeed, that if Hume had been forced to choose between superstition and enthusiasm, he would have chosen superstition, although preferably of a pagan rather than a Christian sort (D. 13).

There are passages in Hume which lend colour to that presumption. So, discussing Bishop Laud's attempt to reinstate ceremonies, Hume remarks that although 'a philosophical mind' will ridicule ceremonies, they have their usefulness 'in a very religious age', as mollifying the 'fierce and gloomy spirit of devotion' to which, in such an age, the 'rude multitude' is subject (H. vii, 57, 36). Nevertheless, Hume's essay 'Of Superstition and Enthusiasm' unmistakably favours enthusiasm over superstition. This comes out even in Hume's description of the character types which each attracts. Most of us, if we had to make the choice, would certainly prefer to suppose that our religion arises from that 'hope, pride, presumption, a warm imagination, together with ignorance' which Hume ascribed to the enthusiast rather than from the 'weakness, fear, melancholoy, together with ignorance' which he ascribes to the superstitious, even if neither description is precisely entrancing (Es. 74).

More important, however, is that Hume sees a very great difference in the long term political consequences of enthusiasm as contrasted with superstition. To sum up the difference briefly: in the long term, enthusiasm encourages liberty, superstition discourages it. So in his *History*, referring to the Puritans, he could write: 'It was to this sect, whose principles appear so frivolous, and habits so ridiculous, that the English owe the whole freedom of their constitution' (H. v, 40, 161). In contrast, superstition renders men 'tame and abject, and fits them for slavery'. Even in his own time, it was the Jansenists, he tells us, who 'preserve alive the small sparks of the love of liberty to be found in the French nation' (Es. 79). The principal reason for this is that the enthusiast, quite unlike the superstitious, rejects the concept of priestly power, the great enemy of liberty; he 'bestows on his own person a sacred character, much superior to what forms and ceremonious institutions can confer on any other' (Es. 76; cf. H. vi, 53, 292).

But what about the violence, the persecutions associated with enthusiasm? That, Hume argues, is only a passing phase. Enthusiasm is like a thunderstorm, short and violent; to complete the metaphor, we might say that superstition is a persistently bad climate. Yesterday's enthusiast, Hume adds, is often today's freethinker or at the very least he comes to adhere to a 'philosophical' religion. As we have already seen, he described the reform movements of the seventeenth century as having issued in his time in a religion 'which being chiefly spiritual, resembles more a system of metaphysics' (H. v, 40, 161). He happily remarks in his essay 'On National Characters' that 'our ancestors, a few centuries ago, were sunk in the most abject superstition, last century they were inflamed with they most furious enthusiasm, and are now settled into the most cool indifference with regard to religious matters, that is to be found in any nation of the world' (Es. 206) – even if later in the century (1776) he is to be found complaining to Gibbon that 'the prevalence of Superstition in England, prognosticates the Fall of Philosophy and Decay of Taste' (L. 516). The fact is that for Hume there are things worse than violence – in particular, servility and credulity. This comes out very plainly in his *History*, describing the Church of Rome. Under the Roman regime, he says, 'violent persecutions, or, what was worse, a stupid and abject credulity' everywhere prevailed (H. iv, 29, 27). Let me emphasise that phrase 'or *what was worse*, a stupid and abject credulity'.

The passage I have just quoted forms part of a lengthy digression in which Hume defends not only toleration but the principle that sects of every kind should be given public support. His argument is typical. If you pay the clergy a salary, they will cease to be diligent in their pursuit of new disciples and will settle down to an amiable mediocrity. To 'bribe their indolence' pays in the long run. It is not surprising that Hume's most favoured church, for all its superstitious weaknesses, was the eighteenth-century Church of England.

In *The Wealth of Nations* (Bk. v. Art. 3, 740–5) Adam Smith quotes this digression and takes the view that the State should permit each sect to find ways of becoming self-supporting, establishing none of them. In Hume's spirit, too, he wryly remarks that 'the sect called Independents, a sect no doubt of very wild enthusiasts' were the great supporters of 'this plan of ecclesiastical government or, more properly, of no ecclesiastical government'. But there is a degree of optimism in Smith's analysis – what people tend to think of as 'Enlightenment' optimism – which Hume did not share. Smith is convinced that if men were left entirely free in these matters, there would, first of all, be no large churches but a multitude of sects and secondly that since these small sects would be forced to make the necessary accommodations with one another, this will 'probably reduce the doctrine of the greater part of them to that pure and rational religion, free from every mixture of absurdity, imposture and fanaticism, such as wise men have in all ages of the world wished to see established'. If Smith is sceptical about this in fact happening, it is only in so far as he questions whether any State will ever surrender the power it can exercise through an established religion.

Hume's scepticism runs far deeper; he believes that superstition and enthusiasm are ineradicable. If you examine the religious principles which have governed the world, he tells us, 'you will scarcely be persuaded, that they are any thing but sick men's dreams' or 'the playsome whimsies of monkies in human shape' (NHR. 362). Of some of those principles, of transsubstantiation, for example, he remarks that 'in a future age, it will probably become difficult to persuade some nations, that any human, two-legged creature could ever embrace such principles'. That may sound optimistic. But then comes the rub: 'it is a thousand to one, but these nations themselves shall have something full as absurd in their own creed, to which they will give a most implicit and most religious assent'. (It is interesting to consider the contrast at this point between Smith and Hume in the light of the history of Christianity in the United States.)

If not enthusiasm, what is, in Hume's eyes, the worst of all religious manifestations? Well, it does not fall neatly within any of the four types we mentioned, the true, the philosophical, the enthusiastic, the superstitious. Rather, it is that admixture of superstition and philosophy which Hume particularly saw in the Roman church. 'Enthusiasts', as he understands the term, feel no need for philosophy. Private revelation, not philosophy, is their starting point; miracles, particular providences, prophesies, inexplicable behaviour their evidence. And if he disputes the conclusions of natural religion, which may fairly be described as a union of philosophy and religion, that is not because he takes it to be monstrous; it is the next best thing, one might say, to 'true' religion. But the union of superstition and philosophy leaves both philosophy and human life in general much worse off than when the minds of human beings were governed by a purely superstitious pagan mythology.[11] Surprising as this may seem, pagan mythology is, on Hume's view, often more reasonable – consisting as it does of a set of stories which 'however groundless, imply no express absurdity and demonstrative contradiction' – than a 'systematical, scholastic' religion (NHR. 352). Worst of all are the Jesuits, although he defends them in his *History* against some of the *political* charges brought against them, for 'by the very nature of their institution, they were engaged to pervert learning, the only effectual remedy against superstition, into a nourishment of that infirmity' (H. V, 41, 209).

Let me now sum up. By 'enthusiasm' – never then equated with 'fanaticism' – Hume sometimes means something like what we now mean by it: an intense interest. In that particular sense he is far from condemning it. He recognises, however, that it can be disastrous when carried to extremes. That happens even in philosophy when a principle is not curbed by common sense. In another sense, as used in the phrase 'poetical enthusiasm', it refers to the capacity of literature to arouse feelings and beliefs in us. That is by no means to be condemned. But it presents difficulties for Hume's epistemology in so far as that regards beliefs as arising only from impressions. So Hume is led to argue that in fact poetry gives rise only to beliefs and to passions which are counterfeits of the real things.

That leaves enthusiasm in its technical, religious, sense, in which Hume does identify it with fanaticism. It is marked by a belief in personal inspiration, ecstasies, particular providences, miracles and the like. Hume attacks it on a wide variety of grounds, rejecting its claims to offer a special kind of certainty, condemning its moral emphases. At the same time, it presents him, as it had presented Locke,[12] with epistemological problems, how to show that the beliefs of the enthusiasts do not in fact have the solidity the enthusiast claims for them. He has to grant, too, that enthusiasts, unlike the superstitious, have advanced the cause of freedom, of constitutional liberties, whether intentionally or not. If the road to Hell is paved with good intentions, the path to a more liberal society – not, of course, to heaven, for that is 'not to be dreamed of' – is paved, it would seem, with bad metaphysics and worse morals. No one is as good as Hume at being disconcerting.

NOTES

The following abbreviations are used:

H   Hume, *The History of England*, Oxford, 1826. Volumes as well as page numbers of this work vary from edition to edition, as does the distribution of material between text and notes.

Essay   John Locke, *An Essay concerning Human Understanding*, ed. P.H. Nidditch, Oxford, 1979.

TE   Meric Casaubon, *A Treatise concerning Enthusiasme as It is an Effect of Nature: but is mistaken by many for either Divine Inspiration, or Diabolicall Possession*, second edition, revised and enlarged, London, 1656.

1. For a fuller account see M.K. Whelan, *Enthusiasm and English Poetry of the Eighteenth Century*, Washington, 1935; S.I. Tucker, *Enthusiasm: A Study in Semantic Change*, Cambridge, 1972; R.A. Knox, *Enthusiasm*, Oxford, 1950.

2. For Hume's religious background in general see André Leroy, *La Critique et la religion chez David Hume*, Paris, 1930. We arrived independently at the Guyon hypothesis – or, more accurately, the hypothesis that Hume had in mind the French school of Mysticism, defended by Fénelon, to which Guyon gave rather strident expression. In his *Hume's Philosophy of Religion*, London, 1978, J.C.A. Gaskin develops and extends some of Leroy's other suggestions, particularly in relation to miracles and to philosophical religion. It is interesting that the first lengthy study of Hume on religion was written by a French scholar; it is equally interesting that Hume refers to the French mystics rather than to those German or Spanish mystics who were the particular targets of earlier critics of enthusiasm. See also Richard Wollheim's introduction to *Hume on Religion*, London, 1963 which usefully collects Hume's major writings on religion, except for his *History of England*.

3. On this point see M. Heyd, 'Robert Burton's sources on enthusiasm and melancholy: from a medical tradition to religious controversy', *History of European Ideas* 5, 1984, 17–44.

4. The first criticisms of enthusiasm of which I am aware came from the Cambridge Platonists. The founder of that movement, Benjamin Whichcote, lays it down in one of his Aphorisms that 'Nothing is more necessary to the interests of religion than the prevention of enthusiasm'. But the aphorisms were not published until 1753; Cudworth's main discussions of enthusiasm still remain in manuscript. On this theme see J.A. Passmore, *Ralph Cudworth* (1951). Henry More's *Enthusiasmus Triumphatus* (1656) was the medium through which the Cambridge Platonist criticism attracted public attention. It appeared in several revised editions and was plagiarised as late as 1739 as *Enthusiasm Explained*, perhaps in response to the rise of Methodism. A year earlier an exiled scholar, Meric Casaubon, son of the more famour scholar, published his *A Treatise concerning Enthusiasme*; my references are to the second edition (1656). Locke added a powerful attack on enthusiasm to the fourth edition of his *Essay on the Human Understanding* (1700). Swift vulgarised – in both the older and the modern sense of the word – More's ideas in *A Tale of a Tub* and *Mechanical Operation of the Spirit*, both published in 1704, although the first had earlier circulated in manuscript. Shaftesbury's typically elusive *A Letter concerning Enthusiasm* first appeared in 1708 and was followed by much else in the way of explanation and extension, all brought together in *Characteristics* (1711). We know from E.C. Mossner's *The Life of David Hume*, Edinburgh, 1954, 31, that Hume owned a copy of this work, acquired as early as 1726. Shaftesbury was a good deal influenced by the Cambridge Platonists; he quotes More extensively. I do not know whether Hume had read Casaubon or More or Locke's

chapter on enthusiasm or these particular writings by Swift. If I nevertheless cite them, that is because they sum up prevalent lines of argument.

5. *A Tale of a Tub*, Section 8.

6. Compare Mossner, *Life*, 570.

7. Quoted in Whelan, *Enthusiasm in English Poetry*, 3, from *The Gentleman's Magazine*, January 1735.

8. Robert Barclay, *Apology for the True Christian Religion*, Eighth edition, London, 1765, iv.

9. Both *The Advancement and Reformation of Poetry* (1701) and *The Grounds of Criticism in Poetry* (1704) are included in E.N. Hooker, ed. *The Critical Works of John Dennis*, Baltimore, 1939. See especially pp. 215–18, from which my first quotation is taken, and the rather clearer account in pp. 338–9, the source of the second quotation.

10. In his *Hume's Philosophical Politics*, Cambridge, 1975, Duncan Forbes draws attention (214–15n.) to an article on superstition and enthusiasm in the *Old Whig* as reported in the *Gentleman's Magazine* (Vol. 8, 148), which takes the same view. But the question still arises why Hume accepted it.

11. Compare Shaftesbury, *Miscellaneous Reflections* (1711) included in *Characteristics*, 2, 206–7. But Shaftesbury speaks of what happened in the early days of Christianity as the malign union of *religion* and philosophy, giving birth to a kind of 'philosophical enthusiasm', rather than, as Hume does, to a union of *superstition* and philosophy.

12. On Locke, see J.A. Passmore, 'Locke and the Ethics of Belief' in A. Kenny (ed.), *Rationalism, Empiricism and Idealism*, Clarendon Press, Oxford, 1986 or *Proceedings of the British Academy*, 1978. Note particularly Locke's appeal to 'professed beliefs'. On a connected theme see J.A. Passmore, 'Hume and the Ethics of Belief' in G.P. Morice (ed.), *David Hume*, Edinburgh University Press, Edinburgh, 1977 or in J.A. Passmore, *Hume's Intentions*, 3rd. ed., Duckworth, London, 1980.

6

KEITH LEHRER

Beyond Impressions and Ideas: Hume vs Reid

Thomas Reid was a persistent and acute critic of the philosophy of David Hume. It is Reid's contention that Hume's theory cannot account for the facts of human conceptualisation and belief.[1] Hume's theory is deficient in that impressions and ideas are inadequate to account for the intentionality of human thought, the fact that human thoughts have objects, ones that may not exist. Impressions and ideas are also inadequate to account for the facts of belief, especially the fact of negative belief. Reid recognises the genius of the attempt to account for human conceptualisation and belief in terms of impressions and ideas. He calls Hume the most acute metaphysician of the age and remarked, in correspondence, that if Mr Hume were to stop writing, he and his cohorts in Aberdeen would have nothing to discuss. Reid remarks as well, however, that it is genius and not the lack of it that leads to false philosophy. Reid is not a mere *modus tollens* critic of Hume. Unlike G.E. Moore, Reid does not rest content with arguing that Hume's theory cannot account for the facts; rather, his philosophy is an attempt to offer a better theory.[2] I shall describe Reid's destructive and constructive efforts to refute the philosophy of Hume.

Reid's theory postulates certain innate conceptual operations of the mind that he considers necessary to account for the facts of human conceptualisation. Some of these operations are operations on other operations of the mind, that is, they are metamental operations based on consciousness of the lower level operations. It is notable that intentionality and consciousness are the two features of the mental that are the most problematic from the standpoint of contemporary cognitive science and philosophy of mind.[3] Reid's theory explains the connection between these two features, namely, that intentionality presupposes consciousness.

To account for intentionality, according to Reid, it is necessary to suppose that we have general conceptions which result from directing our attention to mental operations, what he calls abstracting, and generalising to form general conceptions in ways that are useful for communication and the acquisition of knowledge. Some conceptions and beliefs arise from innate principles of the human mind. Reid argues that the beliefs to which such principles give rise are justified without reasoning, though he admits that all faculties of the mind are fallible. Our original perceptual beliefs concerning the external world are beliefs of this kind, ones that are justified without reasoning, and this fact suffices to refute one sort of scepticism. Reason requires first premises in order to proceed, and some of our beliefs in the external world are first premises, ones that are so evident in themselves that they do not require or admit of justification by reasoning.

There is some similarity to Reid in the later Hume, but Reid remains a powerful critic of the author of the *Treatise of Human Nature*. I agree with Reid that the project of that author was the work of the most acute metaphysician of the age, or any age, and the project to construct a psychology from impressions and ideas was one of the most important of the age, or of any age. It is the brilliance of that project, as well as of the fascination of the alternative Reid presents, which motivates my presentation and evaluation of the controversy. The controversy is of interest because of its relevance to current speculation and construction in the philosophy of mind and cognitive science.

Against Hume on Impressions and Ideas. Reid's interpretation of Hume's doctrine concerning impressions and ideas is and must remain controversial. The reason is the technical and philosophical language in which Hume articulates the doctrine. He says, of course, 'All the perceptions of the human mind resolve themselves into two distinct kinds, which I shall call *Impressions* and *Ideas*'.[4] Reid notes that this use of the term 'perceptions' is technical and that the meaning is unclear. Reid offers a remarkable ordinary-language critique of Hume's use of the words 'perception' and 'impression'; he does not claim that this refutes Hume, only that it shows that his use of the terms is technical and unexplained.

Assuming that *perceptions* are operations of the mind, then all operations of the mind are, on Hume's theory, impressions or ideas. Reid concludes that, according to Hume, what is *immediately* before the mind is always some impression or idea. In the early part of the *Treatise* there is support for attributing to Hume the thesis that what is before the mind, that is, an object of thought, is either some impression or idea, or it is something that is represented by an impression or idea. Let us call this, as Reid does, the Ideal Theory. It is the target of Reid's criticism. Reid regarded the refutation of this doctrine as his greatest contribution. The refutation consists of arguments to show that it does not accord with the facts, as well as arguments to show that a better theory is available.

Reid's basic argument against the Ideal Theory is that it does not account for intentionality. Reid does not present a single refutation. He knew that Hume's doctrine was subtle. One could not knock out the doctrine with a single punch. It is the weight of successive blows, jabs and counterpunches, that is required. The initial jab is clear. It concerns thinking of objects that do not exist, a centaur for example. He notes that it is one of the basic properties of the faculty of conception that it can be employed about things that do not exist. He says:

> The last property I shall mention of this faculty, is that which essentially distinguishes it from every other power of the mind; and it is, that it is not employed solely about things which have existence. I can conceive a winged horse or a centaur, as easily and as distinctly as I can conceive a man whom I have seen. Nor does this distinct conception incline my judgment in the least to the belief that a winged horse or a centaur ever existed. (368)

Impressions and ideas are things that exist, they are operations of the mind, but centaurs are things that do not exist. It is a fact, Reid alleges, that he thinks of a centaur and that what he thinks of does not exist. Since impressions and ideas are things that do exist and centaurs are things that do not exist, what is before the mind is something that does not exist and, hence, is not an impression nor an idea. Now Reid is fully aware that Hume, or a modern defender, would reply that when he thinks of a centaur what is immediately before the mind is some impression or idea constructed by the imagination that represents a centaur. Reid has two replies. The first is that he can tell what is before his mind, and what is before his mind when he conceives of a centaur is not some presently existing impression or idea but a being that is half man and half horse, a being that does not exist. Reid here supposes that attentive reflection reveals to us what is before the mind, because an unconscious thought is like an unthought thought. To the modern mind, this doctrine appears doubtful. It appears perfectly consistent to affirm that there are impressions or ideas before the mind which we cannot introspect and that these represent a centaur. Reid, not content to rest his argument on a controversial philosophical thesis, has another argument.

Before considering his main argument, however, let us consider another example, where the object of thought is a sensation, a prime candidate for the status of an impression or idea. Suppose I smell, Reid says, a tuberose, and, sometime later, remember the sensation. There may be some faded impression of the sensation, but what I remember, what I think of, is not the presently existing idea, the faded sensation, but a sensation that no longer exists, the sensation resulting from smelling the tuberose. The sensation which I had this morning, when I smelled the tuberose, no longer exists when I remember it in the afternoon. The sensation, which is the object of thought, is something that does not exist and, therefore, what is before the mind is not an impression nor an idea. The advantage of this example over the former is it does not presuppose that one can think of external objects and shows that the problem of intentionality is not the problem of thinking of *external* objects that do not exist. The importance of the example is that it shows that every memory of some sensation or experience is a thought of something that does not now exist.

Of course, the same reply might be forthcoming, to wit, that one thinks of something that does not exist by thinking of something that does exist, an impression or idea that represents what does not exist. It is time to turn to Reid's reply. The reply is an attack on the representational theory that is as relevant to contemporary representational theories of thought and conception as to the Ideal Theory. It is an argument to show that representation presupposes conception and, therefore, cannot explain the basic facts of conceptualisation.

Here is the argument. Suppose that what is before the mind is always some impression or idea. Suppose, moreover, that the idea or impression represents something. How does it represent the thing represented or signify the thing signified? It might do so indirectly, by means of some natural relation between the sign and the thing signified, such as similarity. Reid thinks that alternative was refuted by Berkeley. The impression or idea, a sensation whether lively or faded, does not resemble any external object or quality of an object. So our conception of external objects and their qualities cannot be based on impressions and ideas which resemble those objects and qualities. There is no such resemblance. This argument is, however, not fundamental, though the premiss of non-resemblance seems correct.

The principal argument is strikingly simple and, in fact, is derived from reflections that Reid found in Hume himself. Suppose that representation or signification is some natural relation to the thing represented or signified, causation for example. Does it suffice for the sign, S, to signify some object, O, to me that S stand in the natural relation, R, to O? For example, does it suffice for one thing to signify another to me that it stand in a relation of similarity or causation to it? Clearly not. Why? Because I might not *interpret* S as signifying O. Whatever the natural relation between S and O might be, S will not signify O *to me* unless I interpret S as signifying O. The fact, if it were a fact, that some idea or impression resembled some object, that some sensation of smell, for example, resembled an object, a rose, which it does not, or is caused by the object, which it may be, does not mean that it represents that object to me. What else is required?

Obviously, I must have some conception of O, the object represented or signified by S in order for the sign to signify or represent the object *to me*. If I have no conception of O, a rose, or any quality of the rose, for example, then I cannot interpret or even learn to interpret the sign, S, a sensation, impression or idea, as representing or signifying the rose, or any quality of the rose. Or, to leave the matter solely within the realm of sensation, I cannot interpret or learn to interpret any presently existing impression or idea as representing some other impression or idea, one that no longer exists but which I now remember for example, unless I have some conception of that other impression or idea that no longer exists. The conclusion is ineluctable. Representation presupposes conception of the object represented and cannot explain conception of the object.

On the contrary, conception of the object is required to explain representation. Reid concludes that those impressions and ideas postulated to represent all the objects of thought are a mere fiction of philosophers. We cannot discern them by attentive reflection, and they are theoretically otiose for the explanation of our conception of objects. We may, of course, speak of impressions and ideas, using these terms to refer to those operations of the mind we discern by attentive reflection, those of sensation and thought, for example, but the impressions and ideas postulated to represent all the objects of thought do not exist. When Reid asked himself what reason he had for supposing such impressions and ideas to exist, he concluded he had none but the authority of philosophers. As I continue to speak of impressions and ideas in the remainder of the paper, I shall be referring, as Reid often did, not to the elusive creations of philosophers, but to the operations of sensation and thought discernible by attentive reflection.

The foregoing must be qualified. The argument only applies to the most fundamental level of conception. It is, of course, possible, assuming a certain level of conceptual understanding, that contemplation of a sign or representation could conjoin previously understood signs in such a way as to generate some new conception. But the most fundamental level of conception, our original conceptions of objects, cannot be explained by saying some object before the mind represents those objects. In order to learn to interpret signs, we must have some conceptions of objects, for without such conceptions, the so called 'signs' will signify nothing. We must presuppose some original conceptions of objects in order to account for our learning the meaning of any signs. One may put this another way. We must presuppose an innate understanding of some signs. It is not the sign that explains how we conceive of the object, it is, rather, some innate principle of the mind, as Reid put the matter, that gives rise to our conception of the object 'by a natural kind of magic'. In Reid's words,

> A third class of natural signs comprehends those which, though we never before had any notion or conception of the thing signified, do suggest it, or conjure it up, as it were, by a natural kind of magic, and at once give us a conception and create a belief of it. (122)

Reid offers us a theory of this third and most fundamental class of signs and the things signified by them. He attempts to explain how all our conceptions are derived from a frugal supply of original conceptions evoked by innate principles of mind. We shall examine Reid's theory below after examining Reid's discussion of Hume's theory of belief. It is important to note, in concluding this presentation of Reid's critique of Hume, that Reid's criticism of Hume's theory of conception applies to our conception of presently existing ideas and impressions as well as to our conception of those ideas and impressions that do not now exist.

The conception of the operations of our minds, the conception of presently existing impressions and ideas for example, is the result of a conceptual faculty that supplies those conceptions, the faculty of consciousness. Reid holds that we are conscious of all the operations of our mind, but the logical point remains, that we may distinguish between a sensation, a pain for example, and our conception of a pain. For, as Reid often insists, a sensation has no object. I may say that I feel a pain, but here grammar is misleading in that *'feeling a pain* signifies no more than *being pained'* (183). The pain is a modification of me. Unlike a thought or a conception of something, it has no object. Here is Reid's objection to the thesis that intentionality is the mark of the mental, later to be defended by Brentano.[5] There are mental states, sensations, that are not intentional. They have no objects. It follows that there is a distinction between a pain, or any other sensation, and our conception of the pain. The conception has an object, the pain, while the pain has no object.

We can distinguish between presently existing operations of the mind, impressions and ideas, and the conception of those impressions and ideas, even if, as Reid believed, in fact, we are conscious of, that is have a conception of, all the operations of the mind. The conception of our mental operations, of impressions and ideas, takes us beyond the first level of mental operations to a metalevel. Consciousness of mental operations, which implies conception of those operations, is a metamental operation of conceiving of a lower level operation, of sensation for example. To account even for our conception of impressions and ideas, one must assume an innate principle of conception that supplies such conceptions in response to those impressions and ideas. One cannot even account for our conception of presently existing impressions and ideas without assuming something more than impressions and ideas, to wit, the metamental activity of conception resulting from innate principles of the mind, especially the principles of consciousness.

Why must the principles be innate? It is possible to argue as, for example, Sellars has, that our conception of mental operations is derivative from our conception of external objects and, more specifically, from a theory constructed to explain behaviour.[6] All that Reid's argument shows is that *some* conceptions must result from innate principles of the mind. The argument does not tell us which are innately inspired. Reid, a man of his times, thought it was clear empirically that a child has a conception of his own mental operations, of his sensations for example, before these conceptions could be accounted for by tutelage, and, therefore, he assumed that they were the result of innate principles of the mind, those of consciousness.

Reid versus Hume on Belief. It is characteristic of Reid's theory that, in some instances, belief irresistibly accompanies conceptualisation, especially in those instances in which the conceptions arise as responses to signs of the third variety, that is, those that are the results of innate principles. Reid's criticism of Hume was that, starting with just impressions and ideas, it is impossible to give an account of belief. Reid argues that, within the constraints of this starting point, it was impossible to give an account of the distinction between belief and disbelief. The problem is that a faded impression does not yield denial or negation. Reid affirms that belief cannot be defined and that those philosophies that attempt to define it lead to paradox. He says:

Of this kind surely is that modern discovery of the ideal
philosophy, that sensation, memory, belief, and imagination,
when they have the same object, are only different degrees of
strength and vivacity in the idea. Suppose the idea to be that
of a future state after death: one man believes it firmly – this
means no more than that he hath a strong and lively idea of
it; another neither believes nor disbelieves – that is, he has a
weak and faint idea. Suppose, now, a third person believes
firmly that there is no such thing, I am at a loss to know
whether his idea be faint or lively: if it is faint, then there
may be a firm belief where the idea is faint; if the idea is
lively, then the belief of a future state and the belief of no
future state must be one and the same. (107)

Later he remarks, again concerning Hume's theory of belief:

That a strong belief and a weak belief differ only in degree, I
can easily comprehend; but that belief and no belief should
differ only in degree, no man can believe who understands
what he speaks. For this is, in reality, to say that something
and nothing differ only in degree of something.

Every proposition that may be the object of belief, has a
contrary proposition that may be the object of a contrary
belief. The ideas of both, according to Mr Hume, are the
same, and differ only in degrees of vivacity – that is,
contraries differ only in degree; and so pleasure may be a
degree of pain, and hatred a degree of love. But it is to no
purpose to trace the absurdities that follow from this doctrine,
for none of them can be more absurd than the doctrine itself.
(359)

The crux of the argument is clear. To believe that something does
not exist is not just to have an impression or idea of it.
Impressions and ideas do not contain denial or negation. Reid
puts this argument in terms of belief, but he could just as well
have put it in terms of conception. To even conceive of something
as not existing, a future state, for example, cannot be to have a
faded impression. Denial or negation does not fit on the scale of
vivacity or strength of an idea. There is a difference between a
faded or weak sensation of pain, for example, and the happy
conception of the pain as not existing.

The truth, simply put, is that conception has a richer formal
structure than impressions, faded or not. To have a sensation is
not the same thing as to have a conception of the sensation, as we
noted above. Conception is a mental operation on a mental
operation. It is essentially metamental. One kind of mental
operation is denial or negation, the denial of the existence of a

sensation, for example. A less lively idea is not equivalent to a conception of the original impression as not existing nor to disbelief that it exists. Impressions and ideas are inadequate to account for our conception of impressions and ideas.

Hume could have expanded his theory by postulating impressions about impressions, but this would be to introduce the intentionality, or aboutness, of impressions as a fundamental feature. Had he done so, he might have postulated negative impressions of impressions. Whatever the plausibility of such a development, it was contrary to the remarkable metaphysical programme Hume at first undertook, namely, to account for human conceptualisation and belief in terms of impressions and ideas and their natural qualities and relations to each other. Though I think Reid was correct in his criticism of the ideal philosophy, that should not deter us from recognising the metaphysical brilliance and importance of Hume's undertaking. That recognition led Reid to pronounce Hume the most acute metaphysician of the age, even as he sought to show that the consequences of the undertaking were absurd. It did not suffice for Reid to elicit such consequences from the ideal philosophy. It was his aim to show that we need not despair of a better. I now turn to Reid's own theory.

Reid on Conception. I have represented Reid's theory of conception in detail elsewhere, and it is my intention here to present that theory in summary.[7] Reid's theory of conception rests on a metaphysical assumption, to wit, '. . . that every creature which God has made, in the heavens above, or in the earth beneath, or in the waters under the earth, is an individual' (389). What exists is an individual. Universals are not individuals, and, therefore, universals do not exists. Nevertheless, it was clear to Reid that universals or general attributes are involved in knowledge, since what we know, most typically, involves the attribution or predication of a universal or general attribute to a subject. But how can knowledge involve universals in this way if they do not exist? For Reid, this question presupposes the most fundamental error of the Ideal Theory, to wit, that the object of thought must be something that exists. But that is false. We can obviously think of things that do not exist, centaurs, for example. We can also predicate things of things that do not exist, for example, when we affirm that a centaur is half man and half horse. The answer to our question, therefore, is that universals do not exist, but they are, nevertheless, the objects of all our thoughts when we predicate or affirm some universal of a subject. Plato's mistake was to suppose that our thought of universals implied their existence.

The task remains, however, to give a psychological account of

how we come to our conception of universals. Must we suppose
that our conception of universals is obtained from particulars,
that our conception of whiteness is obtained from white stones,
eyes, and so forth? The answer is negative. There are, according
to Reid, individual qualities, which being individuals really exist,
as well as particulars. He distinguishes between the individual
quality of whiteness of an object from the universal whiteness as
follows:

> . . . the whiteness of this sheet is one thing, whiteness is
> another; the conceptions signified by these two forms of
> speech are as different as the expressions. The first signifies
> an individual quality really existing, and is not a general
> conception, though it be an abstract one: the second signifies
> a general conception, which implies no existence, but may be
> predicated of everything that is white, and in the same sense.
> On this account, if one should say that the whiteness of this
> sheet is the whiteness of another sheet, every man perceives
> this to be absurd; but when he says both sheets are white,
> this is true and perfectly understood. The conception of
> whiteness implies no existence; it would remain the same
> though everything in the universe that is white were annihil-
> ated. (395)

Based on this metaphysics, Reid constructs a theory of conception
to account for our conception of universals based on our conception of individual qualities. There are two operations of the mind
required for forming such conceptions. The first is a principle of
abstraction which is somewhat misleadingly named. The operation
of abstraction involves abstracting an individual quality out of the
complexity of our experience. Experience is presented to us as an
undifferentiated whole. Abstraction is the direction of attention
to an individual quality, to the whiteness of a piece of paper lying
among the clutter of objects and qualities on my desk. The result
is a conception of the individual whiteness of that object. Our
conception of the individual quality is automatically acquired
once attention is directed to the quality as the result of an innate
principle of the mind.

The conception of the individual quality is the basis for a
second operation, generalisation, that yields a general conception.
This operation is driven by utility. Against Hume, Reid remarks,

> I apprehend, therefore, that it is utility, and not the associating
> qualities of the ideas, that has led men to form only certain
> combinations, and to give names to them in language, while
> they neglect an infinite number that might be formed. (400)

We form general conceptions for the purposes of communication

and the acquisition of knowledge, and these general conceptions
or universals are meanings of general words. We attempt to use
general words so that they agree with the way others use those
words. Reid says,

> Universals are always expressed by general words; and all the
> words of language, excepting proper names, are general
> words; they are the signs of general conceptions, or of some
> circumstance relating to them. These general conceptions are
> formed for the purpose of language and reasoning; and the
> object from which they are taken, and to which they are
> intended to agree, is the conception which other men join to
> the same words; they may, therefore, be adequate, and
> perfectly agree with the thing conceived. This implies no
> more than that men who speak the same language may
> perfectly agree in the meaning of many general words. (364–5)

Might we not say that we form general conceptions by classing
together things that resemble each other? That would be an error
according to Reid. Though there is an indistinct sort of resemblance
that things have, two faces for example, before we have noted
what feature they have in common, genuine resemblance consists
in having some attribute in common. To note genuine resemblance
is to note some attribute the objects have in common, and,
therefore, our acquiring conceptions of common attributes cannot
be based on an antecedently acquired conception of resemblance.

Reid avers that it is man and not nature that determines how
things are divided into kinds, and this we do according to utility.
He admits, however, that nature may make it useful to divide
things one way rather than another.

> It is utility, indeed, that leads us to give general names to the
> various species of natural substances; but, in combining the
> attributes which are included under the specific name, we are
> more aided and directed by nature than in forming other
> combinations of mixed modes and relations. In the last, the
> ingredients are brought together in the occurrences of life, or
> in the actions or thoughts of men. But, in the first, the
> ingredients are united by nature in many individual substances
> which God has made. We form a general notion of those
> attributes wherein many individuals agree. We give a specific
> name to this combination, which name is common to all
> substances having those attributes, which either do or may
> exist. (401)

The picture should now be clear. It is utility that guides the
manner in which we generalise to form general conceptions. We
attempt to mean what others mean and form general conceptions

that agree with those of others as the meaning of general terms. This leads Reid to remark that our general conceptions are like pictures of pictures, conceptions of conceptions, and that we seek to mean what those mean who are most expert in the language. Reid has obviously anticipated contemporary theories of meaning in a sophisticated way.[8]

What I wish to emphasise, however, is that our formation of general conceptions is, according to Reid, based on our conception of our conceptions of individual qualities and is, therefore, a metamental operation of the mind. Consciousness, for Reid, is the faculty of the mind that gives rise to conception of our own mental operations. Without consciousness, therefore, we would have no conception of our conceptions of individual qualities. Without a conception of our conceptions of individual qualities, we would not be able to generalise and form general conceptions. Without general conceptions we would not be able to conceive of things that do not exist. Therefore, without consciousness and the metamental operations of the mind based upon it, human thought and conceptualisation would not have intentionality. Intentionality and consciousness are thus essentially connected in Reid's philosophy of mind. It should also be noted that semantic plasticity, the freedom to change meanings by changing general conceptions depends, in the same way as does the formation of general conceptions, on consciousness and our metamental conception of our own conceptions.

The fundamental claim of Reid against the Ideal Theory is that conception, particularly general conception, is an operation of the mind that does not resolve itself into impressions and ideas. Any impression, however strong or weak, vivacious or faded, can be distinguished from a conception of such an impression and from a conception of other things as well. Our conceptions must, therefore, be the consequence of first principles of our natural constitution yielding conceptual responses to sensations.

Reid held that there were innate first principles of the mind that yielded original conceptions of the primary qualities of external objects and, at the same time, a relative conception of the external object as that which has the quality. The role of sensation is to give rise to the original conception of the quality. The conception of the primary quality does not have the conception of the sensation as part of its content nor is the conception of the quality inferred from the conception of the sensation. The sensation gives rise to the conception of the quality by a natural kind of magic, that is, immediately and without reasoning. The theory concerning secondary qualities is different. We have initially, Reid alleges, only a relative conception of those qualities as the quality in the object that causes our sensation.

Reid on Belief. It is crucial to our understanding of Reid's theory of belief to note that our original conceptions of qualities carry with them an irresistible conviction or belief that the qualities so conceived really do exist as qualities of external objects. In modern terms, belief is a kind of default attitude toward the original conceptions of the mind. Though conviction and belief irresistibly accompany conception in these cases, conviction cannot be resolved into conception any more than it can be resolved into impressions and ideas. Belief involves the affirmation or denial of a proposition. One can conceive of something without either affirming or denying it in many cases. Thus, even in those cases in which belief irresistibly accompanies conviction, it is clear that conception and belief are distinct operations of the mind and that one cannot be resolved into the other. Reid held, moreover, that belief is basic and cannot be resolved into any other operations of the mind.

Reid holds that we have a natural and irresistible belief in the existence of external objects. This belief is, moreover, implied by our perception of external objects, which involves a sensation giving rise to the conception and irresistible conviction of the qualities of the external object immediately, without reasoning, even reasoning concerning the sensation itself. Reid notes that Hume acknowledges in the *Treatise* the irresistibility of our convictions concerning the external world:

> This, indeed, he (Hume) is so candid as to acknowledge. 'He finds himself absolutely and necessarily determined, to live and talk and act like all other people in the common affairs of life. And since reason is incapable of dispelling these clouds, most fortunately it happens, that nature herself suffices to that purpose, and cures him of this philosophical melancholy and delirium'. (485)

But this concession does not satisfy Reid. He goes on to remark:

> But what pity is it, that nature, (whatever is meant by that personage) so kind in curing this delirium, should be so cruel as to cause it. Doth the same fountain send forth both sweet waters and bitter? Is it not more probable, that, if the cure was the work of nature, the disease came from another hand, and was the work of the philosopher? (485)

The point of the remark requires elucidation. Reid, in opposition to Hume, holds that the beliefs in question are not only natural but evident and justified as they appear irresistibly in us. It might be supposed that Reid in appealing to nature is implicitly

appealing to God for the justification of these beliefs. This Reid
explicitly denies.

> He who is persuaded that he is the workmanship of God, and
> that it is a part of his constitution to believe his senses, may
> think that a good reason to confirm his belief. But he had the
> belief before he could give this or any other reason for it.
> (329)

The beliefs that are the result of first principles of our
constitution occur prior to reasoning and if, as Reid alleges, they
are evident and justified without reasoning as they first appear in
us, then their evidence or justification cannot be the result of
reasoning. In fact, Reid holds that such beliefs, perceptual beliefs
in the existence of what we see directly before us, are justified or
evident in themselves. Their evidence is their birthright.

Reid versus Hume on Reason and Scepticism. We have turned, of
course, from psychology to epistemology, but, for Reid, the two
are closely intertwined. The first principles of conception and
belief are also the first principles of evidence. His argument
against Hume's form of scepticism is simple. Hume has assumed
that the deliverances of consciousness and reasoning are trustworthy. But Hume can give no proof that these faculties are
trustworthy and that perception, memory, and the other faculties
are not.

Concerning consciousness, Reid asks:

> Can any man prove that his consciousness may not deceive
> him? No man can; nor can we give a better reason for
> trusting to it, than that every man, while his mind is sound,
> is determined, by the constitution of his nature, to give
> implicit belief to it. (100).

He then goes on to ask why reason should be given priority
among our faculties.

> Reason, says the sceptic, is the only judge of truth, and you
> ought to throw off every opinion and every belief that is not
> grounded on reason. Why, sir, should I believe the faculty of
> reason more than that of perception? – they came both out of
> the same shop, and were made by the same artist; and if he
> puts one piece of false ware into my hands, what should
> hinder him from putting another? (183)

The philosophical argument behind these remarks might be put
as follows. Every person has a natural trust in their faculties, that
is, they regard them as trustworthy by nature. If, however, we
call one faculty into question – perception, for example – then
what justification do we have for trusting another?

Reid is aware that Hume has argued that the faculty of

perception is particularly untrustworthy. Hume's argument is that as we move away from a table the appearances change, the apparent size changes, for example, in that the table appears smaller as we move away, and this shows that we do not perceive the table but only the appearances, since the table must remain unchanged in size. It is easy enough for Reid to reply to this specific argument. For, as he notes, assuming that we really do perceive the table, we can conclude from what we know about the eye, that the apparent magnitude of the table must change. The change of appearances, Reid notes, is what must occur if we do see the table, and, therefore, rather than leading to the conclusion that we do not perceive the table should confirm us in our original conviction that we do see it.

The foregoing argument summarises the difference between Reid and Hume. Reid assumes that it is hopeless to attempt to account for our belief or the justification for our belief in the external world by appeal to sense impressions. The belief arises immediately as the result of a first principle of our faculties. If we do not trust the first principles of our faculties, then we should not trust reason or consciousness. If, on the contrary, we trust those faculties, then consistency requires that we trust the rest. If we trust the faculty of perception, then the arguments against the trustworthiness of the faculty fail. Our faculties are, Reid admits, fallible, but we must trust all our faculties or none at all as our starting point in philosophy.

In fact, we have no choice. All but lunatics and some philosophers, Reid remarks, trust their faculties. It is a first principle of our nature that our faculties are not fallacious. He writes, 'Another first principle is – *That the natural faculties, by which we distinguish truth from error, are not fallacious*'. Hume's error was to suppose that it made sense to justify first principles of our faculties. It does not. The justification assumes the thing to be proven, that our faculties are trustworthy and not fallacious. The total sceptic offers no argument and cannot be answered. The sceptic who uses reason to argue against another faculty has assumed without justification that the faculty of reason is trustworthy. An adequate reply is that we assume without justification that all our faculties are trustworthy. To attempt to justify the first principles of our faculties by reasoning is to attempt to justify what is the most evident by appeal to less evident premises, those of philosophers. The attempt fails, not because reason is deficient, but because the principles are the first premises of reason. Philosophy, properly understood, does not impugn these principles but grows from them, as a tree grows from its roots. So stood the dispute between Hume and Reid in the eighteenth century. It was a dispute of genius.

NOTES

1. Page references to Reid in this paper refer to *The Works of Thomas Reid, D.D.*, ed. S. Hamilton. Eighth Edition, Edinburgh, 1895. I use this edition only because it is the one that is most commonly available. I gratefully acknowledge that research for this paper was supported by a grant from the National Science Foundation and a fellowship from the John Simon Guggenheim Memorial Foundation.

2. I trace the relationship between Moore and Reid in 'Reid's Influence on Contemporary American and British Philosophy', in *Thomas Reid: Critical Interpretations*, eds. S.F. Barker and T.L. Beauchamp, *Philosophical Monographs*, 1976, 1–7.

3. Cf.J. Searle, *Intentionality*, Cambridge, 1983; J. Fodor, *Language of Thought*, 1975; and D.C. Dennett, *Brainstorms*, Montgomery, 1978.

4. Hume, *A Treatise of Human Nature*, Book I, London, 1739–40, first sentence.

5. Cf.R.M. Chisholm, 'Brentano on Descriptive Psychology and the Intentional', in *Phenomenology and Existentialism*, eds. E.N. Lee and M. Mandelbaum, (Baltimore 1967), 1–23.

6. Cf.W.F. Sellars, 'Empiricism and the Philosophy of Mind', in *Minnesota Studies in the Philosophy of Science*, Vol. 1, eds H. Feigl and M. Scriven, (Minneapolis 1956), 309–20.

7. *Thomas Reid*, 1989.

8. H. Putnam, 'Meaning and Reference', *Journal of Philosophy*, 1983, 699–711, made the division of labour theory of meaning famous.

MANFRED KUEHN

Reid's Contribution to 'Hume's Problem'

Hume presented a problem to Kant. Indeed, Kant himself admitted that 'Hume's problem' was *the* problem that awoke him from his 'dogmatic slumber', and thus set him on his way to work out the theory he later put forward in his *Critique of Pure Reason*. All this seems to be very straightforward. Since Kant's theory itself continues to present a problem to philosophical scholars, however, it is still far from clear what problem Hume presented to Kant. This is one of the reasons why Kant's relation to Hume is a frequent topic of discussion. Though most of the papers in this genre approach the topic by asking whether or not Kant succeeded in his attempt to 'answer' Hume – assuming that the two were radically opposed – more recently there have been attempts to show that this assumption itself may be false, and that it may be philosophically fruitful as well as historically correct to argue that their positions can be accommodated on some fundamental points.[1]

Reid, by contrast, is almost never mentioned when Kant's philosophy is discussed. One of the most important reasons for this seems to derive from statements by Kant himself. For, though he found it necessary, in the very context of Hume's problem, to refer also to Reid, he actually seemed to have nothing good to say about him, claiming that

it is positively painful to see how utterly his opponents, Reid, Oswald, Beattie, and lastly Priestley, missed the point of the problem; for while they were ever taking for granted that which he doubted, and demonstrating with zeal and often with impudence that which he never thought of doubting, they so misconstrued his valuable suggestion that everything remained in its old condition, as if nothing had happened.[2]

I have tried to show elsewhere that the real target of Kant's criticism is not the Scots themselves, but a certain group of their followers in Germany, and that this passage does not preclude influence of the Scots upon Kant.[3] Indeed, I believe that it can be shown that, in insisting upon a necessary *a priori* component in all

human knowledge, Kant begins his first *Critique* at the very point
at which Reid had ceased his inquiry. For Reid and his followers
had already 'generalised' Hume's problem, had attempted to
show that all human perception presupposes a certain *a priori*
component, and had tried to uncover 'such of them as occurred in
the examination of the five senses'.[4] Furthermore, while they
themselves had nowhere given a systematic table of the categories,
Priestley in his critique of Reid, Beattie, and Oswald had given
one for them.[5] Since the Scots were frequently discussed by
German philosophers, Kant could not only have learned from
them, but *did* learn from them *at least indirectly*.

In this paper I would like to pursue this argument further and
show how Kant may also have received other suggestions from
Reid in solving another important aspect of 'Hume's problem'. I
shall argue that Kant also received impulses from Reid in his
theory of perception. To accomplish this, I shall first try to show
how, in spite of Kant's own pronouncements, it is possible to see
Reid as being relevant to Kant's project. Secondly, I shall give a
brief account of Hume's and Reid's respective positions concerning 'sensation' and 'simple apprehension'. Thirdly, I shall examine
Kant's relation to Hume and Reid with regard to the doctrine of
perception, showing that Kant is closer to Reid than to Hume.
Fourthly, I shall argue that this may not be an incidental parallel,
but could be an effect of Reid's influence upon Kant through
Tetens. Fifthly, I shall argue that, after a German translation of
the *Inquiry* was published in 1782, and after his contemporaries
had attacked him with Reidian weapons, Kant must have studied
Reid more closely, and I shall suggest that this may have been
important when he reformulated some parts of his first *Critique*
for a second edition. In any case, it is easy to show that the more
'realistic' bent of the second edition, and its de-emphasis of the
'idealistic' conclusions does have to do with Reid's influence.

I

On most interpretations of Kant it does not make sense to speak
of 'Reid's contribution to "Hume's problem"'. This is due to the
fact that most philosophers have opted for a rather *narrow*
construal of 'Hume's problem'. For some, it is nothing but the
'problem of causality' that is raised by Hume's analysis. The
question at issue between Kant and Hume must have been
whether Kant's theory of the categories and principles does, or
does not, provide an adequate answer to Hume's doubts in that

regard.[6] Whatever Kant is seen as having to offer here, it must be rather different from a simple appeal to common sense. A philosophical *justification* of the principle of causality requires something stronger than that. Those who take this line usually concentrate on the 'Second Analogy' and related passages. However, it is more frequent to view the problem of causality as part of a wider context, namely, as a central aspect of the 'problem of scepticism'. According to this construal, Kant's answer to Hume and other epistemological sceptics includes such passages as the 'Refutation of Idealism' and the 'Transcendental Deduction', but it also leaves out as irrelevant to the Kant–Hume relation many other parts of Kant's work.[7] Furthermore, this conception of the problem tends to make a possible influence of Reid upon Kant still more unlikely. If common sense does not suffice to justify our use of the principle of causality, it cannot, *a fortiori*, suffice to justify all knowledge claims against the epistemological sceptic.

Both these interpretations, however, construe 'Hume's problem' more narrowly than Kant does himself. For he actually claimed that the *Critique of Pure Reason* as a whole should be seen as 'the execution of Hume's problem in its widest extent'.[8] If we take him seriously – as I think we must, if we want to understand him – it is not enough to identify a particular passage, or a small number of particular passages, as Kant's answer to Hume. We must show how Kant's philosophy as a whole is related to Hume, and thus construe Hume's problem much more broadly. Among other things, we must also include Kant's 'Dialectic' as part of Hume's problem. Furthermore, we have to look not only at the developments up to the publication of the first *Critique*, but also consider what happened after.

Yet, even a broad construal that would take into account *all* of Kant might still fail to do justice to 'Hume's problem' as understood by Kant. If Kant's critical enterprise is still understood as a 'response' or 'reaction' to Hume, some of its most significant aspects will very likely be misconstrued.[9] Kant *did not* see himself as engaged in a philosophical dispute with Hume. He saw his task not as one of disproving certain of Hume's claims, and he did not mean to give an *ad hominem* argument against Hume, or an internal criticism that would show his philosophy to be inconsistent. For him, it was not a question of undercutting an opponent, but one of solving a problem that really required a solution. Hume's problem had, he thought, a special status. Like a genuine problem in mathematics, it could not be bypassed once it was raised. It had to be either solved or shown to be unsolvable. Furthermore, since he believed that it was not a peripheral problem, but *the* problem that every metaphysician must face, it was more important than any particular philosophical feud. The *Critique* is meant to be neither 'anti-Humean', nor 'anti-sceptical'.[10] The adversarial model of doing philosophy fails to do justice to Kant's understanding of his relationship to Hume. It is inadequate as an interpretation of Kant, and must be replaced by a different view – one that is less dependent upon merely personal preferences of Kant or Hume. If Kant was right, Hume's problem is independent of such subjective factors, but intersubjectively valid.

While Kant believed that he was the first since Hume who *really* understood Hume's problem and what was required for its solution, he did not have to rule out entirely that others before him made positive (or negative) contributions to the *status questionis*. Indeed, given the broadest possible construal of Hume's problem as independent of his own personal preferences, Kant *could not* consistently have ruled out such contributions. Though he could (and did) say that those before him were themselves not aware of what they really did, he could (and did) also view some of his predecessors as having put forward ideas that took on a new and interesting meaning when they came to be seen in the context of his 'execution of Hume's problem in its widest extent'. For this reason it would, from a Kantian point of view, make a great deal of sense to speak of contributions by others to Hume's problem. Since Kant himself gives credit to Lambert and Tetens, for instance, it would not be inappropriate to speak of Lambert's and Tetens's contribution to Hume's problem.[11]

However, it may well be asked whether it makes any sense to speak of '*Reid's* contribution to Hume's problem'. The famous passage in which Kant refers to Reid and his followers seems to preclude such a contribution. Yet, while this passage has usually been taken to mean that Kant could not possibly have learned anything from Reid, it need not be taken to imply that. It can actually be interpreted as affirming a special interest of Kant in these Scots. Indeed, it can be argued that the entire passage constitutes a kind of argument *for the historical* importance of Reid. For Kant clearly claims:

(1) Hume's work constitutes the most important event in the history of metaphysics.

(2) Hume's work should have instigated the 'good minds' among his contemporaries to work on the task he proposed.

(3) Reid, Oswald and Beattie [as well as Priestley] completely misunderstood Hume.

This leads him to claim that:

(4) *Therefore* metaphysics was not reformed.

(5) To observe this is decidedly painful.

This suggests to me that, though Kant felt the Scots had failed, he also believed *they* were the ones particularly well-equipped to solve 'Hume's problem'. Why else would he say that they were responsible for the state of metaphysics at his time? And why else would he find reading them so painful? At the very least, this gloss of Kant's judgement of Reid and his followers (and critic) should show that we need a more subtle account of the Kant–Reid relation than has been given so far. We must determine what exactly Kant rejected in Reid's philosophy, and what could have led him to pay Reid such an under-handed compliment. The first issue can easily be settled; the second one is more difficult to deal with.

Kant's *Critique of Pure Reason* has two different 'sides'. It is first and fundamentally a *normative* enterprise, being concerned with establishing the criteria for genuine knowledge in metaphysics. As Kant says in the 'Preface' to its first edition, 'the chief question is always simply this:– what and how much can the understanding and reason know apart from all experience' (A xvii)?[12] He thinks that it is necessary to answer this question in order to decide the fate of metaphysics. For, if there were nothing to be known *a priori*, metaphysics would be altogether impossible. In trying to answer the question 'What, or, how much, can we know *a priori?*' Kant finds it necessary to discuss the further question of how knowledge is possible. This question, however, has essentially two different (though related) senses. First, it can be conceived as a fundamentally logical question. If we take it in this sense, we are concerned with the logical presuppositions that all knowledge must fulfil, and we ask ourselves what the necessary conditions of knowledge claims are. Kant answers this question in his transcendental logic, saying that the categories, as *a priori* concepts of objects, are necessary but not sufficient conditions for knowledge claims. They are essentially related to sensations, and cannot be used to make knowledge claims apart from sensations. Thus his answer to the question as to how much we can know apart from experience is 'Nothing'.[13] Metaphysics is possible only as a discipline that deals with the *a priori* presuppositions of experience. This is the most important result of Kant's discussion of Hume's problem. Because it does rule out the very kind of transcendent metaphysics that Hume also contested, it leaves him also in rather close proximity to Hume.

Closely connected with this transcendental enterprise is a

second one that can easily be confused with it, namely, Kant's attempt to uncover and describe the *psychological* sources of knowledge. In this context, the question 'How is knowledge possible?' requires a factual, or descriptive account as an answer. We ask, at least in the Kantian scheme of things, how the different 'faculties of the human mind actually work together to produce knowledge', or we aim at a *genetic* account of the mental actions that give rise to knowledge. Kant claims that an answer to this psychological question, although 'of great importance for [his] chief purpose, . . . does not form an essential part of it' (A xvii).

Furthermore, the psychological question 'How is knowledge possible?' amounts to a demand for 'the search for the cause of a given effect, and to that extent is somewhat hypothetical in character (though as I shall show elsewhere, it is not really so)' (A xvii). But whether or not it is hypothetical does not matter according to Kant because he claims that his normative theory about *a priori* knowledge is independent of his psychological theory of the workings of the human mind. Even if somebody were to succeed in showing that his psychology was nothing but 'opinion', this should not cast any doubt upon his logical or objective account.

Though many philosophers have doubted that Kant actually succeeded in keeping these two questions entirely separate (and even whether he himself was always aware of the difference between them), it is clear that he thinks he has done so in his first *Critique*. But it is also clear that this was not always so. Indeed, the normative question was at first identical with the psychological question. Thus he himself says that Hume's problem was at first 'solely a question concerning the origin' of the concept of cause, and never one 'concerning the indispensable need of using the concept'. Hume, as well as Kant in his 'quasi–Humean' period, believed that if the question concerning the origin 'were decided, the conditions of the use and the sphere of its valid application would have been determined as a matter of course'.[14] The problem became really pressing only when Kant came to believe that the concept of causality really did not originate from experience, but was independent of it.

Reid clearly did not understand the importance of the *normative* aspect of Hume's theory. Reid simply took for granted that, because the concept of causality could not be *derived* from experience, but had to be *a priori*, it had not only empirical, but also metaphysical application. Therefore, he also uncritically used it in theological contexts, and this was one of the things that Kant found so annoying in Reid and his followers, as well as in their critic Priestley.[15] Kant, by contrast, argued that the 'question was not whether the concept of cause was right, useful, and even indispensable for our knowledge of nature, for this Hume had never doubted'. For him, the question was whether the concept of cause 'possessed an inner truth, independent of all experience, implying a perhaps more extended use not restricted merely to objects of experience'.[16] It was the logical question concerning 'the conditions of use and the sphere of its valid application' that was of central importance to Kant.[17]

However, Kant's rejection of Reid's uncritical use of *a priori* principles and concepts in metaphysics, does not rule out that he may have found Reid of interest in his own analysis of their function in *experience*.[18] Indeed, it may well be that, precisely because he found that Reid had much to offer in that regard, he experienced it as painful that Reid never realised the importance of what he himself considered to be the more important question. In any case, that is what I shall argue in what follows.

II

Reid was radically opposed to what he called the 'theory of ideas', or the 'ideal system'. This theory, as he saw it, involved the claim that we do not know objects directly, but only through some kind of mediating mental entities. He denied the very existence of ideas. His reasons for doing so were essentially twofold: first, he believed that an acceptance of 'ideas' necessarily led to scepticism. If Hume had any merit in his eyes, it was that he had made this perfectly clear. Secondly, and more importantly, he thought that such entities as ideas were an arbitrary invention that were not only unnecessary to explain perception, but which would necessarily distort in such account.

Reid's rejection of ideas went hand in hand with the assertion of certain 'original principles of the human mind' that allow us to have beliefs, make judgements, or obtain knowledge. Indeed, his assertion of such original principles seems to be the complement of his rejection of the most central claim of the theory of ideas: the doctrine of simple apprehension, or the view that

> the first operation of the mind about its ideas is simple apprehension, that is, the bare conception of a thing without any belief about it; and that, after we have got simple apprehensions, by comparing them together we perceive agreements or disagreements between them; and that this

perception of the agreement or disagreement of ideas is all that we call belief, judgment, or knowledge.[19]

Reid rejected this view for phenomenological reasons. It is simply false as a descriptive account, he claimed. We do not have access to objects in this way. 'Simple apprehension', or its correlate, the 'simple impression', or 'simple idea' is neither temporally nor logically prior to our experience of objects. Simple introspection assures us that we first see a table, and then its parts. It takes considerable effort to see the 'parts' first, and even if we see them as parts, we do not have a 'bare conception' of a thing without any belief about it. In so far as we must see everything 'as' something, judgement and belief are always implicitly present. Reflection upon what is introspectively given to us shows that before we 'see' anything, we must be aware of quite a lot. Experience, as we have it, is not atomistic, but is of objects. To speak of experience without speaking of objects is nonsense. Experience is *necessarily* experience of objects; and these objects are given independently of 'simple apprehension'. Indeed, 'simple apprehension' itself is dependent upon a prior apprehension of objects.[20]

This apprehension of objects, however, is dependent upon judgements, beliefs and concepts. While most of these judgements, beliefs, or concepts are 'artificial', or dependent upon prior judgements, some are basic in the sense that we could not have any other beliefs without having them. For Reid, all perception involves judgement or belief. In fact, he thinks that certain kinds of perceptions necessarily involve certain kinds of judgement. Thus a present sensation necessarily 'suggests' both an object, of which it is a sensation, and a self which has this sensation. That we have these original judgements is the fact of common sense for Reid. Common sense is a repository of these principles; and his 'appeal to common sense' is thus an appeal to principles or beliefs which have a sense-like certainty. By this, he does not mean that they are only subjective beliefs in Hume's sense, but rather that they are intuitively certain.

It is important to realise in all of this that Reid was not making a 'temporal' claim. He was not saying that we 'first' must have the principles of common sense, and 'then' have experience. Rather, he claims that whenever we can speak of perceiving something, we must also speak of having made a judgement of some sort or other. There is a 'logic' or 'grammar' of perception. And anything that does not, or cannot, conform to the rules of this logic or grammar cannot be called perception either.[21] It is also important to understand that he *therefore* also believes that it is impossible to give a descriptive, or psychological account of how exactly the principles of common sense make experience possible. We must be content with pointing out and describing the principles of common sense as they are required by knowledge and action.[22]

Reid's account of what is primary in perception is thus radically opposed to Hume's from its very beginnings. It bypasses the problem of how a unified experience of objects can arise from the fragmentary material that is given to us through our impressions. While Hume clearly saw the difficulty of this problem, he did not abandon his own account. Thus in the 'Appendix' to the *Treatise*, he points out that

> there are two principles which I cannot render consistent; nor is it in my power to renounce either of them, viz. *that all our distinct perceptions are distinct existences*, and *that the mind never perceives any real connexion among distinct existences*. Did our perceptions either inhere in something simple and individual, or did the mind perceive some real connexion among them, there would be no difficulty in the case. For my part, I must plead the privilege of a sceptic, and confess that this difficulty is too hard for my understanding.[23]

Reid, while admitting that he could not explain *how* exactly the principles of common sense brought about the 'real connexion' between our perceptions, nevertheless argued that there was such a real connection, and that it could only be brought about by what he called the 'principles of common sense'.

III

H.J. Paton observed fifty years ago that it was 'the commonly accepted view that Kant took over Hume's doctrine of sensation as isolated and unrelated atomic entities'.[24] While the influence of this view may have weakened somewhat, it is still very influential (especially among English-speaking philosophers).[25] Kant's (and Hume's) problem, according to this interpretation, was to explain how a unified experience can arise from such isolated representations. This way of looking at Kant's project is not altogether unreasonable. It can be defended by referring to many passages by Kant that do seem to commit him to this view. Such claims are especially prevalent in the first edition of the *Critique of Pure Reason*. Thus, the 'Introduction' to the first edition begins with the claim that experience 'is, beyond all doubt, the first product to which our understanding gives rise, *in working up the raw material of sensible impressions*' (A. 1).[26] This might suggest a view for which knowledge is a synthesis of 'things' that are *first* given as

fragmentary and unrelated entities. The 'Transcendental Deduction' in the first edition also contains many statements that seem
to make such a view likely. Among other things, Kant seems to
claim in it that knowing an object involves three different, and
perhaps even *successive*, acts of synthesis. Especially his description
of the first act of the 'synthesis of apprehension in intuition' can
be taken as maintaining that 'at every moment we are given a
single undifferentiated sense-impression, and that we go on to
join up undifferentiated atomic sense impressions into an intuition
containing a manifold'.[27] Furthermore, in the Second Analogy,
Kant actually seems to say that objects are 'aggregates' of
representations[28] Many more examples could be given.

However, while the Humean view of Kant's theory of sensation
can be defended, Paton thought it was seriously mistaken. He
traced the Humean view of Kant's theory of sensation to what he
called a 'psychological interpretation of Kant', or the tendency to
construe as psychological descriptions what were meant to be
merely logical distinctions between different aspects of what we
encounter in perception.[29] For Paton

> the whole *Kritik of Pure Reason* may be described as an
> analysis of our experience into its formal and material
> elements. An analysis of this kind need not imply that we
> have first the matter and then the form, or first the form and
> then the matter, and I see no sufficient ground for attributing
> such a mistaken psychological theory to Kant.[30]

Paton is quite right. Such Kantian distinctions as those between
matter and form, intuition and concept, appearance and phenomenon, appearance and thing in itself were not meant to be
psychological differentiations of numerically distinct entities, but
were designed to bring out different aspects of one and the same
perception. Accordingly, it might be said that Reid was not the
only one who failed to see the significance of the distinction
between the psychological and the logical aspects of Hume's
problem. Those readers of Kant who see him as beginning from
the Humean conception of sensation make a mistake that is
similar to the one Kant accused Reid of making. But they seem to
compound their mistake by ascribing to Kant a psychological
view that Reid already rejected as false.

That the 'psychological interpretation' does not capture Kant's
considered view on such issues as those relating to form and
matter, intuition and concept, appearance and phenomenon, and
appearance and thing in itself, for instance, can be easily shown.
Thus Kant insists again and again that such 'forms' as space and
time are conditions 'under which alone' intuition 'is possible for

us'. It makes no sense to try to determine how these forms 'get' imposed on things because we cannot, in principle, take a point of view that would allow us to determine this. Intuitions and concepts also mutually require each other. For 'thoughts without content are empty, intuitions without concepts are blind' (A 51: B 75). Only when both are present do we know anything. Though we can observe how some concepts are applied to some sensations, it would be just as impossible to have concepts without any intuition as to have a completely unconceptualised intuition.[31]

The same point can also be supported by reference to Kant's doctrines of the 'transcendental unity of apperception' and the 'affinity of appearances'. Thus Kant claims that 'nothing can come to our knowledge save in terms of . . . original apperception' (A 113). But, whatever else it may be, it is necessarily conceptual or judgemental. So apprehension (or apperception) without judgement would be a contradiction in terms for Kant. And the doctrine of association, which is the complement of that of simple apprehension in Hume and his predecessors, and which is not entirely rejected by Kant, is specifically founded by Kant on an objective unity. Association does not *produce* unity, but is a 'mere consequence' of a 'thoroughgoing connection according to necessary laws' that must be assumed as already existing beforehand.[32] Norman Kemp Smith characterised this aspect of the Kantian view very clearly, finding

> that it amounts to the assertion that *consciousness is in all cases awareness of meaning*. There is no awareness, however rudimentary or primitive, that does not involve the apprehension of meaning . . . And inasmuch as meaning is a highly complex object of apprehension, awareness cannot be regarded as ultimate or as unanalysable.[33]

Accordingly, it should be clear that Kant does *not* begin his analysis of experience at the same point at which Hume begins his. This interpretation, though not unreasonable, is seriously mistaken. Kant did not have a Humean understanding of sensation. Rather, the doctrine of sensation seems to mark one of the greatest differences between the two thinkers. Kant starts at a point much more closely related to Reid's theory, claiming that we begin with an experience of objects, not with one of isolated, unrelated, or atomic impressions. Just like Reid, Kant rejected 'simple apprehension' and everything that goes with it.[34]

It is thus not *necessary* for Kant to explain how we get from fragmentary impressions to unified objective experience. His task is rather to explain what are the psychological and logical presuppositions of the unified experience that is given to us. It might appear that in such a context an account of the actual *origin* or *genesis* of our knowledge is not only unnecessary and superfluous, but even harmful. For, if we truly can describe *how* experience originates from more primitive components, it must be a 'compound' of separable and therefore different entities or acts. Only if we can observe these components both in conjunction and in isolation from one another can we make the kinds of claims that genetic psychology requires. But, if we take Kant's transcendental analysis of knowledge seriously, we cannot do the latter. It must therefore appear most peculiar that Kant is not content with his analysis of knowledge, but also wants to give a psychological account of how experience originates. But since he does, Paton is clearly misleading when he claims that 'the whole *Kritik* may be described as an analysis of our experience into its formal and material elements' that implies no claim about 'before' and 'after'. This also means that we cannot really say that Kant and Reid start from the same point of view. As far as psychology is concerned, they seem to be rather different. For Reid clearly did believe that a *genetic* account of experiential knowledge is impossible.

IV

In discussing alternatives to the 'commonly accepted view' that Kant, like Hume, considered sensation to be made up of isolated and unrelated impressions, Paton suggests that Kant's psychology is 'closely related to that of Baumgarten and Tetens, and in certain respects to that of Leibniz, rather than to that of Hume'.[35] Kant clearly learned from all three. He was deeply influenced by Leibnizian philosophy, the dominant force in German philosophy during the time he was a student in Königsberg, and he knew Baumgarten's theories quite well, if only because he used some of the latter's works as textbooks for his lectures. We also know that Kant was well acquainted with Tetens. Thus Hamann writes to Herder on 13 October 1777 that he has heard that Kant is 'full of Tetens', and on 17 May 1779 he tells him that Kant is busy writing his *Critique*, having Tetens's work always open on his desk.[36] Accordingly, it is not surprising that much of the psychological terminology employed by Kant in this work can be traced back to Tetens, and that it is not an exaggeration to say that Tetens was especially important for Kant's formulation of critical philosophy. Since Tetens does not only mention, quote and discuss Reid often, but is also demonstrably influenced by Reid in his own position, it is also reasonable to argue that Reid may also have exercised an *indirect* influence upon Kant through Tetens.[37]

But what could Kant have learned from Reid through Tetens? He might, for instance, have profitted from Tetens's discussion of Reid's doctrine of the principles of common sense. After all, he argues in his preparatory notes to the *Prolegomena* that the first reviewer of the *Critique of Pure Reason* never really thought about 'the possibility of knowledge *a priori*, even though Herr Tetens could have given him occasion to do so'.[38] While it is not altogether unlikely that Tetens and/or Reid exercised, in 1777, a significant positive or negative influence on Kant in this regard, Kant had already thought much about that problem. He had, for instance, more or less completed his 'Table of the Categories'. But when he himself says that Tetens had nothing important to say to him in this matter, he may actually be misleading. It may be true that after reading Tetens, he no longer concerned himself 'with the evolution of concepts, like Tetens (all actions by means of which concepts are created) . . . but only with their objective validity'.[39] But it is also true that the reflections prior to his reading of Tetens actually show him to be engaged in pursuits that very much resemble those of Tetens. Accordingly, Tetens, and therefore also Reid, could very well have been important to Kant for clarifying his distinction between his essential task and the one that, though 'of great importance for [his] chief purpose', does not 'form an essential part of it' (A xvii).

Tetens's psychology is much more detailed and extensive than Reid's. He did not simply take over Reid's account of sensation and perception, but actually rejected many of Reid's most characteristic claims as premature conclusions. Indeed, his theory is based upon the belief that he can push his analysis farther than Reid did.[40] Thus, where Reid was content to point out that there must be certain basic principles that are presupposed in all perception and knowledge and to describe them, Tetens wants to explain how they originate. While agreeing with Reid that general laws of judgement exist, he did not accept Reid's view that these are instinctual. They are only 'instinct-like', and they only seem to be immediately suggested by our sensations. In reality, they are not immediate at all. We can, Tetens claimed, reduce them further to general rules of *reason*. Thus, though Tetens accepted Reid's principles of common sense as explanatory devices at some stage of his account, he rejected them as the ultimate principles. For him, they were prematurely accepted as basic, since they can be shown to originate from more general laws of thought.

Thus Tetens also rejected Reid's criticism of simple apprehension:

> Reid is of the opinion that some of our first judgments must precede the *simple apprehension* of objects, that is, precede the ideas of subject and predicate. He was led to this, without doubt, because of the rapidity with which the actions of thought follow the actions of sensation in several cases, so that they merge into one noticeable activity of the soul. It is difficult to observe the real limits, to say where the preceding *sensation* and *representation* ends and where *thought* begins.[41]

For Tetens, it made sense to speak of 'simple apprehension'. The unity and objectivity of experience are created only by our faculty of thought. And, while he thought that it might be difficult to isolate a mere sensation, it is not impossible in principle. For him, perception was a complex process with stages that are actually separate from one another. Sensation represented one stage in this process, reason and its judgements another. While the succeeding stages were understood as being dependent upon the preceding ones, what is first given to us in sensation is essentially independent of our judgements.

Accordingly, Tetens was in some respects closer to Hume than he was to Reid.[42] He begins with sensations which, in themselves, are isolated and unrelated. His problem is the same as Hume's: he must explain how unity and objectivity can arise from the fragmentary material given to us by sensation. To be sure, he disagreed with Hume, who thought that belief or judgement is more properly an act of the sensitive, than of the cogitative part of our natures, and who argued that it is ultimately a matter of subjective conviction. Instead, he wanted to show, against Hume, that it was objective, and founded upon reason. But he accepted Hume's starting point, agreeing that order and unity were the result of reflection upon these sensations. Furthermore, his method of psychological descriptions, resulting in genetic accounts of the origin of mental contents remained also essentially Humean. It is very far removed from Kant's 'transcendental' and logical approach. While both Kant and Tetens wanted to show that our rational faculties are more important than Hume was willing to admit, their way of showing this was rather different. Thus the critical Kant must have *disagreed* with Tetens on 'simple apprehension', and must have found himself in *agreement* with the view criticised by Tetens. Kant, in reading Tetens, actually must have sided with Reid on simple apprehension.

This is most interesting. For as late as 1775 Kant held a view that implies a version of the theory of 'simple apprehension', a view according to which sensations actually consist of unrelated, unconnected and arbitrary items that are brought into order only by subsequent acts of the understanding. This is shown by the so-called 'Duisburg Nachlass', which consists of reflections which were written around 1774–75. In these reflections, Kant claims that appearances need to be brought under certain 'titles of the understanding', and that without 'such concepts the appearances would be separate and not belong to one another'. The 'titles of the understanding' make possible 'connections in that which is composite'.[43] Other reflections from roughly the same time support this view as well. Thus Kant notes in several places that 'mere appearance does not yet provide an object', and that appearances are 'in themselves accidental and without unity'.[44] They are transformed into objects only by subsequent acts of the understanding. But in the first *Critique* appearances themselves are already objects.[45] Though they need to be further determined by judgements of the understanding, they are already ordered and unified into objects when we first encounter them. In fact, it appears that in a famous passage in the Transcendental Deduction of the first edition, Kant is hypothetically putting forward his earlier view in order to point out why we must view sensation itself as ordered and connected already:

> appearances are themselves actually subject to . . . a rule, and . . . in the manifold of these representations a co-existence or sequence takes place in conformity with certain rules. Otherwise our empirical imagination would never find opportunity for exercise appropriate to its powers, and so would remain concealed within the mind as a dead and to us unknown faculty. If cinnabar were sometimes red, sometimes black, sometimes light, sometimes heavy, if a man changed sometimes into this and sometimes into that animal form, . . . my empirical imagination would never find opportunity when representing red colour to bring to mind heavy cinnabar. (A 100f)

So Kant clearly changed his mind on 'simple apprehension' between 1775 and 1777, and his doctrine of 'the synthesis of apprehension in intuition' is a result of this. Since 'apprehension' played a large part in Tetens's discussion of Reid, and since the later doctrine is clearly a result of Kant's reading of Tetens, it is not unreasonable to think that Reid also was important for it.[46] Indeed, it is more than reasonable because Kant moved from a position more closely related to Tetens to one more closely related to Reid.

V

One of the results of accepting a theory that implies a rejection of 'simple apprehension' very much like Reid's, should have been a rejection of the kind of genetic psychology Tetens wanted to offer. Kant *should have* rejected as false Tetens's criticisms of Reid, and since these criticisms were actually implied by his developmental account of human knowledge, he should also have rejected parts of that psychology. While it is difficult to know what he rejected, we know that he did not reject it in its entirety. The subjective deduction as well as the psychological passages in the first edition of the first *Critique* amply testify to this.

Not surprisingly, perhaps, precisely these more psychological passages got him into trouble with his contemporaries. Thus the Feder-Garve review advanced the claim that Kant 'transforms the world and ourselves into representations, and lets all objects originate from appearances that the understanding connects to a series of experiences'. The understanding '*makes* objects' from what is at first unconnected and isolated. 'For it first unites several successive small changes of the soul into entire and complete sensations'.[47] The reviewers tried to trace Kant's 'transcendent idealism' to Kant's theory of sensation, which they thought was very similar to that of Berkeley and Hume and amounted really to the attempt to eliminate the difference between external and internal sense. It disputes 'the rightful title and character of external sense in comparison with inner sense'.[48]

The reviewer of a book by Johann August Ulrich was still more explicit. He claimed that the 'main foundation of the entire Kantian system' was questionable. The Transcendental Deduction is not only circular, but it also involves the kind of idealism Kant wanted to reject. Kant has not proved how the categories make experience possible. He left himself open to the following objection:

> If the appearances were indeed an irregular heap, a mere aggregate of *simultaneis* and *successivis* that appears only regular to us because their being has in such a way been extensively pre-established by the will of the creator that certain appearances (which, in any case, are nothing but certain modifications of our consciousness) are always followed by certain others, without there being the slightest real connection between the two . . .[49]

This seemed to imply to the reviewer that Kant's transcendental idealism is compatible with that of Leibniz. From the assumption that Kant's appearances are equivalent to Humean impressions, it follows that Kant is committed to idealism. Accordingly, Kant is accused of idealism not so much on the basis of his logical or transcendental account of knowledge, but on the basis of the psychological passages in the first *Critique*.

Kant's response to this criticism is interesting. He still argued that the question of what the categories allow us to know *a priori* is most important. And he still believes that he has proved 'that the categories . . . can have no other employment whatever than that merely with reference to objects of experience (in such a way that in this experience the categories make possible merely the form of thought)'. But he now also finds that 'the answer to the question *how* they make such form of thought is indeed important enough for completing this deduction, where possible; but with reference to the main purpose of the system . . . the answer is in no way necessary but is merely meritorious'.[50] Whereas he had earlier claimed that the psychological 'exposition is of *great* importance for my chief purpose' (though 'not an essential part of it'), he now considers it only as 'important enough', if completeness is at issue, and if it can be done. The subjective, or psychological question has become less important. But it has not only become less important, it has also become more questionable. For, while Kant admitted already in 1781 that his psychological account might be 'somewhat hypothetical in character', he also promised to 'show elsewhere, it is not really so' (A xvii). In 1786, he casts doubt on the possibility of giving a complete account. Thus he says not only that it is important where it is possible to complete the deduction, but also considers a little later the possibility 'that the manner as to *how* experience is thereby possible in the first place could never be adequately explained', finding that it would make no difference to his normative enterprise.[51] Accordingly, he is now, under the pressure of criticism, trying to de-emphasise the importance of the psychological side of the *Critique*.

This tendency away from psychological explanation and towards a still greater emphasis of logical analysis is still more apparent in the second edition of the *Critique of Pure Reason* that appeared in the following year. Thus Kant completely rewrote the 'Preface', the 'Transcendental Deduction', and the 'Paralogisms of Pure Reason', he added a 'Refutation of Idealism', and made extensive changes in a number of other places.[52] All these places were designed to emphasise Kant's 'empirical realism'. But they were also designed to downplay the importance of the psychological side of the first *Critique*. In fact, to a large extent, they amount to an elimination of precisely these passages.

The combined effect of all these changes was to bring Kant, with regard to empirical psychology, much closer to Reid.[53] This might be an accident. But it might also be the result of a closer study of Reid's *Inquiry*. Since a German translation of this work had appeared in 1782, since the translator called attention to parallels between Kant and Reid in his Preface, and since many of those who were critical of Kant used essentially Reidian arguments against him, it is almost certain that Kant read it before working on the second edition of the *Critique of Pure Reason*. Therefore, his modified stance with regard to psychology could very well also be influenced by Reid. In any case, he saw now what he should perhaps already have seen in 1781: the 'subjective side' of the *Critique* was not only not necessary, but perhaps even harmful.[54]

Accordingly, Reid could have made a contribution to Kant's attempted solution of Hume's problem. Even if the historical account given here – which after all is, like Kant's psychology, 'the search for the cause of a given effect, and to that extent somewhat hypothetical in character' – should turn out to be not entirely convincing, I hope that I have succeeded in showing that a discussion of Reid's relation to Kant is not only reasonable, but perhaps even fruitful. Indeed, if Gerold Prauss is correct in claiming that the 'problem of the objectivity of appearance as such' is one of the most basic problems of the *Critique*, Reid may be *extremely* important for any discussion of Kant's critical philosophy.[55]

NOTES

1. Thus Professor Beck has tried to show that even on the problem of causation a 'surprising degree of accommodation between them is possible'. See Lewis White Beck, 'A Prussian Hume and a Scottish Kant' in *Essays on Kant and Hume* (New Haven: Yale University Press, 1978), 111–29. My interpretation should be looked upon as an attempt to extend Beck's line of interpretation (which is not to say that he would agree with its details or even with its general direction).

2. Immanuel Kant, *Prolegomena to Any Future Metaphysics*. Ed. Lewis White Beck (Indianapolis/New York: Bobbs Merrill Publishing Co., 1950), 6.

3. See Manfred Kuehn, *Scottish Common Sense in Germany, 1768–1800: A Contribution to the History of Critical Philosophy* (Montreal/Kingston: McGill-Queen's University Press, 1987), 167–207.

4. The quote is taken from the conclusion of Reid's *Inquiry into the Human Mind*. He also points out in this context that a

'clear explication and enumeration of the principles of common
sense, is one of the chief *desiderata* in logic'. See Thomas Reid,
Philosophical Works, 2 vols., Sir William Hamilton (Edinburgh,
1895), Vol. 1, 209.

5. Joseph Priestley, *An Examination of Dr. Reid's Inquiry into
the Human Mind on the Principles of Common Sense, Dr. Beattie's
Essay on the Nature and Immutability of Truth, and Dr. Oswald's
Appeal to Common Sense in Behalf of Religion* (London, 1774),
9. His 'Table of Dr. Reid's instinctive principles' is, of course,
rather different from Kant's 'Table of the Categories'. Among
the twelve principles we find not only 'belief in the present
existence of an object' (when sensed), and 'the idea of extension
and space', but also the 'parallel motion of the eyes, as
necessary to distinct vision'. Priestley is not interested in
improving on Reid's 'Table', since his work is extremely critical
of his theory. Nevertheless, even his characterisation of the role
of these principles shows that they play a role roughly similar to
Kant's categories and the principles based upon them.

6. For references as well as a more extensive discussion of
this interpretation and its shortcomings, see Manfred Kuehn,
'Kant's Conception of Hume's Problem', *Journal of the History
of Philosophy* 21 (1983), 175–93, and 'Hume's Antinomies',
Hume Studies 9 (1983) 25–45.

7. For a criticism of such views see Manfred Kuehn, 'Kant's
Transcendental Deduction: A Limited Defense of Hume', in
New Essays on Kant, ed. Bernard den Ouden and Marcia Moen
(New York: Peter Lang Publishing, 1987), 47–72.

8. Kant, *Prolegomena*, ed. Beck, 9.

9. Thus W.H. Walsh claimed that a 'good way to approach
the central doctrines of the analytic is to see them as an
intended answer to Hume'. See W.H. Walsh, 'Kant' in *The
Encyclopedia of Philosophy*, ed. Paul Edwards.

10. This is *not* to say that Kant did not succumb to polemics.
Nor do I want to claim that Kant was entirely successful in
doing what he set out to do (nor even that philosophy can
become a science in this sense). But before those questions can
be discussed, we must know what it was that Kant actually
wanted to accomplish.

11. In fact, Kant makes clear that 'Hume's problem' is not
Hume's 'personal' concern, but has a history older than Hume,
and a significance that goes beyond the latter's empiricism. See,
for instance, Kant, *Prolegomena*, ed. Beck, 5: 'Since the *Essays*
of Locke and Leibniz, or rather since the origin of metaphysics
so far as we know its history, nothing has ever happened which
could have been more decisive than the attack made upon it by
David Hume'.

12. Quotations followed by a page number in the text

(preceded by an 'A' and/or 'B') are from Kant's first *Critique*. 'A' indicates the first edition 'B' the second. I quote in accordance with Kemp Smith's translation.

13. See Kuehn, 'Kant's Transcendental Deduction' for a fuller discussion of this point.

14. Kant, *Prolegomena*, ed. Beck, 7.

15. In his first *Critique* he calls philosophers who subscribe to this approach 'naturalists of pure reason' (A 855: B 883).

16. Ibid.

17. I think that Kant interprets Hume correctly in this regard. It is this normative question that is most important to him, since he is intent on destroying an uncritical use of experiential concepts in theology.

18. When Kant argued in his *Prolegomena* that 'to satisfy the conditions of the problem [Hume's, that is], the opponents of the great thinker [i.e. Reid, Oswald, Beattie and Priestley] should have penetrated very deeply into the nature of reason, so far as it is concerned with pure thinking – a task which did not suit them' (*Prolegomena*, ed. Beck, 7), he may actually be suggesting as much. In any case, Reid himself had pointed out that he had discussed such *a priori* principles 'as occurred in the examination of the five senses'. Kant seems to construe this as a fault. Superficially, Kant's criticism is very similar to that offered earlier by Tetens, who asked: 'Why were *Barkley* [sic], *Hume* and the *heroic* skeptic of the *Treatise of Human Nature*, who pursued skepticism to its non plus ultra, not attacked with their own principles? Why was reason not allowed to judge its own transgressions? However, for this it would have been necessary to investigate the nature of human cognition up to its first beginnings, and even more to explicate the procedure of the faculty of thought in the attainment of knowledge more exactly and more carefully than *Reid* or *Beattie* or *Oswald*, in spite of their otherwise superior perspicuity, appear to have done' (Johann Nicolaus Tetens, *Über die allgemeine speculativische Philosophie* (1775), 16f.). However, their criticisms of the Scots are actually quite different from each other. Though both agree that rational principles are the solution to Hume's problem, Tetens agrees with the Scots that Hume *needs* to be attacked, while Kant thinks that if they had looked at the problem more closely, they would have come to see it as genuine. Both accuse the Scots of not having gone far enough in their explication or rational principles. But, whereas Tetens has in mind a psychological account of what rational principles contribute in our acquisition of knowledge, Kant is concerned with their lack of critical discussion of the 'objective validity of rational principles'. Whereas Tetens finds them falling short in their psychology, Kant finds them falling short in their logic.

19. Reid, *Works*, ed. Hamilton, Vol. 1, 106.

20. Reid identifies 'simple apprehension' with imagination. See Reid, *Works*, ed. Hamilton, Vol. 1, 106.

21. See also Bernard E. Rollin, 'Thomas Reid and the Semiotics of Perception', *The Monist* 61 (1978), 257ff.

22. For this he was taken to task by Joseph Priestley. See, for instance, *Examination*, p. 22: 'who should have asserted that these principles are *simple*, original, and therefore *inexplicable acts of the mind*, and that they *cannot* be produced by any principle of human nature that has ever been admitted by philosophers. This is asserting that it is impossible to advance any farther in the investigation, for who can ever get beyond *simple, original*, and *inexplicable acts of the mind*'.

23. David Hume, *A Treatise of Human Nature*, 2nd. ed. L.A. Selby-Bigge, revision and notes P.H. Nidditch (Oxford: Clarendon Press, 1978), 636.

24. H.J. Paton, *Kant's Metaphysic of Experience*, 2 vols. (London: George Allen & Unwin Ltd., 1970), 1, 138.

25. Today this discussion is usually framed in terms of what kind of phenomenalist Kant was. And there are at least two different conceptions of 'phenomenalism' that are considered. The first one, which also has been called 'ontological phenomenalism', or 'idealism', is the theory according to which objects are literally composed of ideas. Objects *are* 'collections of ideas'. Berkeley is assumed to have held this theory, and Hume is sometimes accused of having held a version of it. A second form of phenomenalism does not involve the ontological claim that objects are actually made up of representations or ideas, but only the claim that statements about objects can always be shown to be 'logically equivalent' to statements that are exclusively about representations or ideas. This theory has been called 'linguistic' or 'analytical phenomenalism'. See, for instance, James Van Cleve, 'Another Volley at Kant's Reply to Hume', in *Kant on Causality, Freedom and Objectivity*, ed. William A. Harper and Ralf Meerbote (Minneapolis: University of Minnesota Press, 1984), 42–57, 43f. See also Jonathan Bennett, *Kant's Analytic* (Cambridge: Cambridge University Press, 1966), 126f. Van Cleve finds that the first *Critique* 'contains many explicit statements of ontological phenomenalism', though he also encounters 'occasional implicit statements of analytical phenomenalism' ('Another Volley', 43). Kant is confused about the difference between the two, or so he thinks. It would be no exaggeration to characterise the phenomenalist reading of Kant as having been the standard interpretation of Kant in English-speaking countries. Recently it has been challenged most vigorously and persuasively by Henry E. Allison, in his *Kant's Transcendental Idealism. An Interpretation and Defense* (New Haven: Yale University Press, 1983). Much of this discussion

goes back to Gerold Prauss's *Erscheinung bei Kant: Ein Problem der 'Kritik der reinen Vernunft'* (Berlin: de Gruyter, 1971) and his *Kant und das Problem der Dinge an sich* (Bonn: Bouvier Verlag Hermann Grundmann, 1974). Kant's distinction between knowable 'appearances' and unknowable 'things in themselves' is not one between 'two objects' or 'two worlds', but rather one of 'two aspects'. It is a 'transcendental distinction between the ways in which things (empirical objects) can be "considered" at the metalevel of philosophical reflection rather than between the kinds of thing that are considered in such reflection' (Henry Allison, 'Transcendental Idealism: The "Two Aspect" View', in *New Essays on Kant*, ed. den Ouden/Moen, 155–78, 155). The 'dual aspect' interpretation has considerable appeal, if only because it disposes of many of the difficulties that have plagued the 'phenomenalist' way of reading Kant.

26. Emphasis mine.

27. Paton, *Kant's Metaphysic*, 1, 358.

28. A 191:B 236: 'That which lies in the successive apprehension is here viewed as representation, while the appearance which is given to me, notwithstanding that it is nothing but the sum of these representations, is viewed as their object'. This is a central passage for the phenomenalist way of reading Kant. See Van Cleve, 'Another Volley'. See also Paul Guyer, *Kant and the Claims of Knowledge* (Cambridge: Cambridge University Press, 1987), 262–6.

29. Paton, *Kant's Metaphysic*, 1, 138.

30. Ibid.

31. For the other two distinctions see Allison, *Kant's Transcendental Idealism*. See also note 25 above.

32. See A 113. What precisely Kant means by these doctrines is very difficult to determine, but it is clear, I think, that they presuppose a rejection of 'simple apprehension'. For Kant, 'apprehension' is anything but simple.

33. Norman Kemp Smith, *A Commentary to Kant's Critique of Pure Reason*, 3rd ed. (Atlantic Highlands, N.J.: Humanities Press, 1984), xli. However, he turns what he has just said into a psychological claim in the very next sentence, saying that it 'can be shown to rest on a complexity of generative conditions and to involve a variety of distinct factors'. See also pp. 270ff. There he actually accuses Kant of being confused, and of having wavered between a Humean view (subjectivism) and his best theory (phenomenalism).

34. Kant would have subscribed to Reid's claim that 'nature does not exhibit these elements separate, to be compounded by us; she exhibits them mixed and compounded in concrete bodies; and it is only by art and chymical analysis that they can be separated' (Reid, *Works* 1, 107).

35. Paton, *Kant's Metaphysic*, 1, 138. Here it seems to be

Paton who is confusing the logical and the psychological, or the transcendental and the physiological.

36. Tetens's *Philosophische Versuche über die menschliche Natur und ihre Entwicklung* appeared in 1776 and 1777. Kant probably also knew the anonymous *Über die allgemeine speculativ-ische Philosophie* of 1775. For more on the evidence concerning Kant's relation to Tetens, see Manfred Kuehn, 'Dating Kant's Vorlesungen uber philosophische Enzyclopadie', *Kant-Studien* 74 (1983), 302–13, especially 308–10.

37. For a discussion of the general outlines of Reid's influence upon Tetens see especially Chapter 7 of Kuehn, *Scottish Common Sense in Germany*.

38. Kant's 'Vorarbeiten zu den Prolegomena' in *Kant's Schriften* (Academy edition), *Handschriftlicher Nachlass*, Vol. 10, 57. This brings Tetens into the immediate context of 'Hume's problem'. There is another passage about Tetens that is ungrammatical and lacks punctuation. It says 'common sense as a principle causes enthusiasm *Tetens* namely one that attempts to rage with reason, the only one that can become a fashion in an age of reason' (59). Kant seems to be referring to the eighth essay 'On the Relation of Higher Cognitions of Discursive Reason to the Cognitions of Common Sense', where Tetens argues that 'to put aside reasoning altogether, and to follow only the so called *sensus kommunis [sic]* is a principle that leads to *enthusiasm*'. To declare in certain cases the 'question "whether we sometimes mistake true subjective and natural necessity with merely received custom" as entirely unnecessary, and to surrender, following *Reid, Beattie,* and *Oswald's* prescription, completely to unexamined common sense, would amount to abandon rational investigation' (Tetens, *Philosophische Versuche,* 584). This passage seems to me to *prove* that Kant was influenced by Tetens in his analysis of Reid as late as 1782.

39. Kant, *Werke* (Academy edition), Vol. 18, 23. He also found '*Tetens* investigates the concepts of pure reason merely subjectively (human nature), I do so objectively. His analysis is empirical, mine is transcendental'. For the date of these reflections see Kuehn, 'Dating Kant's Vorlesung', 308f. See also 'Vorarbeiten', 57, where, after having pointed out that Tetens could have given occasion for the reviewer to think about the possibility of *a priori* knowledge, Kant goes on to say: 'Thus he is far behind. Even a failed attempt of this kind would have deserved his respect and approval, for, at the least it would have called attention to the problem'.

40. Tetens's criticism of Reid is similar to Priestley's. This is due to the fact that both want to give a psychological explanation of how knowledge *originates*. The very title of Tetens's main

work' *Philosophical Essays on Human Nature and its Development,* already indicates the importance of 'development' for him.

41. Tetens, *Philosophische Versuche,* 473. See also 377ff, where he considers the question whether we must be first 'egoists' before we can become convinced of the existence of external things. He denies this, claiming that in the development of the concept of self the concept of something external to it necessarily must also arise.

42. Accordingly, Paton's attempt at distancing Kant from Hume by reference to Tetens is not very promising.

43. Kant, *Werke* 17, 664. Paul Guyer seems to be correct when he claims that 'the fundamental idea of 1774–5 is that certain rules can be shown to be necessary conditions for thinking of objects, as opposed to merely having sensations' (Guyer, *Kant and the Claims of Knowledge,* 25. His entire discussion of the Duisburg Nachlass is most interesting.).

44. Kant, *Werke* (Academy edition), 18, 123, 267.

45. See, for instance, Kant, *Critique,* A 20: B 34 and A 90: B 122ff.

46. See H.-J. Vleeschauwer, *The Development of Kantian Thought,* tr. A.R.C. Duncan (London: Thomas Nelson and Son, Inc, 1962), 85–8. However, Vleeschauwer neither sees the importance of Reid in this nor the differences between Tetens and Kant.

47. Review of Kant's *Critique of Pure Reason* in the *Göttingische Anzeigen von gelehrten Sachen,* Zugabe, 3. Stück, 19 January 1983, 41.

48. Ibid., 48.

49. Review of Johann August Ulrich, *Institutiones Logicae et Metaphysicae* (Jena 1785) in *Allgemeine Literatur-Zeitung,* 13 December 1785, 299. I quote after Reinhard Brandt, 'Eine neu aufgefundene Reflexion Kants "Vom inneren Sinne" (Loses Blatt Leningrad 1)' in *Neue Autographen und Dokumente zu Kants Leben, Schriften und vorlesungen,* ed. R. Brandt and W. Stark, Hamburg: Meiners, 1987.

50. Immanuel Kant, *Metaphysical Foundations of Natural Science,* tr. James Ellington (Indianapolis/New York: The Bobbs Merrill Co., Inc, 1970), 12n.

51. Ibid., 14n.

52. Most notably in the 'Introduction', and in the chapter on the 'Distinction of All Objects in General into Phenomena and Noumena'.

53. This is especially true of the 'Refutation of Idealism', as I have tried to show in my 'Kant and the Refutations of Idealism in the Eighteenth Century', in *Man, God and Nature in the Enlightenment,* ed. D.C. Mell, T.E.D. Braun, and L.M. Palmer

(East Lansing: Colleagues Press, 1988), 25–35.

54. For a more systematic discussion of the relation of psychology and transcendental philosophy, see W.H. Walsh, 'Philosophy and Psychology in Kant's Critique', *Kant-Studien* 57 (1966), 186–98; and Lewis White Beck, 'Toward a Meta-critique of Pure Reason', in *Essays on Kant and Hume*, 20–37.

55. Prauss, *Erscheinung bei Kant*, 14.

8

RÜDIGER SCHREYER

'Pray what Language did your wild Couple speak, when first they met?' – Language and the Science of Man in the Scottish Enlightenment

I. WHY STUDY EIGHTEENTH-CENTURY THEORIES ON THE ORIGIN OF LANGUAGE?

Writing the history of a scientific discipline is in some ways like describing a Cheshire cat: Now you see it, now you don't! It is both a well-known fact and an ever new surprise, that what we consider a pretty well defined field of study looses its shape or disappears altogether the further back we go in time.

Thus with linguistics. The eighteenth century has produced an enormous number of works explicitly dealing with language. However, perhaps an even greater number of linguistic reflections will be found embedded in some larger context. By the time the historian has reached the eighteenth century, linguistics has disappeared as an academic discipline, it has even disappeared as an autonomous field of study. Its subject, language, much like the grin of the Cheshire cat, is still there, but it appears on branches of the tree of knowledge we would not, by any stretch of the imagination, call linguistic.

The historian of linguistics can and often did perform some mental surgery by amputating and examining those passages of larger works that discuss language. But if he does, he runs the risk of missing the point, and he often has. A case in point is the much maligned, derided and often ignored debate on the origin and development of language, perhaps the major issue in eighteenth-century linguistic thought. Why, it has been asked (Kuehner 1944:24,44; Teeter 1966), did so many thinkers of the Enlightenment waste their time with developing theories on a subject for which they must have known there was no shred of evidence?

The answer is, that they did not consider the problem of glottogenesis a waste of time and they did believe they had evidence, but above all, that they tried to explain language in the same way they tried to explain all cultural objects, namely by writing their theoretical history. It does not take much ingenuity to recognise this: a glance at the context of glottogonic theories is sufficient. Mandeville (1670–1733) in his *Fable of the Bees* (1729), Condillac (1715–1780) in his *Essai sur L'origine des connoissances humaines* (1736), Rousseau (1712–78) in his *Discours sur l'origine de l'inégalité parmi les hommes* (1755) discuss language only as part of a larger inquiry into cultural phenomena. And even in works whose titles suggest a more single-minded concern with the origin of language, such as Herder's (1744–1803) *Abhandlung über den Ursprung der Sprache* (1772) or Adam Smith's (1723–90) *Dissertation upon the origin of languages* (1761) reveal on closer inspection that they are inextricably bound up with questions concerning the development of the human mind or of society.

The glottogonic question would probably not have acquired such urgency, if language did not play an essential part in the theoretical history of other societal phenomena whose evolution was investigated at the time. Eighteenth-century thinkers were alive to the fact that none of the arts, sciences and institutions could have developed without the aid of communication, and thus of language. Indeed, society could not even exist without communication. Furthermore, the progress of society would be impossible without the transmission of knowledge from one individual to the other and from one generation to the next: progress is largely due to the knowledge accumulated during the history of mankind. Thus theoretical history is impossible without the theoretical history of language.

Language also plays an essential part in the progress of the human mind. Nature has given man reason only as a faculty, the operation of this faculty must be developed by continual practice – a practice that includes the use of language.

Sociability and reason had always been considered the two *specificae* of the human animal. Eighteenth century linguistic thought is inextricably bound up with the problem of human nature, perhaps *the* problem of Enlightenment philosophy. Two interrelated questions were of major interest in these reflections on man (Formigari 1974; Viertel 1966):
 – the relation between language and mind
 – the relation between language and society.
Here, it seems to me, is the intellectual *locus* of linguistic and glottogonic theories: I believe that the eighteenth-century study of language and its origin must be understood as one part of a greater endeavour, viz. the scientific approach to the study of man. Approaching eighteenth-century linguistics from this point

give it the coherence that I believe it has (Schreyer 1984, 1985, 1986).

2. MORAL PHILOSOPHY AND THEORETICAL HISTORY

The study of nature and the study of man, natural and moral philosophy, were considered two parts of the same discipline. It was the overruling scientific endeavour of the time to establish a science of man that was to be as certain and methodologically sound as the natural philosophy of a Boyle or Newton. Moral philosophy was international, systematic and scientific – by contemporary standards.

Moral philosophers adopted the scientific method of analysis and synthesis and adapted it to moral subjects. The underlying assumption was that there was no basic difference in the subject matter of natural and moral philosophy, that the science of man like the science of nature ultimately rested on observation and experience, that it was the task of the philosopher to establish a causal relationship between the principles of nature and observable phenomena. For moral philosophy, this meant that a causal relationship was assumed between the principles of human nature and man's cultural achievements, a relationship that – given identical circumstances – would result in a uniform pattern of human development. Within this framework of moral philosophy a huge number of inquiries into all manner of social institutions was made, with the aim of providing a typical, generalised history of these institutions from their presumed origins to the present.

The first step, analysis, was concerned with the discovery of the basic principles of human nature by employing the familiar method of observation and comparison, first the comparison between man and animal, later the comparison of societal man and man in the state of nature, specimens of whom were believed to exist in savage societies, ancient cultures, feral man, very young children and deaf-mutes. Analysis is indispensable, and this is why most works in moral philosophy begin with a discussion of the motives of human behaviour, trying to derive them from as few principles as possible.

Analysis having yielded the essential features of man's nature, genetic reconstruction could begin, and ideally it would result in a theoretical or conjectural history of human society by establishing a causal chain of development from savage to societal man. The inquiry into the origin of language and all the other 'artificial' acquisitions of society can be understood as the equivalent of the synthetical step of the scientific method in moral philosophy.

Synthesis thus could enlighten us about periods in the history of mankind that seemed irretrievably lost, but it could do more than that: if convincing, such a history could be taken as a confirmation of the hypothesised basic human characteristics – and sometimes, mistakenly, as reality.

Clearly, theories of the origin of language fall under the general heading of theoretical history (Schreyer 1986). In keeping with the tenor of theoretical history, it was the aim of glottogonic theories to demonstrate how man, left to his natural faculties, would be able to invent language, an art deemed essential to the further progress of human civilisation towards this most wonderfully complicated state called polite society. All the arts and sciences were perceived as conditioned by, and in their turn conditioning, language.

Theories of the natural origin of language usually begin with the postulation of a couple of savages without language, without society, without culture. The question is whether and how they could create a language. 'Pray what Language did your wild Couple speak, when first they met?' was not only the question Mandeville's Cleomenes (Mandeville 1957 II:284) was trying to answer, but in his wake also less fictitious philosophers such as Condillac, Rousseau, in France, Maupertuis, Herder, Süssmilch (1707–67) in Germany, and Monboddo (1714–99) and Adam Smith in Scotland.

Inquiries into the origin of language were not an exclusively Scottish affair. Neither was theoretical history in general. Although Scottish writers in this field did not suffer from exaggerated modesty, they acknowledged that their work formed part of the general European effort of creating a science of man. With respect to theoretical history in general, and the theoretical history of language in particular, the Scottish Enlightenment is an Enlightenment in Scotland and the Scots knew it.

But I will devote my attention exclusively to two Scots. Monboddo will be ignored. Adam Smith has been given some attention in recent literature (Berry 1974; Coseriu 1970; Land 1977; Lindgren 1969; Noordegraaf 1977; Salvucci 1982; Smith 1970, Stam 1976; Windross 1980), but he deserves more. And Thomas Reid (1710–96) has, in this context, not had any, although he makes interesting use of glottogonic ideas.

In the following investigation I shall not be concerned with the merits of individual solutions to the problem of glottogenesis, but rather with the way the problem presented itself to eighteenth-century thinkers and with the way they approached it.

3. THE DEFINITION OF LANGUAGE

The difficulties these philosophers encounter derive, so it seems to me, from the necessity of reconciling the genetic question with the received definition of language.

James Harris (1709–80) in his *Hermes* (1751), the famous eighteenth-century standard work on universal grammar, offers the following definition of language: 'A system of articulate voices, the symbols of our ideas, but of those principally, which are general or universal' (1751:347–8). Symbols are derived 'from Accidents quite arbitrary', they are only known by habit or institution: all language is founded in compact (Harris 1751:337).

These are then the main components of a definition of language:
- Language serves the communication of ideas.
- Words are the signs of ideas, most of them general.
- The relation between words and ideas is arbitrary, conventional, by institution or compact.

To this must be added:
- Language is the tie that holds society together.

This definition of language was commonplace and uncontroversial. In the sphere of a scientific moral philosophy, language had to be viewed as the product of the uniform laws of human nature. Clearly, language was not innate as it had to be learned anew by every individual: in this sense there was no natural connection between language and ideas. However, as man was the only speaking animal, language in some sense, had to be natural to man. In this respect language was no different to all the arts, sciences and institutions found in society. These were obviously not innate or god-given, but the product of society. On the other hand, they must have their foundation in the psychology of man: man must have faculties animals do not possess. Thus for language the following two questions arise:
- Which are the faculties or principles of human nature responsible for the creation of language?
- How might language have evolved by natural means?

4. PROBLEMS OF A THEORETICAL HISTORY OF LANGUAGE

The theoretical history of any societal phenomenon must start at a point before this phenomenon existed: usually theoretical histories take as their point of departure the so-called state of nature, a hypothetical pre-societal state when man was endowed with nothing but the principles of his nature. The theoretical historian then proceeded to deduce society and all the societal phenomena from these principles and the circumstances of the environment.

The principles were seen as causes, the phenomena as their effects. Each stage of societal evolution presented man with changed circumstances, to which he would react as his nature demanded by further changing his natural and social environment. Thus the evolutionary process is a process without end.

The theoretical history of language conforms to this general pattern: Man in the state of nature is pre-societal and pre-linguistic man. Accounts of the origin of language usually begin with the philosophical fiction of a primordial couple devoid of speech. This starting point immediately creates difficulties: it is not compatible with the definition of language. The history of glottogonic theories can be written in terms of the solutions adopted to solve these difficulties. For my immediate purpose it will be enough to list, and comment upon, these problems. This will allow me to put the contributions of Reid and Smith in perspective.

Most of the problems are of the chicken-and-egg type: they can be stated in the form of a paradox.

Problem 1:

No language without society, no society without language.

Language is the result of a compact between the members of a society to use certain articulate sounds to express a given idea. Thus society must precede language.

Language is the instrument of society. The need to create such an instrument would not arise unless man lived in society. Thus society must precede language.

Language is the common tie of society: there can be no society without language. Thus language must precede society.

Problem 2 (assuming the existence of society):

No compact without language, no language without compact.

Language is the result of a compact between members of a society. This compact involves the declaration of purpose. This is necessarily linguistic. Thus language must precede any compact.

Problem 3:

No language without reflection, no reflection without language.

Man's reason is a latent power; the operations of the reasoning faculty develop through application, particularly in language. Nearly all words of a language are general words. General words are the signs of general ideas. General ideas are the product of the mental operations of generalization

and abstraction. Thus man would have to apply his mental
operations before he has the use of them.

Not all thinkers of the Enlightenment are theoretical historians,
and not all theoretical historians address problems of language.
Some theoretical historians and some thinkers, who are not
theoretical historians, address some of these problems. Put in a
less syllogistic form: Reid, who is not a theoretical historian,
discusses the first two problems, and Smith, who is, discusses the
last.

5. THOMAS REID: LANGUAGE AND THE ANALYSIS OF HUMAN NATURE

5.1 The argument from language

Observations on language, sometimes of considerable length,
occur scattered throughout Reid's works. But these observations
are always subservient to his main concern, his 'anatomy of the
mind', an attempt to discover its powers and principles. Analysis
is, in Reid's view, the necessary preliminary to the construction of
a system of the mind, 'that is, an enumeration of the original
powers and laws of our constitution, and an explication from
them of the various phenomena of human nature' (Reid 1812
I:11). Reid (1812 I:84) stresses that the chief and proper source
from which to draw the knowledge of the operations of the mind
is accurate reflection. But he points out again and again that one
important source subservient to such reflection is 'attention to the
structure of language'.

> Language is the express image and picture of human thoughts;
> and from the picture we can draw some certain conclusions
> concerning the original. (Reid 1812 II:290)

or

> Language being the express image of human thought, the
> analysis of the one must correspond to that of the other.
> (Reid 1812 I:XLIIX)

Thus the philosopher would be well advised to pay heed to 'the
common opinions of mankind, upon which the structure and
grammar of all languages are founded' (Reid 1812 I:51), for, says
Reid (1812 I:37), 'I believe no instance will be found of a
distinction made in all languages, which has not a just foundation
in nature'.

It is plain that Reid, for his analysis of the faculties of the mind,
is trying to enlist the support of universal grammar. What is
common to all languages, so the argument goes, cannot be
accidental: it must be the manifestation of the mind's operations

common to all human beings, and thus embody the 'common sense of mankind'.

> Now what is common in the structure of all languages, indicates an uniformity of opinion in those things upon which that structure is grounded. (Reid 1812 II,291; cf. I:51)

Reid's argument from language is a sub-category of the argument from consent: he states explicitly that, to lend authority to his first principles, the moral philosopher can refer to the 'consent of ages and nations, of the learned and unlearned' (Reid 1812 II:285–6). Universal grammar embodies this consent and is thus often appealed to:

> We shall have frequent occasion to argue from the sense of mankind expressed in the structure of language; and therefore it was proper here to take notice of the force of arguments drawn from this topic. (Reid 1812 I:67–8)

Often Reid uses the argument from language in rather a crude way, as for instance, when he asserts that 'all mankind' distinguish between the operations of the mind, which are expressed by active verbs, and 'the mind itself, which is the nominative to these verbs' (Reid 1812 I:36).

5.2 *Glottogenesis and the social operations of the mind*

Linguistic ideas are, however, exploited in a more subtle way in Reid's reflections on the origin of language. He begins by describing what he considers the received opinion:

> Language is commonly considered as purely an invention of men, who by nature are no less mute than the brutes, but having a superior degree of invention and reason, have been able to contrive artificial signs of their thoughts and their purposes, and to establish them by common consent. (Reid 1801:92)

Dissatisfied with this account, Reid (1801:92) suggests 'that the origin of language deserved to be more carefully inquired into', as such an inquiry 'tends to lay open some of the first principles of human nature'. He distinguishes two types of mental operations, the solitary and the social operations.

> I call those operations solitary, which may be performed by a man in solitude, without intercourse with any other intelligent being. I call those operations social, which necessarily imply social intercourse with some other intelligent being who bears a part in them. (Reid 1812 III:537)

Seeing, hearing, remembering, judging and reasoning are among the solitary acts. Asking a question, testifying a fact, giving a command, making a promise, entering into a contract, refusing, threatening and supplicating 'are social acts of the mind, and can have no existence without the intervention of some other intelligent being, who acts in part of them' (Reid 1812 III:537). The difference between these two types of act is that solitary acts can exist and be complete without being expressed. Their expression by words or other signs is purely accidental. In social acts, however, expression is essential: 'They cannot exist without being expressed by words or signs, and known to the other party' (Reid 1812 III:538). In fact, Reid (1812 I:37) claims, that 'it is the primary and direct intention of language' to express the social operations of the mind.

> If nature had not made man capable of such social operations of mind, and furnished him with a language to express them, he might think, and reason, and deliberate, and will; he might have desires and aversions, joy and sorrow; in a word, he might exert all those operations of mind, which the writers of logic and pneumatology have so copiously described; but, at the same time, he would still be a solitary being, even when in a crowd; it would be impossible for him to put a question, or to give a command, to ask a favour, or testify a fact, to make a promise or a bargain. (Reid 1812 III:538)

On the other hand, Reid maintains that 'a man who had no intercourse with any other intelligent being, would never think of language. He would be as mute as the beasts of the field'. Social intercourse cannot be taught, for teaching presupposes social intercourse. As social intercourse is of necessity carried out by sensible signs, it also presupposes 'language already established between the teacher and the learner' (Reid 1812 III:539). Thus we arrive at Reid's version of the classical paradox: no social intercourse without language, no language without social intercourse. Reid uses this paradox in a formal proof of the necessary existence of a natural language prior to the artificial language of words.

> . . . I think it is demonstrable, that if mankind had not a natural language, they could never have invented an artificial one by their reason and ingenuity. For all artificial language supposes some compact or agreement to affix a certain meaning to certain signs; therefore there must be compacts or agreements before the use of artificial signs; but there can be no compact or agreement without signs, nor without language; and therefore there must be a natural language before any artificial language can be invented: Which was to be demonstrated. (Reid 1801:93)

Natural signs are 'such as, previous to all compact or agreement, have a meaning which every man understands by the principles of his nature' (Reid 1801:93; III:540). Scanty as it may be, this common language of modulations of the voice, gestures and features, must be sufficient to enter into a contract – the precondition for the creation of artificial language. This presupposes the existence, in the mind of man, of 'a notion of contracts or convenants, or of moral obligation to perform them' (Reid 1801:94).

Animals lack social intercourse: they cannot plight veracity by testimony nor can they lie, they cannot plight fidelity by any engagement or promise nor are they sensible of the obligation of a promise or contract, and therefore they could not develop artificial signs.

> . . . none of them, as far as we know, can make a promise, or plight their faith, having no such notions from their constitution. And if mankind had not these notions by nature, and natural signs to express them by, with all their wit and ingenuity they could never have invented language. (Reid 1801:94)

Signs need not resemble the thing signified by them. It is, however, necessary and sufficient that there should be a real connection established between them 'either by the course of nature, or by the will and appointment of men' (Reid 1801:383). In the former case Reid speaks of natural, in the latter of artificial signs. The natural signs of human thoughts, purposes, and desires make up the natural language of mankind.

This language is immediately understood by the spectator. The knowledge of natural signs is latent in the mind. The understanding of the signs is like reminiscence in that it is immediate. Although there is no necessary connection between 'looks, changes of the features, modulations of the voice, and gestures of the body' (Reid 1812 III:540) and such operations of the mind as consenting, refusing, affirming, denying, threatening and supplicating 'the operations become visible as it were by their natural signs' (Reid 1812 III:542). It must therefore be concluded that this connection and thus the social intercourse of mankind 'is the gift of God, no less than the powers of seeing and hearing' (Reid 1812 III:540).

Social intercourse is based on the principles of fidelity on the one hand, and trust and reliance on the other. Reid (1812 III:543–4) leaves it open whether these are 'original powers, or resolvable into other original powers', but he insists on their innateness, for promises, compacts, testimonies and the whole system of social intercourse would not be possible without them.

> Without fidelity and trust, there can be no human society.

There never was a society, even of savages, nay even of robbers and pirates, in which there was not a great degree of veracity and fidelity among themselves. Without it man would be the most dissocial animal that God has made. His state would be in reality what Hobbes conceived the state of nature to be, a state of war of every man, against every man; nor could this war ever terminate in peace. (Reid 1812 III:545)

Reid (1812 III:544) thus concludes that the social operations, as much as the social affections, of man make it evident that man was made for living in society.

Reid devotes far more attention to the language of nature than to artificial language, whose evolution receives short shrift. The transition from natural to artificial signs, for instance, a thorny problem in glottogonic theory, does not cause him much headache:

Mankind having thus a common language by nature, though a scanty one, there is no great ingenuity required in improving it by the addition of artificial signs, to supply the deficiency of the natural. (Reid 1801:95)

Reid is clearly aware of the complexities of artificial language, as we can glean from the following, intriguing simile:

This art, if it were not more common, would appear more wonderful, than a man should dance blindfold amidst a thousand burning ploughshares, without being burnt. . . . (Reid 1812 III:142)

Nevertheless, Reid gives no thought to the question of how this complex system of rules may have evolved. His interest in the origin of language derives from his interest in proving the innateness of what he calls the social operations of the human mind. Language in general interests him only inasmuch as it provides him with an argument for a potential principle of human nature. As a moral philosopher, Reid is a self-confessed analyst.

Not so Adam Smith! He does not so much as mention the problems involved in accounting for the origin of language from compact, although it is highly unlikely that he was not familiar with them. His attention is focused entirely on a problem Dugald Stewart (Smith 1980: 292–6) formulated as follows: 'Whence has arisen that systematical beauty which we admire in the structure of a cultivated language . . .?'

6. SMITH: THE OPERATIONS OF THE MIND AND THE DEVELOPMENT OF THE PARTS OF SPEECH

6.1 Rousseau's problem and Smith's problem

Smith's DISSERTATION ON THE ORIGIN OF LANGUAGES or Considera-

*tions Concerning the First Formation of Languages and the Different
Genius of Original and Compounded Languages* was first published
in 1761 in the *Philological Miscellany* and in 1767 appended to the
third edition of the *Theory of Moral Sentiments*. The ideas put
forward in the *Dissertation* were also discussed in Smith's Glasgow
Lectures on Rhetoric and Belles Lettres (1762/63), which only
survive as a set of student's notes (Smith 1963).

My purpose here is not a re-interpretation of the *Dissertation*,
but an investigation into the principles underlying Smith's account
of the evolution of the parts of speech. For a more precise
formulation of Smith's problem, we shall have to look in Rousseau's
Discours sur l'origine de l'inégalité parmi les hommes (1755) since
Smith himself suggests that he solved the problem 'the ingenious
and eloquent M. Rousseau, of Geneva,' found himself unable to
solve (Smith 1970:509). If we look up the relevant pages we find
that Rousseau's problem was a version of Problem 3: '. . . si les
hommes ont eu besoin de la parole pour apprendre à penser, ils
ont eu bien plus besoin de savoir penser pour trouver l'art de la
parole' (1971:189–90). Rousseau conjectures that, in the beginning
of language, each word had the meaning of an entire proposition,
that the distinction between subject and attribute, verb and noun
was quite an effort of genius, that the first nouns were proper
nouns, the infinitive the only form of the verb, and that the
notion of the adjective was difficult to develop since every
adjective is an abstract word and 'abstract thinking is a painful
and not very natural operation' (Rousseau 1971:192).

Rousseau (1971:193) then asks his readers to reflect on the time
and knowledge needed to discover the numerals, abstract words,
aorists, verb tenses, particles and syntax – and, convinced of the
almost demonstrable impossibility of a natural explanation, he
leaves all further speculation to others – or at least he says he
does.

Smith seems to have taken up the challenge: his main issue is
the same as was adumbrated by Rousseau, viz. the explanation of
the 'invention' of the parts of speech in their natural order
(Windross 1980:283).

6.2 Smith's method

Smith's *Dissertation* is clearly hypothetical. It is about probabilities
and therefore written in the subjunctive mood throughout. The
question of why and how his fictitious savage couple would hit on
speech as a means of communication did not trouble Smith
unduly. Apparently he has endowed his savages with enough
reason to think of the possibility of language by themselves. What

they are clearly incapable of is complicated feats of ratiocination: to Smith, reason is a faculty whose use can only be learned through frequent application.

The question is: what do the faculties of the mind have to do with language and with a theory of its invention? To answer it, we have to remember the dominant view of eighteenth-century semantics, that words are the signs of ideas, that the great majority of words are general terms, that general terms are general because they stand for general ideas. However, as Smith states in one of his early essays 'to explain the nature, and to account for the origin of general Ideas, is, even at this day, the greatest difficulty in abstract philosophy', a difficulty two thousand years of reasoning have not brought to a satisfactory solution (Smith 1967:130–31). John Locke (1632–1704) in his influential *Essay Concerning Human Understanding* (1690) had suggested that:

> Words become general by being made the signs of general *ideas*; and ideas become general by separating from them the circumstances of time and place and any other *ideas* that may determine them to this and that particular existence. By this way of abstraction they are made capable of representing more individuals than one: each of which, having in it a conformity to the abstract *idea*, is (as we call it) of that sort.
> (Locke 1961:17)

The importance the Enlightenment attached to general ideas for the progress of society can hardly be overestimated. It is a commonplace of the eighteenth century that the motor of progress is the acquisition and accumulation of knowledge and that knowledge is only possible if there are general ideas. The argument runs something like this: knowledge can only be gained through propositions. Propositions can be about particular or about general ideas. If about particular ideas, the only possible proposition is that no particular idea is identical with any other particular idea. Such a proposition clearly does not advance knowledge. Propositions, to be useful, presuppose the existence of general ideas. Thus there can be no knowledge withough general ideas.

The main purpose of language is the communication of knowledge. This presupposes the existence of words standing for general ideas. Thus there can be no communication of knowledge without general words. This proves that without general ideas there would be neither knowledge nor communication of knowledge.

It is plain that, in Locke's philosophy, matters of great

importance depend on the existence of general ideas. General ideas being the result of abstraction, this becomes one of the key faculties of the human mind. It is, for instance, the faculty which most clearly distinguishes man from the rest of the animal kingdom. Animals cannot abstract; consequently they have no general ideas, consequently no language, consequently no communication of knowledge, consequently no progress.

Locke himself did not raise the problem of glottogenesis. If the problem were discussed within a Lockean framework, however, and it often was, the question of the origin of general words, of general ideas, and thus of abstraction would have to play a central role. In fact abstraction is one of the key concepts both in Rousseau's and Smith's discussion, as well as one that leads immediately into difficulties. One of the problems Rousseau could not solve was how the names of particulars could become general by abstraction. Abstraction is precisely the problem Smith singles out in his *Lectures* (Smith 1963:8):

> This is what chiefly difficults Mr Rousseau, to wit, to explain, how general names were first formed, as they require abstract thought and what is called generalization, before they can be formed, according to his way of thinking: which he thinks men at first hardly capable of.

The eighteenth century generally agrees that abstracting is a 'painful operation'. Berkeley (1685–1753), in his *Principles of Human Knowledge* (1710) even goes so far as to deny the possibility of abstract ideas altogether, a proposition hailed by Hume (T. 17) as 'one of the greatest and most valuable discoveries that has been made of late years in the republic of letters'. One argument in support of this contention is the acknowledged difficulty of forming abstractions:

> . . . it is on all hands agreed that there is need of great toil and labour of the mind, to emancipate our thoughts from particular objects, and raise them to the sublime speculations that are conversant about abstract ideas. From all which the natural consequence should seem to be, that so difficult a thing as the forming of abstract ideas was not necessary for *communication*, which is so easy and familiar to all sorts of men. (Berkeley 1962:54)

Smith nowhere mentions the learned Bishop (although he knew his writings), but it seems that he took heed of his advice. As one bewildered commentator remarks:

> It seems as though Smith wants to explain the parts of speech without having recourse to abstraction, for having seemingly

admitted that this operation forms the basis of adjectives, he then argues that in the formation of languages men adopted another expedient, which required no abstraction. (Windross 19° ?:285)

In his hypothesis of the *beginning* of language, Smith indeed tries to do without abstraction for the very reasons adumbrated by Rousseau and Berkeley. But he can and will not do without it altogether: denying the possibility of abstraction entirely would have meant denying the possibility of abstract ideas and thus of abstract terms, like the names of qualities and relations.

The operations of the mind most essential for the invention of language are generalisation, comparison and abstraction, to which Land (1977:680) adds systematisation, an activity derived from Smith's 'love of analogy'. Smith is not entirely lucid in explaining the function and the sequence of these operations. The most interesting interpretation is to be found in Land (1977). It is true one might take issue with certain points of his analysis, particularly his unsatisfactory treatment of abstraction, which is for Smith without doubt the most important mental operation. What Locke, Berkeley and Hume and many less important thinkers had to say about abstraction profoundly influenced the linguistic thought of, say, James Harris or Horne Tooke. It could also be shown to have exerted a great influence on Adam Smith's assumed parallelism between the development of language and the faculties of the mind. But here is neither the place nor the time to discuss the problem of abstraction, however central to eighteenth-century linguistic theory.

These operations, so important for the development of language, Smith calls 'metaphysical'. As he takes the 'metaphysicalness' of a word as an index of its place on a temporal scale, his task boils down to explaining the transition from the least to the most metaphysical parts of speech. Basically, his entire theory of the rise of the parts of speech rests on the assumption that the different parts of speech represent different stages of abstraction, stages which he correlates with stages of the development of the human mind: those parts of speech which emerge first must be the least abstract and vice versa.

The basis for this assumption is his belief in the gradual unfolding of the faculties of the mind during the history of society: all men are endowed with the faculty of abstraction but they have to learn to apply it. The faculties of the human mind and language develop in a dialectic process, and thus the faculties that develop late will become manifest in language equally late.

This is how Smith's arrangement of the parts of speech along an abstract/concrete scale is related to his view of the origin of language.

If we order the parts of speech on Smith's scale of 'metaphysicalness' we arrive at roughly the following sequence (cf. Haggblade 1983:16; Land 1977:682–3):

- impersonal verbs, signifying one type of fact or event (Smith 1970:524–6)
- proper names, signifying one particular object (Smith 1970:507–09)
- combination of appellative noun and impersonal verb
- general nouns, signifying a species
- personal verbs
- general nouns inflected for gender (Smith 1970:514)
                                    case (Smith 1970:519)
                                    number (Smith 1970:529)
- personal verbs inflected for person, number, etc. (Smith 1970:528–30)
- adjective, signifying quality (Smith 1970:509–12)
- preposition, signifying relation (Smith 1970:515–21)
- numbers (Smith 1970:521–2)
- pronouns (Smith 1970:528–9)

6.3 The evolution of verbs and substantives

Smith's treatment of the rise of verbs and substantives will serve to illustrate his argument.

. . . in the beginnings of language, men seem to have attempted to express every particular event, which they had occasion to take notice of, by a particular word, which expressed at once the whole of the event. (Smith 1970:527)

Clearly, Smith's original language (like Rousseau's 1971:190) consisted of utterances referring to one individual concrete event, i.e. one particular proposition. These utterances had the character of impersonal verbs 'which suppose no abstraction or metaphysical division of the event into its several constituent members of subject and attribute' (Smith 1970:524). The impersonal verbs 'express a complete affirmation, the whole of an event, with that perfect simplicity and unity with which the mind conceives it in nature' (Smith 1970:524). The division of an event into subject and predicate 'is altogether artificial, and is the effect of the imperfection of language, which, upon this, as upon many other occasions, supplies, by a number of words, the want of one, which could express at once the whole matter of fact that was meant to be affirmed' (Smith 1970:524).

When, after a period of linguistic progress, names of particular substances had been invented, speakers would begin to join the name of an object (i.e. thing) to the verb. Now the verb no longer denotes a particular, distinct event, but rather an event of a certain type (Smith 1970:526). From the moment the impersonal verb ceases to refer to a single event, the name of an object would have to be attached to the verb to determine the signification of the expression. The result is thus a sentence with a subject and a verb.

Smith's account of the evolution of the rudimentary sentence presupposes the prior independent creation of the substantive. For both Rousseau and Smith, substantives developed from proper names, as these require the least amount of metaphysical thinking. The two savages would use these names to denote a very small number of individual objects 'to make their mutual wants intelligible to each other' (Smith 1970:507). With their experience enlarged, these savages would observe, and need to communicate about, other objects similar to the one referred to by a proper name. The recognition of the similarity of an object B to an object A would recall the idea of A and the proper name attached to it. The name of A would be extended to B by a process of antonomasia, i.e. the use of a proper name to express a general idea. Thus antonomasia is based on the psychological process of the association of ideas, a term actually used in Smith's lecture (Smith 1963:7).

> It was impossible that those savages could behold the new objects, without recollecting the old ones; and the name of the old ones, to which they bore so close a resemblance . . . And thus those words, which were originally the proper names of individuals, would each of them insensibly become the common name of a multitude. (Smith 1970:508)

Man, according to Smith, has a natural propensity to 'give to one object the name of any other, which nearly resembles it, and thus to denominate a multitude, by what was originally intended to express an individual'. Thus antonomasia, in Smith's opinion, is the key to the problem Rousseau was unable to solve:

> In this application of the name of an individual to a great multitude of objects, whose resemblance naturally recalls the idea of that individual, and of the name which expresses it, that seems originally to have given occasion to the formation of those classes and assortments, which, in the schools, are called genera and species, and of which the ingenious and eloquent M. Rousseau, of Geneva, finds himself so much at a loss to account for the origin. What constitutes a species is

merely a number of objects, bearing a certain degree of
resemblance to one another, and, on that account, denomi-
nated by a single appellation, which may be applied to
express any one of them. (Smith 1970:509)

A more precise formulation of Smith's definition of general terms
would thus be: a general term is a term which signifies indifferently
any of a set of similar, particular ideas. Smith seems to believe
that the recognition of similarity does not presuppose abstraction.

Neither Smith's problem nor his solution are new. Berkeley
and Hume offer virtually the same solution in order to save
general terms, while denying that they are names of abstract
ideas: '. . . a word becomes general by being made the sign, not
of an abstract general idea, but of several particular ideas, any one
of which it suggests indifferently to the mind' (Berkeley 1971:52;
cf. Hume, T. 20–1). Thus defined, general words need not signify
abstract ideas and still allow the communication of knowledge
(Berkeley 1971: 55–6). It seems, then, as if Smith had adopted
Berkeley's solution of the problem of general terms in order to
avoid an all too early introduction of abstraction in the glottogonic
process.

6.4 *More metaphysical parts of speech*

Denoting classes, general names have the peculiar disadvantage
that they cannot be used to refer to individuals. Thus, any
individual comprehended under the same general name must be
distinguished from other individuals of the same species 'either,
first, by its peculiar qualities; or, secondly, by the peculiar
relation which it stood in to some other things. Hence the
invention of general terms necessitates the creation of two other
sets of words, of which the one should express quality; the other
relation' (Smith 1970:510). Adjectives express quality, prepositions
relation. Prepositions serve to distinguish particular objects of the
same species when they have no distinguishing qualities of their
own.

Prepositions are very metaphysical, but even the invention of
adjectives would require 'mental operations of arrangement or
classing, of comparison, and of abstraction' that Smith (1970:512),
like Rousseau, is not willing to concede to the inventors of
language. Smith elaborates at length his arguments in support of
the increasing degree of metaphysical acumen required in the
formation of the ideas of quality, relation, number and deixis, and
thus of adjectives, prepositions, numerals and personal pronouns.
However, since the arguments always follow the same pattern I
will not discuss them in detail.

Smith's account of the development of the parts of speech shows that, unlike Berkeley, he does not seem to deny the possibility of abstract ideas on principle: abstraction is the single most important mental operation in the formation of most parts of speech, and the degree of abstraction required in their formation allows the arrangement of the parts of speech on a quasi-temporal scale. But Smith introduces abstractive processes as late as possible in his theoretical history of the parts of speech.

6.5 Forestalling abstraction

Nevertheless, Smith seems to have created a dilemma for himself: the introduction of general terms makes it impossible to specify particular objects of the same species. To individuate them, it will be necessary to mention their peculiar qualities or their relations to other objects. Similar considerations support the need for numerals or personal pronouns. Owing to the increasing degree of metaphysical thinking required in the invention of adjectives and prepositions, in numbers and personal pronouns, it seems unlikely that the early inventors commanded the mental aptitude to form such ideas. Is Smith then caught again between the horns of Rousseau's dilemma? Not so! There is, in his opinion, a more 'natural' way of expressing all these metaphysical ideas, i.e. a way involving less comparison, generalisation and abstraction.

For qualities, such an expedient is 'to make some variation upon the noun substantive itself, according to the different qualities which it is endowed with' (Smith 1970:512): the introduction of gender forestalls the need to create adjectives denoting sex. The creation of case endings does the same for prepositions denoting relations. Substantives inflected for gender and case exhibit a close analogy to the idea/object they denote.

> . . . quality appears in nature as a modification of the substance, and as it is thus expressed in language by a modification of the noun substantive which denotes that substance, the quality and the subject are in this case blended together, if I may say so, in the expression, in the same manner as they appear to be in the object and the idea. (Smith 1970:513)

This expedient, according to Smith (Smith 1970:513), requires 'no abstraction, nor any conceived separation of the quality from the subject'. Thus endings can, and in other languages may, be used to express any kind of quality (cf. Bergheaud 1984:34–5).

Similar reasons are given to explain the evolution of case in nouns or number and person in verbs. Thus both declension and conjugation owe their creation to 'the difficulty of forming, in the beginnings of language, abstract and general terms', a difficulty which explains the structure of the ancient languages (Smith 1970:522–3).

From the above it is clear that in the development of language an inflective stage precedes the compositive stage: gender before adjective, case before preposition, number before numerals, person before pronoun. In all cases the argument is the same. Variation of the substantive is easier or more natural than the invention of the corresponding parts of speech; it requires less comparison, generalisation and abstraction. It is easy to see why Smith needed to interpolate a synthetic stage in the theoretical history of language: as far as Smith was concerned, the oldest languages, i.e. Greek and Latin, were highly inflecting languages. Thus his first task was to explain the origin of inflections and all the parts of speech found in these languages on the basis of as few principles as possible.

Notice, however, that in Smith's view no fully developed language can be totally synthetic: it is mixed in the sense that only some qualities are expressed via declension, some relations via case etc., but the vast majority of these concepts is expressed by separate words. Smith repeatedly stresses the complexity of inflecting languages. Substantives, he claims for instance, would altogether lose their original form, if they were to undergo the enormous number of variations necessary to express that almost infinite number of qualities and relations that might be necessary to distinguish them. Inflection can only 'forestall' the invention of the more metaphysical parts of speech (Smith 1970:514), it cannot prevent it.

New parts of speech were thus introduced in order to keep the complexity of a language within tolerable limits. If tolerable, at least for the native speaker, there is no reason to assume why the structure of the language should change. There is even less reason why existing 'terminations' of words should be replaced by prepositions (Smith 1970:530). Smith's very first principle is: no change without a cause. And the inflectional system works. In order to explain why the modern languages did away with inflections another explanation needs to be found. Notice, however, that abolition of inflection in French, Italian etc. is a historical fact and thus needs a historical rather than a theoretical explanation. The question is not how it could have happened but how it did happen. And this is what Smith is concerned with in the so-called second part of his *Dissertation*.

It would, of course, be easy to pick holes in Smith's argument (cf. Coseriu 1970; Funke 1934, Land 1977). Understanding an argument and picking holes in it are, however, different activities, the latter being logically dependent on the former. I find understanding difficult enough. And therefore I will, finally, offer you my understanding of an important, but misunderstood metaphor, which may throw new light on Smith's *Dissertation*.

6.6 The machine metaphor

As we have seen, a language passes through several stages: from the unitary expression of individual events (one-word propositions) through an inflectional to an analytical phase. This development corresponds to a progress in the speakers' metaphysical abilities. Thus in the beginning of language an utterance expressed a whole event, and as the event was analysed into its components the linguistic expression became analytical, or as Smith calls it, compounded. In this respect languages are like machines.

> It is in this manner that language becomes more simple in its rudiments and principles, just in proportion as it grows more complex in its composition, and the same thing has happened in it which commonly happens in regard with mechanical engines. All machines are generally, when first invented, extremely complex in their principles, and there is often a particular principle of motion for every particular movement which it is intended they should perform. Succeeding improvers observe, that one principle may be so applied as to produce several of those movements; and thus the machine becomes gradually more and more simple, and produces its effects with fewer wheels and fewer principles of motion. In language, in the same manner, every case of every noun, and every tense of every verb, was originally expressed by a particular distinct word, which served for this purpose and for no other. But succeeding observation discovered, that one set of words was capable of supplying the place of all that infinite number, and that four or five prepositions, and half a dozen auxiliary verbs, were capable of answering the end of all the declensions and of all the conjugations in the ancient languages. (Smith 1970:535)

Although Smith's comparison of language with a machine is rather striking, historians of linguistics have had very little to say about it. Some even ignore it altogether. It is, however, well-known that the machine analogy plays an important part in Smith's description of scientific inquiry, as well as in the whole of moral philosophy (e.g. Shaftesbury, Butler in Raphael 1969: 169–77, 326–7, 356). A less linguistic, and therefore less myopic view of Smith, the moral philosopher, would have shown that he uses the machine analogy whenever he discusses the concept of system.

Consider the close similarity of the following passage with the one above:

> The machines that are first invented to perform a particular movement are always the most complex, and succeeding artists generally discover that, with fewer wheels, with fewer principles of motion, than had originally been employed, the same effects may be more easily produced. The first systems, in the same manner, are always the most complex, and a particular connecting chain, or principle, is generally thought necessary to unite every two seemingly disjointed appearances: but it often happens, that one great connecting principle is afterwards found sufficient to bind together all the disconnected phenomena that occur in a whole species of things (Smith 1967:66).

Here Smith uses the machine analogy to elucidate his concept of a philosophical, i.e. scientific, system. We can, therefore, conclude that the common denominator of a machine, a language and a philosophical system is that all are man-made systems which have taken a similar course of development. The machine metaphor is particularly apt to illustrate the other systems because a machine has not only an imaginary but also a real existence. It is inspectable. Thus it can elucidate nature, which is not. The comparison is not new. Berkeley (1971:97), for instance, compares the formation of ideas with that of machines in the following curious statement:

> . . . the reason why ideas are formed into machines, that is, artificial and regular combinations, is the same with that for combining letters into words. That a few original ideas may be made to signify a great number of effects and actions, it is necessary they be variously combined together.

Here is Smith's definition of a philosophical system:

> Systems in many respects resemble machines. A machine is a little system, created to perform, as well as to connect together, in reality, those different movements and effects which the artist has occasion for. A system is an imaginary machine invented to connect together in the fancy those different movements and effects which are already in reality performed. (Smith 1967:66)

In this interpretation language, like the other arts and sciences, is a man-made system, the result of a long process of system-building. We may, therefore, expect that the linguistic system and its evolution will exhibit certain similarities with other systems and their evolution. Smith does not draw out the analogy, but we know enough about his view of the development of philosophical systems to be able to compare the system building processes in philosophy and in language.

In the first place, Smith's 'inventors' of language proceed by a method which bears more than a chance resemblance to the scientific method of analysis and synthesis. They begin with utterances expressing one single event, utterances subsequently analysed into two parts, the substantive and the verb, both of which are general words; i.e. they refer to a class of objects and a class of events. To distinguish any member of a class of objects, these are analysed into qualities and their underlying substance by comparison and abstraction, thus arriving at a further set of general terms. The continuing process of dissolving complex ideas into their elements allows the establishment of taxonomy of ideas, the parts of speech denoting certain classes and sub-classes of this taxonomy. All elements in this taxonomy are given names, which are general as they denote general ideas. For this reason they cannot be used to refer to a particular object or event: to do so, they have to be connected like the elementary ideas such an event or object consists of. In this sense language may be considered as a theory of nature, a popular system, which joins in 'the fancy' the multitude of unconnected phenomena of this world, which are, strictly speaking, the only objects of perception. The linguistic system-builders thus resemble philosophical system-builders, who endeavour 'to find out something which may fill up the gap, which, like a bridge, may so far at least unite those seemingly disjointed objects, as to render the passage of the thought betwixt them smooth, and natural, and easy' (Smith 1967:40).

We can note yet another similarity in Smith's description of the evolution of philosophical and linguistic systems: evolution proceeds by trial and error towards the most simple system. A philosophical system breaks down when, by accommodating new facts and observations, it has become too complicated. It is eventually replaced by a simpler system, able to account for the same facts. In the evolution of language, the event-word system breaks down when the number of events to be communicated becomes too large. The inflectional system is supplemented by the analytical system of adjectives, prepositions etc. when a society needs to make and express a larger number of distinctions than the system can easily accommodate. A language is apt to become completely analytic, when through language mixture, non-native speakers cannot even cope with the complexities of the prevailing inflectional system.

There can be no doubt that Smith interprets the evolution of language as the evolution of a system:

The expression of every particular event became, in this manner, more intricate and complex, but the whole system of the language became more coherent, more connected, and more easily retained and comprehended. (Smith 1970:527)

Let me, however, stress that Smith does not compare language evolution directly with the evolution of scientific systems. He does liken both to the development of machines, his standard metaphor for any type of system. Thus taking Smith's description of the development of the parts of speech as an illustration of his general view of the development of systems may not be unjustified: this interpretation would allow us to view Smith's *Dissertation* as an instance of his overall concern with the evolution of societal systems, thus 'making the passage of thought betwixt them smooth, and natural, and easy'.

7. CONCLUSION

Neither Reid nor Smith are linguists or even grammarians. But they are both concerned with the origin of language. Reid uses glottogonic ideas to gain support for his analysis of the principles of human nature. Smith uses the principles of human nature in order to write a theoretical history of the parts of speech. What we might be inclined to call mere speculation was to them an important contribution to the science of man.

Glottogonic theories held an important place in the philosophical endeavours of the European Enlightenment and some of the greatest thinkers of the time contributed to the debate about the origin of language. The historian of linguistics cannot close his eyes to their theories and wish they would go away, simply because they upset his preferred ancestry of linguistics. It can hardly be argued that a historian will gain a better understanding of the history of his subject by ignoring certain areas of research altogether. Expurgated history is no history. But 'unexpurgated' history will remain an ideal, an elusive standard by which written histories may be measured. I am perfectly aware that this brief look at Smith's and Reid's treatment of glottogenesis falls short of the ideal, but I do hope I have shown that modern researchers who approach this fascinating aspect of eighteenth-century linguistic thought both as linguists and intellectual historians will gain a deeper understanding of eighteenth-century linguistic theory and

its place in the larger scientific issues of the time.
N.B. You cannot reconstruct a Cheshire cat from its disembodied grin alone.

REFERENCES

AARSLEFF, H. (1967) *The Study of Language in England 1780–1860*. Princeton, N.J.: Princeton University Press.

AARSLEFF, H. (1982). 'An Outline of Language-Origins Theory since the Renaissance'. Aarsleff 1982. 278–92.

AARSLEFF, H. (1982) *From Locke to Saussure: Essays on the Study of Language and Intellectual History*. Minneapolis: University of Minnesota Press.

ALLEN, D.C. (1949) 'Some Theories of the Growth and Origin of Language in Milton's Age'. *Philological Quarterly*, 28, 5–16.

AUROUX, S. et al. (eds) (1984) *Matériaux pour une historie des théories linguistiques*. Lille: Université de Lille III.

BARKER, S.F. AND BEAUCHAMP, T.L. (eds) (1976) *Thomas Reid: Critical Interpretations*. Philadelphia: University City Science Center.

BECKER, J.F. (1961) 'Adam Smith's Theory of Social Science'. *Southern Economic Journal*, 28, 13–21.

BERGHEAUD, P. (1979) 'De James Harris à Horne Tooke: Mutations de l'analyse du langage en Angleterre dans la deuxième moitié du xviie siècle'. *Historiographia Linguistica*, 6, 15–46.

BERGHEAUD, P. (1984) 'Tensions paradigmatiques et objets polémiques chez Adam Smith et Lord Monboddo: le pluralisme epistémologique du 18e siècle comme objet d'histoire'. Auroux et al. 1984, 31–43. Lille: Université de Lille III.

BERKELEY, G. (1685–1753). 1948–1956. *The Works of George Berkeley Bishop of Cloyne*. Ed. A.A. Luce and T.E. Jessop. London: Th. Nelson.

BERKELEY, G. (1971) (1710/1713) *The Principles of Human Knowledge. With other writings*. Edited with an introduction by G.J. Warnock. Glasgow: Collins/Fontana.

BERRY, C.J. (1974) 'Adam Smith's "Considerations on Language"'. *Journal of the History of Ideas*, 35, 130–138.

BRYSON, G. (1945) *Man and Society: The Scottish Inquiry in the Eighteenth Century*. Fairfield, N.Y.: Kelly.

CAMPBELL, R.H. AND SKINNER, A. (1982) *Adam Smith*. London and Canberra: Croom Helm.

CHITNIS, A.C. (1976) *The Scottish Enlightenment: A Social History*. London: Croom Helm.

COLLINGWOOD, R.G. (1960) (1945) *The Idea of Nature*. Oxford University Press.

COLLINGWOOD, R.G. (1961) (1946) *The Idea of History*. Oxford: Oxford University Press.

CONDILLAC, E.B.A. DE (1715–1780). (1947) *Oeuvres Philosophiques*. Texte établi et présenté par Georges LeRoy. 3 vols. (Corpus Général des Philosophes Français). Paris: Presses Universitaires de France.

CONDILLAC, E.B.A. DE (1977) (1746). *Essai über den Ursprung der menschlichen Erkenntnisse*. Aus dem Französischen übersetzt von Ulrich Ricken. Leipzig: Reclam.

COSERIU, E. (1970) 'Adam Smith und die Anfänge der Sprachtypologie'. Narr 1970, 15–25. (Repr. 'Adam Smith and the Beginnings of Language Typology'. Transl. E. Haggblade. *Historiographia Linguistica*, 10 (1983), 1–12.

COSERIU, E. (1974) *Die Geschichte der Sprachphilosophie von der Antike bis zur Gegenwart. Teil II: Von Leibniz bis Rousseau*. Tübingen: Gunter Narr.

DINNEEN, F.P., S.J. (ed.) (1966) Report of the 17th Round Table Meeting on Linguistics and Language Studies. (Georgetown Monograph Series on Languages and Linguistics, 19). Washington: Georgetown University Press.

FORMIGARI, L. (1974) 'Language and Society in the Late Eighteenth Century'. *Journal of the History of Ideas*, 35, 275–92.

FUNKE, O. (1934) *Englische Sprachphilosophie im späteren 18. Jahrhundert. Teil I: Von Harris bis Lord Monboddo. Teil II: Horne Tooke als Sprachphilosoph*. Bern: Francke.

FUNKE, O. (1945) (1941) 'Sprachphilosophie und Grammatik in den englischen Sprachbüchern des 17. und 17. Jahrhunderts'. Funke 1945, 185–99.

FUNKE, O. (1945) (1941) *Wege und Ziele. Ausgewählte Aufsätze und Vorträge*. Bern: Franke.

GRAVE, S.A. (1960) *The Scottish Philosophy of Common Sense*. Oxford: Clarendon Press.

GRIMSLEY, R. (ed.) (1971) *Maupertuis, Turgot et Maine de Biran. Sur l'origine du langage*. Trois textes presentés par R. Grimsley. Geneve: Librairie Droz.

HAGGBLADE, E. (1983) 'Contributors to the Beginnings of Language Typology'. *Historiographia Linguistica*, 10, 13–24.

HARRIS, J. (1709–80) (1751) *Hermes: or a Philosophical Inquiry Concerning Language and Universal Grammar*. Menston: Scolar Press.

HAYEK, F.A. VON (1969) 'Dr. Bernard Mandeville'. Hayek 1969, 126–43.

HAYEK, F.A. VON (1969) *Freiburger Studien. Gesammelte Aufsätze*. Tübingen: J.F.C. Mohr.

HERDER, J.G. (1744–1803). n.d. (1772) *Abhandlung über den Ursprung der Sprache.* Text, Materialien, Kommentar. Ed. Wolfgang Pross. München/Wein: Carl Hanser.

HEWES, G.W. COMP. (1975) *Language Origins. A Bibliography.* The Hague/Paris: Mouton.

HEWES, G.W. (1977) 'Language Origins Theories'. *Language Learning by a Chimpanzee. The Lana Project.* (Ed.) Duane M. Rumbaugh, 3–53. New York: Academic Press.

JACK, M. (1978) 'One State of Nature: Mandeville and Rousseau'. *Journal of the History of Ideas*, 39, 119–24.

KAYE, F.B. (1922) 'The Influence of Bernard Mandeville'. *Studies in Philology*, 19, 83–108.

KAYE, F.B. (1924) 'Mandeville on the Origin of Language'. *Modern Language Notes*, 39, 136–42.

KUEHNER, P. (1944) 'Theories on the Origin and the Formation of Language in the Eighteenth Century in France'. Dissertation. Philadelphia: University of Pennsylvania.

LAND, S.K. (1975) 'Berkeley's Theory of Meaning'. *Historiographia Linguistica*, 2, 191–206.

LAND, S.K. (1977) 'Adam Smith's "Considerations concerning the first formation of languages"'. *Journal of the History of Ideas*, 38, 677–90.

LINDGREN, J.R. (1969) 'Adam Smith's Theory of Inquiry'. *Journal of Political Economy*, 77, 897–915.

LOCKE, J. (1632–1704). (1961) (1690) *An Essay Concerning Human Understanding.* 2 vols. With an introduction by John W. Yolton. London: Dent & Dutton.

MANDEVILLE, B. (1670–1733) (1957) (1729). *The Fable of the Bees: or, Private Vices, Publick Benefits.* 2 vols. With a commentary critical, historical and explanatory by F.B. Kaye. Oxford: Clarendon Press.

MCREYNOLDS, P. (1980) 'The Clock Metaphor in the History of Psychology'. *Scientific Discovery. Case Studies.* Ed. T. Nickles. 1980, 97–112. Dordrecht: Reidel.

MONBODDO, J.B., LORD (1714–1799) (1773–1792) *Of the Origin and Progress of Language.* Menston: Scolar Press.

NOORDEGRAAF, J. (1977) 'A Few Remarks on Adam Smith's Dissertation (1761)'. *Historiographia Linguistica*, 4, 59–67.

RAPHAEL, D.D. (ed) (1969) *British Moralists 1650–1800.* Vol. 1: *Hobbes–Gay.* Vol 2: *Hume–Bentham.* Oxford: Oxford University Press.

REID, T. (1710–1796) (1872) *The Works of Thomas Reid now fully collected with selections from his Unpublished Letters, Preface, Notes. . .* by Sir William Hamilton. 2 vols. Edinburgh: Maclachlan & Stewart.

REID, T. (1801) (1764) *An Inquiry into the Human Mind on the Principles of Common Sense.* Prefixed by Stewart's Life of Reid. London: Bell, Bradfute & William Creech.

REID, T. (1812) (1785/1788) *Essays on the Intellectual Powers of Man*. Edinburgh: Bell and Bradfute.

RENDALL, J. (1978) *The Origins of the Scottish Enlightenment 1707–1776*. London: Macmillan.

RODIS-LEWIS, G. (1967) 'L'art de parler et l'Essai sur l'origine des languages'. *Revue Internationale de Philosophie*, 21, 407–20.

ROUSSEAU, J.-J. (1712–1778). (1971) (1751/1755). *Discours sur les sciences et les arts. Discours sur l'origine de l'inégalité parmi les hommes*. Paris: Garnier-Flammarion.

SALMON, P. (1968/69) 'Herder's Essay on the Origin of Language, and the Place of Man in the Animal Kingdom'. *German Life and Letters*, 22, 59–70.

SALVUCCI, R. (1982) *Sviluppi della problematica del linguaggio nel XVIII secolo: Condillac, Rousseau, Smith*. Rimini: Maggioli.

SAPIR, E. (1907/8) 'Herder's Ursprung der Sprache'. *Modern Philology*, 5, 109–46. (Repr. in *Historiographia Linguistica* 11 (1984), 355–88).

SCHREYER, R. (1986) 'The Use and Method of Theoretical History'. Paper presented at the IPSE Conferences 1986 (Hume Conference), Institute for Advanced Studies, University of Edinburgh, Edinburgh. Mimeo. Forthcoming.

SCHREYER, R. (1985) 'The Origin of Language: A Scientific Approach to the Study of Man'. *Topoi*, 4, 181–86.

SCHREYER, R. (1978) 'Condillac, Mandeville and the Origin of Language'. *Historiographia Linguistica*, 5, 15–43.

SCHREYER, R. (1984) 'Evidence and Belief. Arguments in the 18th Century Debate on the Origin of Language'. Auroux et. al. (eds) 1984, 325–36.

SKINNER, A.S. (1972) 'Adam Smith: Philosophy and Science'. *Scottish Journal of Political Economy*, 29, 307–19.

SMITH, A. (1723–1790). (1970) (1761) *A Dissertation on the Origin of Languages or Considerations Concerning the First Formation of Languages and the Different Genius of Original and Compounded Languages*. Herausgegeben und mit einer Einleitung versehen von Gunter Narr. Tübingen: TBL Gunter Narr.

SMITH, A. (1963) *Lectures on Rhetoric and Belles Lettres. Delivered in the University of Glasgow by Adam Smith. Reported by a student in 1762–63*. Ed. By John M. Lothian. London etc.: Th. Nelson & Sons.

SMITH, A. (1967) *The Early Writings of Adam Smith*. Ed. by J.R. Lindgren. New York: Kelly.

SMITH, A. (1976–1983) *The Glasgow Edition of the Works and Correspondence of Adam Smith*. 6 vols. General editors D.D. Raphael and A.S. Skinner. Oxford: Clarendon Press.

SMITH, A. (1980) *Essays on Philosophical Subjects*. Ed. by

W.P.D. Wightman and J.C. Bryce. With Dugald Stewart's Account of Adam Smith. Ed. J.S. Ross. (= Vol. 3 of *The Glasgow edition of the Works of Adam Smith*, ed. by D.D. Raphael and A.S. Skinner) Oxford: Clarendon Press.

STAM, J.H. (1976) *Inquiries into the Origin of Language: The Fate of a Question*. New York/London: Harper & Row.

STAROBINSKI, J. (1966) 'Langage, nature et société selon Rousseau'. *Le langage*. Actes du congrès des sociétés de philosophie et de langage française. Vol. 1. 1966, 143–46. Neuchâtel: La Baconnière.

STAROBINSKI, J. (1967) 'Rousseau et l'origine des langues'. *Europäische Aufklärung: Herbert Dieckmann zum 60. Geburtstag*. (Eds) Hugo Friedrich and Fritz Schalk. 1967, 281–300. München: Fink.

STEWART, D. (1753–1828). (1877) *The Collected Works of Dugald Stewart*. (Ed.) Sir William Hamilton. Edinburgh: T. & T. Clark.

STEWART, D. (1808) (1792) *Elements of the Philosophy of the Human Mind*. London: T. Caddell & W. Davies.

SÜßMILCH, J.P. (1766) *Versuch eines Beweises, daß die erste Sprache ihren Ursprung nicht vom Menschen, sondern vom Schöpfer erhalten habe*. Berlin: Akademie Verlag.

TEETER, K. VAN D. (1966) 'The History of Linguistics: New Lamps for Old?' Dinneen 1966, 83–95.

THOMSON, H.F. (1965) 'Adam Smith's Philosophy of Science'. *Quarterly Journal of Economics*, 79, 212–33.

VIERTEL, J. (1966) 'Concepts of Language Underlying the 18th Century Controversy about the Origin of Language'. Dinneen 1966, 109–32.

WEST, E.G. (1971) 'Adam Smith and Rousseau's Discourse on Inequality. Inspiration or Provocation?' *The Journal of Economic Issues*, 5, 56–70.

WINDROSS, M. (1980) 'Adam Smith on Language'. *Linguistica Antverpiensa*, 14, 277–88.

9

THOMAS CRAWFORD

Boswell and the Tensions of Enlightenment

At one point in *James Boswell and his World* David Daiches quotes a passage from Boswell's 'Memorabilia' of 1767 which shows him trying to explain the contradictory tendencies in himself: 'I have the whim of an Englishman to make me think and act extravagantly, and yet I have the coolness and the sense of a Scotsman to make me sensible of it'.[1] Daiches comments that Boswell is not describing the English and Scottish national characters at all, but the tendency to which the name of 'Caledonian antisyzygy' has been given, a trait which is found in Scots of many different centuries ('fier comme un ecossais', the 'perfervidum ingenium Scotorum' coexisting with the qualities of solidity and perseverance shown by McWhirr in Conrad's *Typhoon*). The term has become a reach-me-down formula among the literati of the late twentieth century in spite of the ridicule it has attracted among practising poets.[2] What does the expression mean and how useful is it in plumbing the enigma of Boswell's character and achievement?

Let me begin with the OED's definition of 'syzygy': 'in astronomy, conjunction, but now extended to include both the conjunction and opposition of heavenly bodies, or, in gnostic theology, a couple or pair of opposites or of "aeons"'. 'Antisyzygy' is defined simply as 'union of opposites', and the OED's solitary example comes from a certain F.H. Hall in 1863: 'Zoroastrianism . . . fuses together – in what Clement of Rome would have denoted an "antisyzygy" – the Deity and Satan'. The adjective 'Caledonian' was tagged on to it in 1919 by Gregory Smith,[3] in the first place during a discussion of Scottish imaginative literature, whose whole history he described as 'almost a zig-zag of contradictions'. Smith noted two main oppositions in Scottish writing:

(1) 'the talent of close observation', allied to 'the power of producing by a cumulation of touches, a quick and perfect image to the reader'. In Scots, he ambiguously says (he is either talking about writing in the Scots language, or else about Scots people whatever language they happen to be writing in), 'the zest for

handling a multitude of details rather than for seeking broad effects by suggestion is very persistent', and he sums up the realistic trend in the Scottish tradition in a telling phrase – 'this gluttony of the particular' (5–6).

(2) 'the airier pleasure to be found in the confusion of the senses, in the fun of things thrown topsyturvy. . . . It is a strange union of opposites, alien as Hotspur and Glendower; not to be explained', he says. Smith saw this characteristic as 'not a mere accident, or wantoning, no matter how much of its extravagance may be a direct protest against the prose of experience'. He goes on to make a leap from literature to life – to national character itself, for his next sentence reads: 'It goes better with our knowledge of Scottish character and history to accept the antagonism as real and necessary' (19). And he continues in a sentence which seems an apt description of at least one side of Boswell, the artist in life: 'The Scot is not a quarrelsome man, but he has a fine sense of the value of provocation, and in the clash of things and words has often found a spiritual tonic'. Finally, let me quote what is probably the best known of Smith's pronouncements: 'There is more in the Scottish antithesis of the real and fantastic than is to be explained by the familiar rules of rhetoric. The sudden jostling of contraries seems to preclude any relationship by literary suggestion. The one invades the other without warning. They are the "polar twins" of the Scottish Muse' (20).

Everything just quoted, it is clear, applies to literature alone. But Smith also sees the antisyzygy at work in life, as an essential part of the Scottish national character. In the 1920s Hugh MacDiarmid gleefully took up the concept as a weapon in his struggle for a new national literature and culture. In his hands and those of his followers a number of subsidiary ideas were developed: that a disastrous split in the Scottish consciousness arose from the sixteenth century onwards, with which both Calvinism and the spread of the English language were causally connected. Scots folk, for whom the vernacular was the natural medium for the expression of feeling, could only *think* in the alien southern Standard because they had no other suitable medium for abstract thought after Latin ceased to be the language of intellectual discourse. The seventeenth-century wizard Major Weir; Deacon Brodie, burglar by night and respectable burgess by day; Dr Knox the anatomist, James Hogg's Justified Sinner, Dr Jekyll and Mr Hyde, despite their London milieu – all were seen to illustrate the formula.

Now it must be admitted that it is possible to attach many of the characteristics of Boswell the man to the model of the antisyzygy as it has been developed by the *literati* not of the eighteenth but of the twentieth century. His swings from exuberant elation to the depths of despair, which Frank Brady, his most recent biographer, significantly refuses to categorise as 'manic depressive';[4] his association, especially in the earlier journals, of gloom and hypochondria with Calvinism;[5] his delight in the particulars of everyday experience and his pleasure in the onward flow of sense-impressions and their variety (but not, I think, in 'things thrown topsy-turvy' in quite Smith's sense) – all seem to fit the pattern. To measure Boswell, or indeed any other individual, against the antisyzygy, is a strangely mechanical proceeding, like first designing a mould for the tragic hero, then denying the title to Othello or Macbeth or Willy Loman because they don't fit your schema. The antisyzygy tends to be seen as an entity, mysteriously 'given', like an archetype, and the very term, which seems so dialectical at first sight, is made to refer to a peculiarly static oscillation. Perhaps another approach is preferable – not from swings on a dial plate, but from contradictions, conflicts, and their resolution.

The principal contradiction in every person's life can be described as that between the genotype[6] – the bundle of general and particular human potentialities which emerges from the womb – and the environment, familial and other, to which he must adapt and which he must try to understand and if possible dominate. In Boswell's case the genotype included a large penis and a weak will; an intense sensibility open to every sense-impression and directed, one presumes accidentally, towards persons rather than things, to social groups rather than to natural scenes; a talent for languages; a remarkable memory; whatever inherited characteristics lie behind those whom we call 'born newspapermen'; and a prodigious histrionic gift which was the source of his exploits as a mimic and his ability to *empathise* with almost everybody he met. On the positive side we must list his rage for collection, which Freudians might well ascribe to an adaptive neurosis, not to inherited characteristics, and which in Boswell's case was directed towards collecting people, or rather images of people and relationships with them, and not botanical specimens, pictures, or *objets d'art*. It is a characteristic which unites him with his age – with the virtuosi, the connoisseurs, and the gatherers of scientific data, not in Scotland only, but all over Europe. On the negative side must be put his shortcomings in philosophical reasoning power, though not in the ability to frame a legal argument. Nor was he lacking in organisational ability; in daily living he could plan events like the meeting of Johnson and

Wilkes or the entire Hebrides tour, and in art work out the total structure of the *Life of Johnson*, the supreme example of its genre in English.

I propose to call the society in which Boswell was born an 'Enlightenment' one – in other words, I am using 'Enlightenment' as shorthand for 'the Age', just as a century ago people used 'the Age of Reason' for the same period and the same sort of social organisation. When examining Boswell, then, I mean by 'Enlightenment' a very broad category indeed: the entire complex of conditions surrounding a scion of the Scottish legal establishment born in 1740, familial, social and intellectual. Inevitably, the family at Edinburgh and Auchinleck was the primary medium in which the enlightenment first impinged on young Boswell and which saw his earliest attempts to adapt to it. Frederick Pottle imagines him carrying from his infancy an image of his father 'as Sheriff, stern, sentencing, the bench handing out whippings and imprisonments to rioters and thieves'. From Mundell's private academy in the West Bow the child could presumably hear the procession of sentenced criminals go down the Bow to the gallows in the Grassmarket, the tramping of the City Guard, the shouts and roars of the crowd. As Pottle says, 'though the master would not have let [the boys] run down to the Grassmarket, where they might have got hurt in the press, he may well have allowed them to crowd to the windows of the schoolroom to see the condemned man go by'. The image of his father as a stern Sheriff (he did not become a Lord of Session till Boswell was fourteen) was complemented by that of his mother – and here I quote Pottle once again – as shining 'in the murk of his childish terrors like a guardian angel or saint, something to hold on to, to trust, to turn to as an intercessor'.[7] The primary familial contrast in our culture between a patriarchal father and a gentle, loving mother was present in an extreme, concentrated form; and it was complicated still further by the fact that it was from this loving mother and the Catechism she put in his hands that he derived 'the gloomiest doctrines' of Calvinism, as he called them in his autobiographical letter to Rousseau – hellfire and all. It was from his mother, a *victim* of patriarchy as we must assume, that he imbibed a *religion* of patriarchy. In a draft outline of the letter to Rousseau, in a part not used in the finished copy, Boswell summed up his childhood like this:

> Spirit crushed. No noble hope. Terribly afraid of ghosts. Up to eighteen could not be alone at night. Got over it by a habit of not thinking, not by reasoning about it. Afraid of the cold and everything else. A complete poltroon in the streets of

Edinburgh. . . . Black ideas even at that age. Ignorant –
terrified by everything I did not understand.[8]

To the feeling-structure within the family, with its own special
variants of the general patriarchal structure, there was added the
tensions produced by an education at Edinburgh University in the
1750s. The course which made by far the greatest impression on
Boswell was John Stevenson's logic class, which he attended in the
session of 1756–57. The positive impact of the course came from
the section on rhetoric (among the works studied were Aristotle's
Poetics and Longinus' *On the Sublime*); the negative part was the
metaphysics, which made him think seriously about the problem
of God's foreknowledge and man's free will.[9] It is clear from the
letter to Rousseau that the 'terrible hypochondria' that seized him
at the age of sixteen was mediated by his worries about determinism;
in early manhood it seemed to him that the worries were the cause
of his depression, though others – and presumably these included
Lord Auchinleck – ascribed it to genetic factors, an inherited
mental instability. His adolescent crisis resulted in what might be
called an adolescent peripety. His first response was to go back to
the emotional religiosity of conversion and the doctrines of the
new birth which his mother had introduced him to in early
childhood, only this time he turned to them in their Methodist
form. To quote the revealingly sentimentalist terminology of a
journal retrospect in which the self is automatically felt to be
passive: 'Methodists next shook my passions'.[10] His second
response was equally emotional, and equally religious: a brief
conversion to Roman Catholicism in his nineteenth year, under
the influence of an actress with whom he was infatuated. Lord
Auchinleck packed him off to Glasgow, where he came under
another important Enlightenment influence, Adam Smith's lectures on moral philosophy: once more, it was those on rhetoric
which made the greatest impression.[11] By now, the adolescent
peripety had transformed the quiet, grave, studious youth that his
friend Temple remembered from 1755–56 into the Boswell we
know from the London Journal and all later records, responding
chameleon-like to every social scene and every strong personality,
whizzing rapidly from one mood and one way of life to another,
indecisive, a compulsive role-player. To the extent to which he
delighted in these zig-zags he can be fitted into Gregory Smith's
category of taking pleasure in 'the fun of things thrown topsy-
turvy', though Smith's adjective 'airier' is generally inappropriate
to Boswell. He fled suddenly from Glasgow to London, driven on
by two drastically opposing motives; one (so he said), to join the
Roman Church and perhaps take up a monastic life, celibate vows

and all; the other, to see London and experience all the metropolis could offer a provincial. The unity between these opposites is provided by the senses – the colour, the sensual delights and drama of Catholic ritual on the one hand, and the far from 'airy' sensuality of urban pleasures on the other – fine food, fine clothes, sex, aristocratic company, the excitement of the race-course and of meeting royalty. Now the tendency of each of these motives was anti-paternal: Roman Catholicism was as far from Lord Auchinleck's Presbyterianism as could be imagined, while to deny Scotland and sink into the ambience of London, to prefer High English and genteel pronunciation to the Scots-English and occasional racy vernacular of the last generation – all this was a declaration of independence against the domestic tyrant. At the level of language at least, Boswell's revolt was in tune with the spirit of the 1750s and 1760s. It was in 1754 that Allan Ramsay the painter founded the influential Select Society, a centre of religious moderation and gentility with an interest in encouraging southern modes of speech and writing, and in 1761 that the actor Thomas Sheridan came to Edinburgh to give a series of lectures on elocution which involved the teaching of a 'correct' English pronunciation. (Boswell was invited to become a member of the Select Society towards the end of 1761, soon after his twenty-first birthday, and he had attended Sheridan's lectures.)[12]

The rest of Boswell's career is well known: his return to Scotland, his second visit to London in 1763 as written up in the London Journal, Holland, the Grand Tour, Paoli and Corsica, marriage, the years at the Scottish bar interspersed with annual forays to Johnson and London, the Hebridean Tour, heavy drinking and compulsive whoring, the continuing pull of London and the disastrous English bar scheme, Lord Lonsdale and the Recordership of Carlisle, a lifetime of frustrated political ambition, the writing of *The Life of Johnson*, decay and death. It would be pointless to summarise these events in any sort of detail: what is required is to bring out and if possible to explain the contradictions in the pattern.

We have already seen how in Boswell's case familial conflicts are interwoven with the broader social and intellectual contradictions of the age, and it is precisely on these in their most general form that Carlyle concentrates in his review of *The Life of Johnson* in *Fraser's Magazine* in 1832. He ends with a paragraph in which the principal opposition in the intellectual life not just of the eighteenth century but of the early nineteenth century as well is crystallised in the radically different figures of Johnson and Hume:

It is worthy of note that, in our little British Isle, the two
grand Antagonisms of Europe should have stood embodied,
under their very highest concentration, in two men produced
simultaneously among ourselves . . . As Johnson became the
father of all succeeding Tories; so was Hume the father of all
succeeding Whigs, for his own Jacobitism was but an
accident, as worthy to be named Prejudice as any of Johnson's
. . . In spiritual stature they are almost equal; both great,
among the greatest: yet how unlike in likeness! Hume has
the widest, methodising, comprehensive eye; Johnson the
keenest for perspicacity and minute detail . . . They were the
two half-men of their time: whoso should combine the
intrepid Candour and decisive scientific Clearness of Hume,
with the Reverence, the Love and devout Humility of
Johnson, were the whole man of a new time.[13]

Four years later, in his lecture on the Hero as Man of Letters,
Carlyle presented another 'grand Antagonism of Europe' when he
contrasted Johnson with Rousseau. Of Rousseau he wrote: 'Once
more, out of the element of that withered mocking Philosophism,
Scepticism, and Persiflage, there has arisen in this man the
ineradicable feeling and knowledge that this Life of ours is *true*;
not a Scepticism, Theorem, or Persiflage, but a Fact, an awful
Reality'. Voltaire, in contrast, seems to have been a fake hero for
Carlyle; his life, he says, 'was that of a kind of Antichrist. . . .
The unbelieving French believe in their Voltaire; and burst out
round him into very curious Hero-worship, in that last act of his
life when they "stifle him under roses"'.[14]

Hume, Johnson, Rousseau, Voltaire: if we grant that in the
differences between these men we can see some of the principal
contradictions of the Age of Englightenment, then it is surely
suggestive that the young Boswell should have been drawn to
these writers above all others. At some time during their student
days in Edinburgh, Boswell and the youth who was to become
almost his greatest friend, William Johnson Temple, climbed
Arthur's Seat and shouted, one presumes into the wind, 'Voltaire!
Rousseau! Immortal Names'[15] – names which recur again and
again in their correspondence, like a litany. It would seem that
these savants, to the student generation of 1755–60, whether they
had read any of their works of not, symbolised all that was most
forward-looking in the thought of the age; one can only speculate
that by thundering out their names on a piece of almost symbolic
wild nature so close to the centre of Edinburgh they were making
some kind of protest against what they regarded as Scottish,
perhaps even English, cultural provincialism. It looks as if the

young men were indulging in an eighteenth-century precursor of Carlylean hero-worship, with Voltaire the Hero as *philosophe engagé* and Rousseau the Hero of Sensibility.

As for Hume, Boswell got to know him quite early on, and was on friendly terms with him to the day of his death (their last interview is justly celebrated, and a Life of Hume is among Boswell's many unachieved literary projects). Boswell's very first journal – the 'Journal of my Jaunt', 1762 – shows that he was already fascinated by Johnson before he had any chance of meeting him, and records (he was then aged twenty-two) that he had a higher opinion of the *Rambler* papers than either Lord Kames or Adam Smith, with both of whom he had discussed the essays. The 1762 journal contains a summary of an interview with Hume in his house in St James's Court, from which it is obvious that Boswell had questioned Hume closely about Johnson:

> Mr Samuel Johnson has got a pension of £300 a year. Indeed his Dictionary was a kind of a national work so he has a kind of claim to the Patronage of the state. His stile is particular and pedantic. He is a man of enthusiasm and antiquated notions, a keen Jacobite. He yet hates the Scotch. Holds the Episcopal Hierarchy in supreme veneration and said he would stand before a battery of cannon to have the Convocation restored to its full powers. He holds Mr Hume in abhorrence and left a company one night upon his coming in. Garrick told Mr Hume that Johnson past one Evening behind the Scenes in the Green room. He said he had been well entertained. Mr Garrick therefore hoped to see him often. 'No, David,' said he, 'I will never come back. For the white bubbies and the silk stockings of your Actresses excite my Genitals'.[16]

The 1762 'Journal of my Jaunt' is Boswell's earliest experiment in a form he was to attain complete mastery in only a year later, and the conversation with Hume is the first conversation he ever recorded. The dialogue itself lasted an hour and a half, and the record is less than a thousand words in length, yet Boswell states that he 'has preserved the heads and many of the words actually spoken'. I am inclined to think that it was the stimulus of his London foray of 1760 that first gave him the idea of journalising – that it was what he had there heard of Johnson that set him reading or re-reading *The Rambler* and predisposed him for the 1763 meeting in Tom Davies's back parlour, with all that followed.[17] It should be stressed that the first conversation he recorded was with an eminent Scot – indeed, with one whose urbane infidelity was later to haunt him; that his interrogation of

Hume centred on people, not ideas (they included Sheridan and Lord Kames as well as Johnson); and that the savant to impress him most was a Scot-hating Englishman whose personal eccentricities, themselves so obviously proceeding from contradictions, seemed more fascinating even than his ideas.

Boswell, then, on the brink of that manhood he never fully achieved, was already intensely aware of some of the contradictions in the thought and above all in the feeling-structure of the age – through the impact made by personalities or, before he met them, the impact of the mental images he had formed of these savants. He had, of course, first-hand knowledge of Kames's works; of the *Rambler* essays and later on of almost everything Johnson wrote; of Hume's *History* and some of his essays; of Smith, Adam Ferguson, John Gregory, Robertson's Histories, and some others; and he prepared himself for meeting Voltaire and Rousseau by sampling their works, above all Voltaire's historical writings and Rousseau's *Nouvelle Héloise* and *Emile* (particularly the Creed of the Savoyard Vicar).[18] His most lasting achievement was to make the English-speaking world for almost 150 years see the age through *his* eyes, through the intermediary of his full depiction of a character, and to think of the period as predominantly the Age of Johnson.

So far we have been considering the dialectic of Boswell's life and career. But he also gives us a dialectic in his two chief works. In *Tour of the Hebrides* we have Johnson, himself a strange compound of strong rationality, deep emotion, and prejudiced unreason, in confrontation with Scotland the dual nation (part lowland, part Gaelic); in the *Life* we have Johnson throughout his whole career face to face with intellectual England, understanding it according to his lights, and trying to dominate it. In each case the opposition, the contrast, is between a hero and a nation. But it is Boswell's own dialectic with which I am concerned, not Johnson's – Boswell racked by tensions, *Boswell* Agonistes. What, then, were the other main contradictions in Boswell's relation with his world, and how do they unfold?

One of them was in the realm of the Subject/Object relationship: he is almost equally interested in himself (subject) and in other people (object). If the twin poles of Biography are Confessions (dealing with oneself – Pepys, Rousseau) and Lives (Walton, Lockhart, Strachey), then Boswell achieved distinction in both modes, imaginatively making his journal nourish and sustain biography. Certainly Temple was well aware of the subjective–objective dichotomy within the Journal itself. Just as the London Journal had been intended for the eyes of John Johnston of

Grange, so the account of his stay in Holland was written with Temple in mind; and Temple wrote, on 13 September 1763: 'I long to see your Journal. I consider it the History of your mind as well as travels, and shall be as much entertained with its ebbs and flows, its elasticity and lassitude, as with the variety of characters, of places and of objects which you will describe'. Further, in Boswell the contradiction between Subject and Object appears within the realm of the Subjective itself, because he was able to stand back, observe, and indeed marvel at the far from regular procession of his strongly contrasting moods and views. There are several instances of his amazed and often slightly complacent self-contemplation in his letters to Temple, for example:

> Is not thy freind one of the most amazing Existences that has ever walked this Globe? Or are Mankind all amazing. Surely however there are distinctions, and thy freind is one of the most distinguished. Trace me only from the time when first our congenial souls united, when they separated themselves from the profanum Vulgus at College and united in elegant freindship. Since that time what variety has there been in my Mind? Trace me only since I left London. (23 July 1764)

> But it is hardly credible what ground I go over, and what a variety of men and manners I contemplate in a day; and all the time I am [the main part of all I see and know] for my exuberant spirits will not let me listen enough. (17 April 1775)

Sometimes this quality is more aloof, verging on what Frank Brady has called 'dispassionateness' – a quality manifest in any long-drawn-out situation such as his efforts to save the life of Reid the sheep-stealer in 1766 as 'intense involvement' combined with 'extraordinary detachment'.[19]

If we were to seek an explanation for this characteristic in the classic account of the Caledonian Antisyzygy, we might find it in the 'talent of close observation' which Burns displayed in, say, the first stanza of 'To a Mouse', or John Galt throughout *Annals of the Parish*, applied to the details of an individual's life as coloured by his feelings – Gregory Smith's 'gluttony of the particular' united to the delicate discriminations of a gourmet of the senses. But such minute and apparently objective scrutiny of the inner self cannot be so readily pressed into a national mould extending over several centuries. At best, it can be linked to Scottish philosophy in Boswell's own century, with its roots in England and France, in the empiricism of Locke and the sociology of Montesquieu. When Bertrand Bronson addressed himself to this feature, he showed how it appears at the grammatical level in Boswell's use of

the second person singular when reporting his actions and
feelings in the past. An excellent example comes from his journal
report of an interview with Sir John Pringle in London:

> Sir John made you own 36 [36 was Boswell's shorthand for
> an unidentified lady who possibly lived at no. 36 in some
> London street]. He said, 'Add one sin and deny it to Mrs.
> Boswell.' I insisted on preserving my truth. (Journal, 18 May
> 1778)

The change of personal pronouns, and above all that 'my', reflects
a change in Boswell's attitude to himself as he moves from Object
to Subject. The Boswellian 'Subject' is a supremely valuable
consciousness for whom truth is an emanation of his personality
and even something that he owns, a piece of subjective private
property. Bronson sees the Subject–Object dichotomy in Boswell's
consciousness in terms which might at first sight seem to bring
comfort to the antisyzygist: they show a 'double consciousness' of
himself; one, that of the feeler and doer, the other, that of the
spectator for whom the observer's role is the most important. At
this point Bronson makes a highly suggestive connection between
Boswell and Hume: 'His mere existence was the literal exemplifi-
cation of Hume's discontinuous present; but the consciousness
that registered it and brooded over it, and tried to puzzle out of it
a rational pattern and a definable purpose, was a continuous
identity'.[20] That the relevance of Hume to Boswell is even greater
might be deduced from a remarkable paper by Susan Manning, in
which she categorised the problems of one of Hume's *personae* as
'how to overcome the damaging categories of objective and
subjective', and spoke of Hume himself as having 'a chaotic inner
life of solipsism and spleen'.[21]

In other words, a psychobiography of Hume might throw light
on Boswell and *vice versa*: not, I think, because they were racially
or nationally Scotsmen, but because they were men of the
European eighteenth century and men of the sentimental era.
Once more Bronson can be of help; he notes that the quirkiness of
Boswell's presentation of himself as object, his fascination with
his own 'emotional kaleidoscope', is reminiscent of Sterne's in *A
Sentimental Journey*.[22] What is important is not that Boswell's
attitude was identical with Hume's, or Sterne's – quite manifestly
it was not – but that his essentially unphilosophic life-stream had
connections with contemporary philosophy, and that Hume's
structures of abstract thought were related to structures of feeling
experienced by quite untheoretical contemporaries.

One aspect of Bronson's treatment of Boswell's solipsism is, I
think, open to question; his observations on these repeated

adjurations in the memoranda to 'be' someone he admires – 'be Johnson, be West Digges, be Father'. Bronson explains the trait as follows:

> Boswell's habitual mental state has close analogies with the child's faculty of make-believe. Absorbed in his game, the child can tell himself to 'be' any person or thing, and for him it is so. But all the time he remains himself, his divided consciousness poised above the real and ideal states of being. If the child could actually externalize his make-believe, he would be a Boswell. For Boswell is like a child who, in a never-never land, has, to his delighted amazement, seen his make-believe self suddenly projected into a solid physical reality, from which he knows his real self distinct, though inseparable. So long as the spell remains, he can neither wholly resume his own identity nor completely identify himself with the figure he sees.[23]

Boswell's behaviour most closely fits Bronson's description in those many instances, particularly in his youth, when he tried to make his life conform to some literary stereotype. In the period of his search for a wife (1766–69), for example, he put himself in an emotional posture to adore Catherine Blair 'like a divinity' in the 'romantick groves of Auchinleck', and converted the sixteen-year-old 'belle Irlandaise' Mary Ann Boyd into an Arcadian shepherdess with himself as a 'Sicilian swain'. But in both of these escapades he was really at play, indulging in a complicated gamesmanship that turned life into art. The obverse of such idealistic image-building was equally a mixture of compulsive drives and a conscious, posturing will, the *nostalgie de la boue* of his whoremongering. 'I met with a monstrous big whore in the Strand, whom I had a great curiosity to lubricate, as the saying is' (Journal, 13 April 1763). When he argued with his father about the entail on the estate, he saw himself as 'like an old Roman when his country was at stake' (Journal, 13 August 1769), and when he imagined Margaret Montgomerie turning down his offer of marriage, he responded by picturing himself abandoning his prospects, his country, and his career to become a 'wild Indian' in America (Journal, 23 July 1769): this time the image is from the primitivist side of sentimentalism. It must be admitted, however, that there is one incident from these years that perfectly fits Bronson's account: his infatuation with the gardener's daughter at Auchinleck. He wrote about it to Temple on 28 April 1766:

> The Gardener's Daughter who was named for my Mother, and has for sometime been in the family as Chambermaid, is so very pretty that I am entirely captivated by her. . . . I am

mad enough to indulge imaginations of marrying her. Only
think of the Proud Boswell with all that you know of him,
the fervent adorer of a country Girl of Three and twenty. I
rave about her. I was never so much in love as I am now. My
Fancy is quite inflamed. . . . I take every opportunity of
being with her when she is putting on fires or dressing a
room. She appears more gracefull with her besom than ever
Shepherdess did with a Crook. I pretend great earnestness
to have the Library in good order and assist her to dust it. I
cut my gloves that she may mend them. I kiss her hand. I tell
her what a Beauty I think her. . . . And yet is it not being
singularly happy that after the gloom I have endured, the
dreary speculations I have formed, and the vast variety of all
sorts of adventures that I have run through, my mind should
not be a bit corrupted and I should feel the elegant passion
with all the pure simplicity and tender agitations of youth.
Surely I have the genuine Soul of love. When dusting the
rooms with my Charmer, am I not like Agamemnon amongst
the Thracian Girls?

The realisation of the make-believe self is an even more
controlled affair than in Bronson's account. The magic does not
come from outside, as it would to the child, but from within
Boswell himself, from the consciousness brooding over Hume's
discontinuous present and taking on a Prospero role towards his
make-believe self. Throughout his account of the gardener's
daughter he knows his feelings are only temporary: his third
sentence, 'I write to you while the delirium is really existing',
implies he is well aware they will soon pass away. At the end of
the letter, the voice of reason comes uppermost:

All this may do for a Summer. But is it possible that I could
imagine the dear Delirium would last for life? I will rouse
my Philosophic Spirit, and fly from this fascination. I am
going to Moffat for a month. Absence will break the enchantment.

In the context of the present discussion, the word 'enchantment'
is most revealing; Boswell–Prospero manifests himself in a variety
of shapes; and it is only occasionally that he is out of control. At
his most organised, he is the magician behind the mimic. In the
very first of the journals, Boswell mentioned how successful he
was at taking off Hume's idiosyncrasies (Journal, 9 November
1762); he was better at imitating Johnson's very self and voice
than anyone else except possibly Garrick;[24] and in his later life
his talent for mimicry made some people shun his company just
as much as the fear that he would write up their conversations

in his journal.[25] But when in his early memoranda he tells himself to 'be' one of his heroes, something more intense than mimicry is involved; the external audience of his friends has been replaced by the internal audience of himself. By 'being' Johnson or his father he means in the first instance to be *like* them; a moral mimesis is intended and he wishes to act as they would in the circumstances. It is because of his histrionic ability (an outward-looking characteristic) that he can visualise himself *becoming* them – transforming simile into metaphor, as it were, but what is involved is not the child's magical transformation but a moral one.

For my last example of the contradictory links between philosophy and life, I shall take the night of Boswell's arrival in London from Edinburgh on 22 March 1768:

> Upon the whole, it was as good a journey as ever was made; and as in all other scenes, though words do but imperfectly preserve the ideas, yet such notes as I write are sufficient to make the impressions revive, with many associated ones. . . . After unpacking my trunk, I sallied forth like a roaring lion after girls, blending philosophy and raking. I had a neat little lass *in armour*, at a tavern in the Strand (Journal, 22 March).

What did Boswell mean by blending philosophy and raking? The key lies in the sentence about words imperfectly preserving ideas: in addition to the many details of his journal – of places visited, people seen, conversations, fluctuating moods, fears, plans, and literary schemes – there was a host of sense impressions which even he had not the skill or the time to put down on paper, together with other 'associated' ones; reading the journal would call them all up in his memory whether he had recorded them or not. We are reminded of his inability to describe landscape: a phrase like 'the romantick groves of Auchinleck' was presumably sufficient for him to recreate the entire scene in his memory. 'Blending' suggests that he experienced a Joycean rather than a Sartrean thought-stream as he went along; thoughts about the difficulty of recording the surface, let alone the depths of life came to him as he rampaged after night-walkers. My very last instance comes from two years earlier, in Paris, and it exhibits that use of the second person when reporting the past which (following Bronson) I have already commented upon:

> Had been morning with de Tuyll [i.e., with Willem René van Tuyll, brother of that Zélide with whom Boswell had been emotionally entangled in Holland]; made him come to you at night. . . . His melancholy speculations of Supreme

Being did not affect you. Curious consciousness. God may
make you any kind of being. Said to Tuyll, 'When one is too
delicate, door opening offends, and you speculate "Why are
doors made to give wind?" But in health you don't think so.
Thus tender mind is hurt by notions of moral evil' (Notes, 19
January 1766).

The cryptic expression of these rough impressionistic notes, in
which we come closer than usual to Boswell's philosophic centre,
produces some intriguing ambiguities. The first 'you' shows
Boswell objectively looking back at himself as victor in some mild
social manoeuvrings, while the second reinforces the impression
of an internal observer overseeing all the inner parts of the psyche
as well as the total self seen as an entity. But the third is more
complicated in its reference – it denotes both Boswell as a unique
individual, and 'everybody'. When taken in the first sense, the
statement is a theist's assertion of existential freedom as it
concerns himself; when taken in the second, it is a generalisation
about all human beings, giving the lie to determinism as a
doctrine and to everything Boswell understood by 'presbyterianism'. In the sentence of direct speech, the generalisation continues
impersonally with 'one' (?translating the original French that
Boswell used), then particularity takes over with 'you' referring
largely to himself in the role of the archetype of the hypersensitive
– Boswell as Sentimental Man when slightly off-colour. (I take it
that 'delicate' contains both the sense of 'weak constitution',
which has existed since Middle English times, and the more
prominent eighteenth-century ones of 'fine', 'polite', 'unable to
bear hardship', as given in Johnson's *Dictionary*.) The speculation
'why are doors made to give wind?' arrests us because it reminds
us of the convictions of very young children and of some primitive
peoples that it is the waving and groaning trees that cause the
wind to blow, although the sentence is merely a physical parallel
to the last topic of conversation with de Tuyll – the concept of
moral evil as inextricably bound up with human nature. The
theory Boswell puts forward is one of psychophysical parallelism:
a 'tender' mind is analogous to a delicate body. The notion of
man's original goodness was of course a key one for the European
enlightenment and European sentimentalism, and very common
in Scotland, going back via Boswell's teacher Adam Smith
through Francis Hutcheson in Glasgow to the English Lord
Shaftesbury.

It is my contention, then, that Boswell, whose personality at
first sight seems almost a textbook illustration of the 'Caledonian
antisyzygy', can best be explained in terms of the tensions of

enlightenment: of enlightenment as a specific Scottish development, it must be admitted, but nevertheless of a phenomenon
whose leading features are European. Boswell's conflict with his
father has sometimes been seen as a particularly Scottish one, and
parallels have been drawn with some of the best known characters
in Scottish imaginative literature: the weak, sensitive Archie Weir
and the brutal, Scots-speaking domineering Lord Hermiston;[26]
young Gourlay (weak in intellect, strong in sensibility and sense-
perceptions and a drunkard) and the towering dumb-ox Colossus
of Barbie;[27] father and son in John McDougall Hay's *Gillespie*.[28]
It is almost as if the real Boswell, the Boswell of the journals, is
the platonic archetype of all these later fictional anti-heroes, and
Lord Auchinleck the real life prototype of the overbearing,
insensitive fathers. There is, however, another possible explanation
– that Boswell is a *literary* source for the father-son relationship in
Weir of Hermiston, and that Stevenson is a *literary* source for
George Douglas Brown and McDougall Hay, as well as for such
popular exploiters of the theme as A.J. Cronin in *Hatter's Castle*.
There was enough about the real relations between Boswell and
Lord Auchinleck in the *Life of Johnson* and *Tour of the Hebrides*,
and in the oral tradition of Edinburgh legal circles for Stevenson
to have made the imaginative leap to young Archie and the
Hanging Judge (who also owes a great deal to Lord Braxfield);
and Stevenson knew both these works very well indeed: 'I'm
reading . . . Boswell daily by way of a Bible; I mean to read
Boswell now till the day I die', he wrote to Mrs Sitwell (July and
August 1876). And in a letter to his father of 12 December 1880,
Stevenson outlined a plan for a book on Highland history
beginning immediately after the suppression of the 1715 rebellion;
one chapter or section of a chapter was to be on Boswell and
Johnson. A year later (November, 1881) he was contemplating an
article on 'Burt, Boswell, Mrs Grant, and Scott', all of whom had
written about the Highlands.[29] It is at least plausible that
memories of Stevenson's conflict with his own father fused with
memories of Boswell to create the Hermiston confrontation, thus
establishing a *literary* tradition in Scotland that runs from novel to
novel right down to the present day, and which has now begun to
take on some of the attributes of Myth. The Scottish conflicts
between fathers and sons are merely special variants of the general
'Oedipus complex' in western culture. Its classic British expression
is not by a Scot but by an Englishman, Samuel Butler, in *The Way
of all Flesh*; and in real life Kafka's father is just as relevant to
Scotland as Lord Auchinleck. To pass on to other aspects of the
antisyzygy, Byron's comments on Burns, about 'dirt and deity'

and all sorts of other antithetical qualities united in 'that one compound of inspired clay'[30] – such a comment could be passed on many writers of other lands and other times. Neither Galt nor Scott, as men or writers, can easily be pressed into the antisyzygist mould. Neither can Hogg as a person (his insecurities were those of a lower-class intellectual trying to break into the established literary world dominated by commercial publishing), though his writings can: but even these have strong parallels with German Romanticism, as in the often quoted resemblance between *The Private Memoirs and Confessions of a Justified Sinner* and E.T.A. Hoffman's *Die Elixiere des Teufels*.

Nor is it easy to find an extreme antisyzygy in the historians, philosophers and scientists of the Scottish Enlightenment – Hume, Kames, Adam Ferguson, Adam Smith, Hugh Blair, Beattie, Black, Hutton and Reid. Are we to say that most of the luminaries who were the subjects of all those hundreds of seminars and lectures in Edinburgh and Aberdeen during the 'Enlightenment Year' of 1986 were aberrations, not proper Scotsmen at all because they were not well and truly split down the middle? Or does the real division lie between the Enlightenment figures proper – the philosophers, scientific and medical men, engineers, inventors – on the one hand, and the vernacular humanists[31] on the other? Were the Enlightenment men and the vernacular revival poets 'the half-men of their time', to borrow Carlyle's term for the Scottish Hume and the English Johnson? Would they, the revivalists and the literati, have had to be fused together for there to have been a mature *national* culture in eighteenth-century Scotland?

It will be recollected that David Daiches based his attribution of antisyzygist tendencies to Boswell on a passage where Boswell identified volatile and extravagant behaviour with Englishness, and rationality, calculation, and sobriety with Scottishness. I find it hard to believe that so acute and sensitive an observer as Boswell would not have been aware that two entirely and uniquely contradictory tendencies were present in his friends, his mentors, and his fellow advocates if this had really been the case. When Gregory Smith invented the 'Caledonian antisyzygy', he prefixed the term with this phrase – 'the very combination of opposites – what either of the two Sir Thomases, of Norwich or of Cromarty, might have been willing to call ['the Caledonian antisyzygy']'. That the first name to occur to him was that of an Englishman, Sir Thomas Browne, is highly significant; and mention of Browne inevitably makes us think of his contemporaries, the *English* metaphysical poets, whose style and wit have all the violent yoking of contraries heterogeneously together, all the *discordia concors*, that anyone could ever wish for. The antisyzygist qualities that Smith claimed were predominant in Scottish imaginative literature are surely very similar to those that Northrop Frye saw as defining a *genre* in world literature – the Anatomy, which he derived from the Menippean satire of the classical world;[32] they are found in many medieval works from continental Europe, in many works of European romanticism, in some Russian novels and novelists, in the twentieth-century literature of the Absurd, and in works of the sentimental era, in England and Europe as well as in Scotland.

What is new, what is revolutionary in the Tory Boswell has nothing to do with his philosophy (for he had no soberly worked out system) or his political stance; it is rather the consequence of his obsession – the Journal, its extreme particularity following on from his conviction that nothing is truly experienced until it is recorded. The very zig-zags of feeling that the antisyzygists would see as peculiarly Scottish seem to others to be universal: 'It is the biographer's despair', writes Frank Brady, 'that Boswell's fluctuations in mood so faithfully resemble those found in many other lives' (clearly Brady, an American, is not thinking only of Scottish lives). As we have already seen, Boswell's love and hatred of Scotland were profoundly connected with his love and fear of his father. He sincerely wanted all his life to '*be* father', to 'be like father'; yet to be that kind of strong, 'retenu' Scots laird and Judge would go clean counter 'to what he felt were the demands and potentialities of his own nature'.[33] Being true to his basic drives meant being false to Scotland; Boswell increasingly identified his real self and the satisfaction of his real desires with England and with London, and the narrow, rude, provincial Scotland (as he saw it) with his father. It did not matter to him – perhaps he had no inkling of it – that some of those Scotch professors and literati who were so tongue-tied in Johnson's presence, but in whose company Benjamin Franklin was to say he had spent the 'six weeks of the densest happiness I have ever met with in any part of my life',[34] were of more lasting import than any members of the Club except Gibbon, Reynolds and Burke. He never seems to have suspected that the local men Hume and Adam Ferguson might be of far greater *world* importance than Samuel Johnson himself, that it was 'the meikle Ursa Major' who was in the last analysis provincial. Yet pride in Auchinleck and his ancestors remained till the end; it was Margaret Montgomerie he married, not Dutch Zélide or any of the English heiresses he had coveted – Margaret in her homeliness, common sense and loyalty almost the incarnation of Ayrshire and of Scotland. Some works planned but never executed testify to the ambivalence of this anglophile: a 'Dictionary of Words Peculiar to Scotland' (1769), 'A Life of Thomas Ruddiman' the Jacobite and humanist (1773), 'A History of King James IV of Scotland' (1773), 'A Novel on Sir Alexander MacDonald' (1773), 'A History of Edinburgh' (1774), 'A Life of Lord Kames' (1775), 'A life of Sir Alexander Dick' (1775), 'A History of the Civil War in Great Britain in 1745 and 1746' (1777), an edition of 'The Autobiography of Sir Robert Sibbald' (1778), and 'A Collection of Feudal Tenures and Charters of Scotland' (1791), only five years before his death.

Everyone recognises Boswell's volatility, instability, and extreme unpredictability: indeed one biographer of our own century, C.E Vulliamy, could only conclude his profoundly hostile survey by saying (like so many of Boswell's contemporaries, including Hume) that he was 'mad'.[35] Yet this 'madman' produced two epics of lasting sanity and balance, the one deploying the clash of nationalities and cultures, the other recreating imaginatively a representative sector of the intellectual superstructure of eighteenth-century Britain. Nor was this all. Those tensions gave rise to that enormous mass of journals and letters which, in Bronson's words, provide 'possibly the fullest evidence for the study of his inner and private history that exists for any historical human identity'.[36] It is the inner and private history, not of any passive vehicle of some mysterious 'Caledonian antisyzygy' grounded in the germ plasm or historically 'given' from the Middle Ages to the present, but of a unique being whose tensions belong more with Marivaux, Rousseau, Goethe's Werther, Goldsmith, Sterne, and – in Scotland – with Harley in Mackenzie's *Man of Feeling*, than with Jekyll and Hyde or Hogg's justified sinner.

NOTES

1. London, 1976, 59.

2. See e.g. Robert Garioch, 'Ane Guid New Sang in Preise of Professor Gregory Smith, Inventor of the Caledonian Antisyzygy', in *Doktor Faust in Rose Street* (Edinburgh, 1973), 25–7, and Edwin Morgan, 'Caledonian Antisyzygy', in *Themes on a Variation* (Manchester, 1988), 152.

3. In *Scottish Literature: Character and Influence* (London, 1919), 4. Subsequent page references are given in the text.

4. *James Boswell: the Later Years 1769–1795* (New York and London, 1984), henceforth cited as *Later Years*, 561–2.

5. See for example *Boswell in Holland 1763–1764*, edited by F.A. Pottle (London, 1952), 88, 178–9, 188, 191, 196, 307.

6. I owe this use of the term to Christopher Caudwell, *Illusion and Reality* (London, 1937), 124 and *passim*.

7. Frederick A. Pottle, *James Boswell: the Earlier Years 1740–1769* (New York and London, 1966), henceforth cited as *Earlier Years*, 19, 17, 12.

8. *Earlier Years*, 2, 16.

9. The Metaphysics in Stevenson's class came from Devries' *Ontologia*. For the contents of this course, see F.A. Pottle, 'Boswell's University Education' in *Johnson, Boswell and their Circle: Essays presented to L.F. Powell* (Oxford, 1965), 239–40.

10. Journal, 20 March 1768. All Boswell's Journal references are to the originals in the Yale collections.

11. *Earlier Years*, 42–3.

12. *Earlier Years*, 64–5, 473.

13. *The Works of Thomas Carlyle* (London, 1896–99), XXVIII, 133–5.

14. *On Heroes, Hero-Worship, and the Heroic in History* (London, 1897), 186, 14.

15. From Temple,? Spring 1759.

16. Journal, 4 November 1762.

17. Journal, 16 May 1763.

18. Boswell's familiarity with these authors is clear from many passages in the correspondence with Temple and in the Journals.

19. *Later Years*, 191, 101.

20. Bertrand H. Bronson, 'Boswell's Boswell', in *Johnson Agonistes and other Essays* (Cambridge, 1946), 63–5.

21. Susan Manning in 'Eloquence and Evasion: Hume's Elusive Wit', paper read at the British Society for Eighteenth Century Studies Conference in Edinburgh, 28 August 1986.

22. Bronson, 63.

23. Bronson, 65–6.

24. Boswell, *Life of Johnson*, edited by G.B. Hill, revised L.F. Powell (Oxford, 1934), II, 326, n. 2.

25. To his son Sandy, 7 February 1794, quoted in *Later Years*, 455.

26. Robert Louis Stevenson, *Weir of Hermiston* (London, 1896).

27. George Douglas Brown, *The House with the Green Shutters* (London, 1901).

28. London, 1914.

29. *The Letters of Robert Louis Stevenson*, edited by Sidney Colvin (London, 1911), I, 308; II, 19, 66.

30. *Works of Lord Byron, Letters and Journals*, edited by R.E. Prothero (London, 1898), II, 357–8.

31. I owe the term to F.W. Freeman, in *Robert Fergusson and the Scots Humanist Compromise* (Edinburgh, 1984).

32. Northrop Frye, *Anatomy of Criticism* (Princeton, 1957), 309–12.

33. *Later Years*, 125, 202.

34. Franklin to Lord Kames, quoted in Esmond Wright, *Franklin of Philadelphia* (Cambridge, Mass. and London, 1986), 126. Franklin added 'did not strong connexions draw me elsewhere, I believe Scotland would be the country I should choose to spend the remainder of my days in'.

35. C.E. Vulliamy, *James Boswell* (New York, 1933), viii.

36. Bronson, 54.

Index